CIPS Study Matters

Level 6

Graduate Diploma in Purchasing and Supply

COURSE BOOK

Finance
for
Purchasers

© Profex Publishing Limited, 2010

Printed and distributed by the Chartered Institute of Purchasing & Supply

Easton House, Easton on the Hill, Stamford, Lincolnshire PE9 3NZ

Tel: +44 (0) 1780 756 777

Fax: +44 (0) 1780 751 610

Email: info@cips.org

Website: www.cips.org

First edition July 2006
Second edition July 2007
Third edition April 2009
Fourth edition October 2010

Contents

Preface

Welcome to your new Study Pack.

For each subject you have to study, your Study Pack consists of three elements.

- A **Course Book** (the current volume). This provides detailed coverage of all topics specified in the unit content.

- A small-format volume of **Passnotes**. For each learning objective, these highlight and summarise the key points of knowledge and understanding that should underpin an exam answer. Use your Passnotes in the days and weeks leading up to the exam.

- An extensive range of **online resources**. These include a **Quick Start Guide** (a rapid 40-page overview of the subject), practice questions of exam standard (with full suggested solutions), notes on recent technical developments in the subject area, and recent news items (ideal for enhancing your solutions in the exam). These can all be downloaded from the study resources area at www.cips.org. You will need to log in with your membership details to access this information.

For a full explanation of how to use your new Study Pack, turn now to page xv. And good luck in your exams!

A note on style

Throughout your Study Packs you will find that we use the masculine form of personal pronouns. This convention is adopted purely for the sake of stylistic convenience – we just don't like saying 'he/she' all the time. Please don't think this reflects any kind of bias or prejudice.

October 2010

The Exam

The format of the paper

The time allowed is three hours. The exam is in two sections.

Section A – case study scenario, with two application questions based on the case study, each worth 25 marks.

Section B – questions to test knowledge and understanding. Candidates will be required to answer two questions from a choice of four. As with Section A, questions will be worth 25 marks each.

The unit content

The unit content is reproduced below, together with reference to the chapter in this Course Book where each topic is covered.

Unit characteristics

Purchasing managers are responsible for specific activities and processes, which can contribute to achieving corporate strategic goals.

This unit is designed to provide students with an understanding of strategic aspects of finance in relation to the decision-making process and detailed analysis necessary to deliver effective procurement.

Students will understand how to navigate around the world of finance in an effective and efficient manner so they can identify the where, when, how, and what a professional purchaser needs, in order to use and interpret the key financial models and tools required to deliver robust and sustainable procurement solutions.

Students will be expected to propose a range of tried and tested models, as well as innovative tools and techniques, which will allow key business stakeholders to interact and contribute towards developing and exploiting opportunities to grow and expand a business, through new supply arrangements, channels to market, diversification, outsourcing and differentiation strategies.

It will help students to develop an understanding of the terminology and different sectors within the financial and accounting profession which allows an engagement and exchange that will guide and benefit the decision-making process in an efficient manner.

Statements of practice

On completion of this unit, students will be able to:

- Evaluate the appropriate cost and benefit models for a wide variety of scenarios

- Evaluate and assess reports that have their origins in finance and accounting and relate them back to the business

- Compare the value and relevance of financial information in the context of the decision-making process for evaluation and selection of supplier and service providers

- Use the wide variety of finance and accounting terminology

- Propose financial management tools and techniques and be able to apply these in relation to the total procurement and supply chain process

- Evaluate the elements that make up a complex business case for a capital acquisition, including downstream maintenance, service provisions for the life of the acquisition, and disposal

- Assess the non-financial factors that are interrelated with financial modelling and analysis, and predict their impact.

Learning objectives and indicative content

1.0 Financial management tools
(Weighting 10%)

1.1 Evaluate the difference between management accounting and financial accounting.

•	Management accounts	1
•	Company secretaries	1
•	Financial accountants	1
•	Cost accountants	1

1.2 Assess the importance of corporate governance, regulation and corporate social responsibility (CSR) and sustainability in relation to economic performance and value creation.

•	Examples of CSR and sustainability in practice	1
•	Importance of CSR and sustainability to customer satisfaction	1
•	Contemporary developments in the area of CSR and sustainability	1
•	Regulatory mechanisms – EU Directives for Procurement	1

1.3 Understand and use the terminology associated with finance and accounting.

•	Accounting standards and their role	1
•	International issues in accounting standards	1
•	Effects of the convergence of accounting standards and practices	1

1.4 Identify which goods and services can be categorised as capital and which will be expense items.

•	Capital items – plant and equipment, buildings, vehicles, high value office equipment, construction	2
•	Expense items – cleaning materials, stationery, office supplies, consumables, cleaning services, services contracts	2

2.0 Financial and non-financial factors in decision-making
(Weighting 20%)

2.1 Analyse key financial statements to inform decisions.

•	Profit and loss accounts/income statements	2
•	Balance sheet	2
•	Cash flow statement	2
•	Five-year summary	2

2.2 Use descriptive and inferential statistics.

•	Definitions	3
•	How and when to use them	3
•	Assess the outcomes of analysis	3

5.0 Effective capital purchasing plans
(Weighting 20%)

5.1 Evaluate the nature and importance of investment decision-making for home and international markets.

• Accounting rate of return (ARR)	10
• Payback period (PP)	10
• Discounted cash flow (DCF)	10
• Net present value (NPV)	10
• Internal rate of return (IRR)	10
• Opportunity costs of capital	10
• The impact of depreciation on running costs	10

5.2 Assess the impact of external factors upon the decision-making process and how these might be factored into the modelling and ultimate business case.

• Inflation	10
• Customs and Excise	10
• Taxation	10
• Exchange rates and currency management	10
• Social and political factors	10
• CSR and sustainability	10
• PESTLE and regulatory factors	10

5.3 Evaluate the most appropriate decision-making tools for projects across a variety of sectors.

• Whole life costing	9
• Target costing	9
• Value engineering	9
• Value for money (VFM)	9

5.4 Evaluate the roles of the functions of an organisation in the reduction and control of costs.

• Design and engineering	9
• Purchasing	9
• Marketing	9
• Distribution	9
• Finance	9

6.0 Financial risk in procurement
(Weighting 15%)

How to Use Your Study Pack

Familiarisation

At this point you should begin to familiarise yourself with the package of benefits you have purchased.

- Go to www.cips.org and log on. Then go to Study and Qualify/Study Resources. Browse through the free content relating to this subject.

- Download the Quick Start Guide and print it out. Open up a ring binder and make the Quick Start Guide your first item in there.

- Now glance briefly through the Course Book (the text you're reading right now!) and the Passnotes.

Organising your study

'Organising' is the key word: unless you are a very exceptional student, you will find a haphazard approach is insufficient, particularly if you are having to combine study with the demands of a full-time job.

A good starting point is to timetable your studies, in broad terms, between now and the date of the examination. How many subjects are you attempting? How many chapters are there in the Course Book for each subject? Now do the sums: how many days/weeks do you have for each chapter to be studied?

Remember:

- Not every week can be regarded as a study week – you may be going on holiday, for example, or there may be weeks when the demands of your job are particularly heavy. If these can be foreseen, you should allow for them in your timetabling.

- You also need a period leading up to the exam in which you will revise and practise what you have learned.

Once you have done the calculations, make a week-by-week timetable for yourself for each paper, allowing for study and revision of the entire unit content between now and the date of the exams.

Getting started

Aim to find a quiet and undisturbed location for your study, and plan as far as possible to use the same period each day. Getting into a routine helps avoid wasting time. Make sure you have all the materials you need before you begin – keep interruptions to a minimum.

Begin by reading through your Quick Start Guide. This should take no more than a couple of hours, even reading slowly. By the time you have finished this you will have a reasonable grounding in the subject area. You will build on this by working through the Course Book.

Using the Course Book

You should refer to the Course Book to the extent that you need it.

- If you are a newcomer to the subject, you will probably need to read through the Course Book quite thoroughly. This will be the case for most students.

- If some areas are already familiar to you – either through earlier studies or through your practical work experience – you may choose to skip sections of the Course Book.

The content of the Course Book

This Course Book has been designed to give detailed coverage of every topic in the unit content. As you will see from pages vii–xiii, each topic mentioned in the unit content is dealt with in a chapter of the Course Book. For the most part the order of the Course Book follows the order of the unit content closely, though departures from this principle have occasionally been made in the interest of a logical learning order.

Each chapter begins with a reference to the learning objectives and unit content to be covered in the chapter. Each chapter is divided into sections, listed in the introduction to the chapter, and for the most part being actual captions from the unit content.

All of this enables you to monitor your progress through the unit content very easily and provides reassurance that you are tackling every subject that is examinable.

Each chapter contains the following features.

- Introduction, setting out the main topics to be covered
- Clear coverage of each topic in a concise and approachable format
- A chapter summary
- Self-test questions

The study phase

For each chapter you should begin by glancing at the main headings (listed at the start of the chapter). Then read fairly rapidly through the body of the text to absorb the main points. If it's there in the text, you can be sure it's there for a reason, so try not to skip unless the topic is one you are familiar with already.

Then return to the beginning of the chapter to start a more careful reading. You may want to take brief notes as you go along, but bear in mind that you already have your Quick Start Guide and Passnotes – there is no point in duplicating what you can find there.

Test your recall and understanding of the material by attempting the self-test questions. These are accompanied by cross-references to paragraphs where you can check your answers and refresh your memory.

Practising what you have learned

Once you think you have learned enough about the subject, or about a particular topic within the overall subject area, it's good to practise. Access the study resources at www.cips.org, and download a practice question on the relevant area. Alternatively, download a past exam question. Attempt a solution yourself before looking at our suggested solution or the Senior Assessor's comments.

Make notes of any mistakes you made, or any areas where your answer could be improved. If there is anything you can't understand, you are welcome to email us for clarification (course.books@cips.org).

The revision phase

Your approach to revision should be methodical and you should aim to tackle each main area of the unit content in turn. Begin by re-reading your Quick Start Guide. This gives an overview that will help to focus your more detailed study. Then re-read your notes and/or the separate Passnotes accompanying this Course Book. Then return to question practice. Review your own solutions to the practice questions you have had time to attempt. If there are gaps, try to find time to attempt some more questions, or at least to review the suggested solutions.

Additional reading

Your Study Pack provides you with the key information needed for each module but CIPS strongly advocates reading as widely as possible to augment and reinforce your understanding. CIPS produces an official reading list of books, which can be downloaded from the bookshop area of the CIPS website.

To help you, we have identified one essential textbook for each subject. We recommend that you read this for additional information.

The essential textbook for this unit is *Financial Management for Decision Makers* by Peter Atrill, published by Pearson (ISBN: 978–0–273–71764–5).

CHAPTER 1

Finance in the Organisational Framework

Learning objectives and indicative content

1.1   Evaluate the difference between management accounting and financial accounting.

- Management accounts
- Company secretaries
- Financial accountants
- Cost accountants

1.2   Assess the importance of corporate governance, regulation and corporate social responsibility (CSR) and sustainability in relation to economic performance and value creation.

- Examples of CSR and sustainability in practice
- Importance of CSR and sustainability to customer satisfaction
- Contemporary developments in the area of CSR and sustainability
- Regulatory mechanisms – EU Directives for Procurement

1.3   Understand and use the terminology associated with finance and accounting.

- Accounting standards and their role
- International issues in accounting standards
- Effects of the convergence of accounting standards and practices

Chapter headings

1   The relevance of financial analysis to purchasing professionals

2   Financial accounting, cost accounting and management accounting

3   Corporate social responsibility (CSR)

4   Accounting regulations

5   EU procurement directives

Introduction

As its title suggests, the aim of this chapter is to set out the broad framework in which financial professionals carry out their roles.

We begin by examining why a purchasing professional should be interested in financial analysis.

From there, we consider the different types of financial analyses that accountants prepare, in particular distinguishing between the work of financial accountants, cost accountants and management accountants.

An increasingly important influence on the work of professional purchasing and finance staff is the concept of corporate social responsibility and sustainability. In Section 3 of this chapter we explain the nature of the concept and the effects it has on the work of a purchaser.

Finally, we look at the regulatory framework within which a finance professional must carry out his work. This helps to explain both the usefulness of his work to purchasing professionals, and also its limitations. The regulatory framework includes both accounting regulations (Section 4 of this chapter) and the EU procurement directives (Section 5).

1 *The relevance of financial analysis to purchasing professionals*

Why prepare accounts?

1.1 Business accounting is the process of recording financial transactions carried out by an organisation, and summarising them so as to present a financial picture. This process is undertaken by all manner of organisations: commercial businesses (from the very small 'sole trader' to large companies), charities, government authorities and so on. From the buyer's point of view, however, the interest in financial information is very often concerned with assessing the viability of a supplier, so our focus in this text will be primarily on commercial businesses.

1.2 Recording each transaction carried out by a large business is a costly and time-consuming task. For example, imagine the number of sales transactions carried out in a single day – never mind a month or year – in a large department store. Or the number of purchase invoices received from the suppliers of a large business such as British Telecom.

1.3 In order to prepare accounts, all of these transactions must be captured and recorded. Moreover, they must be totalled and summarised at regular intervals (perhaps monthly or annually) so as to display an overall picture. This is an activity of some complexity, and is usually handled by people with professional qualifications in accounting.

1.4 It is clear that a great deal of effort, time and money is required in order to carry out the accounting function. However, there are many reasons why all this effort is justified. It is convenient to distinguish between 'external' reasons for preparing accounts and 'internal' reasons.

External reasons for preparing accounts

1.5 By 'external' reasons we mean reasons relating to people or organisations outside the organisation whose accounts are being prepared. By 'internal' reasons for preparing accounts we mean reasons relating to the needs of the organisation itself, and in particular its managers.

1.6 One reason why organisations prepare accounts is that they are obliged to do so by external regulations. For example, in the case of limited companies there is a legal requirement to prepare accounts annually and to file a copy of those accounts with an official called the Registrar of Companies. The content of the accounts, and the nature of the accounting records supporting the annual figures, is very closely regulated by the Companies Acts. Failure to satisfy the regulations may give rise to fines and in some cases to more serious punishments.

1.7 Another 'external' reason for preparing accounts is to satisfy the tax authorities. The tax payable by an organisation depends on how much profit (if any) it earns. To compute the organisation's profit, and hence its tax liability, we need to prepare accounts.

1.8 Other people too have an interest in the accounts of an organisation. For example, a supplier may wish to ensure that a potential customer is financially stable before he agrees to supply goods on credit terms. A bank may equally be interested, especially if the organisation has requested a loan or overdraft. A buyer will want to know that a potential supplier is financially stable before relying on him for security of supply.

1.9 Finally, the owners of a business will wish to ensure that the business is being managed profitably. This is not a great problem in a small business, where the owner is probably the manager as well. But it is a problem in large companies where there may be many owners ('shareholders') who take no part in running the business. Instead they appoint managers ('directors') to act on their behalf. The annual accounts provide evidence of how well the directors have carried out this function.

1.10 All of these users of accounts can be described as **stakeholders** of the organisation. Table 1.1 shows some examples of stakeholders and what they may expect from the organisation.

Table 1.1 *Examples of stakeholder expectations*

Stakeholder	**Typical expectations**
Customer	Perceived value in the products supplied by the organisation
Supplier	Satisfactory sales volume at an acceptable price
Shareholders	Maximisation of shareholder wealth (see below)
Employees	Security of well paid employment
Lobby groups	Outcomes on specific issues, eg ethics, environment
Community at large	Responsible behaviour

1.11 By 'shareholder wealth' we mean two things in particular: the income stream enjoyed by the shareholders from the organisation (typically in the form of dividends) and an increase in the capital value of shares. Both of these are achieved by earning profits: increasing sales volumes, increasing sales margins, and reducing costs. Managers must therefore pursue policies aimed at long-term profitability (which will lead to shareholder wealth maximisation) rather than short-term profits. This is sometimes expressed by saying that managers should pursue **economic profit**, a measure of profitability which takes account of the value of shareholder capital tied up in the business.

1.12 To satisfy the information needs of all these interested parties, organisations prepare accounts at least annually and make them publicly available. Typically – as in the case of limited companies already mentioned – these accounts are prepared in a defined format and include details specified by the relevant legislation. The process of doing this is referred to as **financial accounting**.

1.13 Often there is a legal requirement that the financial accounts of an organisation are checked ('audited') by an independent expert from outside the organisation. This is to ensure that they present a true picture of the organisation's finances. The annual accounts of limited companies – other than small ones – must be audited in this way. The auditors must usually satisfy themselves that the accounts show a 'true and fair view' of the organisation's financial performance and position. The auditors do not guarantee complete accuracy in the accounts, but they check that the accounts are free from any material misstatement.

Internal reasons for preparing accounts

1.14 This is all fine so far as it goes. However, the annual published accounts do not satisfy all possible information needs. In particular, they are quite inadequate as a basis for managers in the organisation to take financial decisions.

1.15 There are three main reasons for this.

- The financial accounts are published only infrequently – usually every twelve months. In a fast-moving business environment managers cannot afford to wait that long for financial information.

- The financial accounts are historical in outlook. They record how well the business has done over the period just ended. They do not include estimated information relating to the future, and yet that is precisely what managers need when making decisions.

- The form and content of the accounts are dictated by external regulations. They may not be at all in the form that best suits the information needs of managers.

1.16 For these reasons, the management of an organisation will prepare all kinds of accounting statements and analyses in addition to those required by law. They do so to help in taking decisions and running the business.

1.17 This process is called, appropriately, **management accounting**. Management accounts are not regulated by law: managers can prepare whatever accounting statements they think best, with whatever information content they think they need, and at whatever intervals they choose. Such accounts are internal documents, and there is no requirement to make them publicly available. Indeed, commercial secrecy ensures that management accounts are mostly kept confidential.

The buyer's interest in financial analysis

1.18 How does all this relate to purchasing professionals? The simple answer is that buyers need accounting information for similar reasons to those we have already discussed.

- Buyers wish to deal with suppliers who are financially stable. A supplier in financial difficulties cannot be counted on to provide a secure and continuous stream of supply. Much information can be gleaned from the annual financial accounts of suppliers and potential suppliers – provided you know enough about accounting to be able to interpret it.

- Buyers should seek to obtain prices which are fair to their own organisations and also fair to their suppliers. Often negotiation will revolve around the costs that a supplier must incur in providing the goods required. You need to understand costing and accounting principles in order to perform well in this kind of negotiation.

- Buyers are involved with accounts even within their own organisations. For example, most organisations will establish budgets for each operational function, including the purchasing department. You need to understand the principles of budgeting to take part in this process.

2 Financial accounting, cost accounting and management accounting

Financial accounting

2.1 **Financial accounting** is mainly concerned with the production of financial statements for users outside the business.

2.2 The financial accounts record transactions between the business and its customers, suppliers, employees and owners. The managers of the business must account for the way in which funds entrusted to them have been used and, therefore, records of assets and liabilities are required, as well as a statement of any increase in the total wealth of the business. This is done by presenting a statement of financial position (balance sheet) and an income statement (profit and loss account) at least once every year. The law requires that accounts for certain businesses shall be presented in a specific way. In particular, for most organisations it is a requirement that accounts comply with detailed regulations discussed in Section 4 of this chapter.

2.3 Once a company's financial accounts have been prepared and (usually) audited the company must lodge a copy of the accounts with a government official called the Registrar of Companies. The accounts are then available for inspection (for a small fee) by any interested party. There are time limits by which the accounts must be submitted to Companies House. This means that a buyer wishing to check the financial status of a supplier or potential supplier can usually inspect recent financial accounts by applying to Companies House. This process is usually and most conveniently performed by downloading a copy of the accounts from the Companies House website.

Cost and management accounting

2.4 In performing their job, managers need to know about the detailed workings of the business. This knowledge must embrace production methods and the cost of processes, products etc. It is not the function of financial accounting to provide such detail and therefore the managers require accounting information geared to their own needs.

2.5 **Cost accounting** involves the application of a comprehensive set of principles, methods and techniques to ascertain and analyse costs to suit the various information needs of managers. This analysis of costs feeds into the work of the management accountant.

2.6 **Management accounting** is a wider concept involving professional knowledge and skill in the preparation and particularly the presentation of information to all levels of management in the organisation structure. The source of such information is the financial and cost accounts. The information is intended to assist management in its policy and decision-making, planning and control activities.

2.7 An integral part of management accounting is concerned with identifying, presenting and interpreting information used for:

- formulation of strategy
- planning and controlling the activities
- decision taking
- optimising the use of resources.

2.8 To do this, management accountants perform activities such as cost analysis, cost control, budget preparation, budgetary control (ie monitoring actual performance in comparison with budgeted performance), and investment appraisal (the subject of Chapter 10 of this text).

2.9 It would be a mistake to assume that all of the information of interest to managers is financial in nature. Increasingly, companies see the value of non-financial performance indicators and management reports may well take the form of a 'balanced scorecard'. This means that managers monitor performance by reference to a range of indicators, covering both financial and non-financial factors.

2.10 Table 1.2 summarises some of the main differences between financial accounts and management accounts. (And remember that cost accounts are just one element of management accounts.)

Table 1.2 *Financial accounts and management accounts*

Financial accounts	Management accounts
In many instances are required by law (eg in the case of limited companies).	Records are not mandatory, and may be kept in any form.
Accordingly the cost of record keeping is a necessity.	Accordingly the cost of record keeping needs to be justified.
Objectives and uses of financial accounts are general (to provide information).	Objectives and uses of management accounts can be laid down by management.
Are mainly concerned with profits	Are mainly concerned with cashflow, profits and business management generally.
Are mainly an historical record	Are regularly concerned with predictions
Information should be computed in accordance with legal and accounting requirements.	Information should be computed as management requires, the key criterion being relevance.

The role of the company secretary

2.11 Somewhat oddly, the syllabus for this paper lumps the company secretary in with the financial accountants, cost accountants and management accountants. Although the role of this official has very little connection with the preparation of accounts, we follow the syllabus by including the topic here.

2.12 Every public company must have a company secretary. The secretary must be suitably qualified to carry out the role, either by his knowledge or experience, or (more usually) by holding an appropriate professional qualification, such as an accounting or legal qualification. A private company need not have a company secretary, but many choose to do so.

2.13 The main task of a company secretary is to ensure that the company complies with the various regulations laid down by the Companies Acts. For example, the secretary's responsibilities will usually include the following.

- Making arrangements for meetings of the board of directors
- Making arrangements for meetings of the shareholders (the annual general meeting, or any extraordinary general meetings)
- Maintaining the minutes for meetings of the directors and of the shareholders
- Filing appropriate notices with the Registrar of Companies. Such notices are required in a wide variety of circumstances, eg when a director resigns or a new director is appointed, when the company changes its share capital etc.

Corporate governance

2.14 The company secretary also has an important role in **corporate governance**. This term refers to the mechanisms for ensuring an ethical approach to directing and controlling a business. In particular, it is important that directors of a company (responsible for day-to-day management) behave in the interests of the company owners (the shareholders), rather than pursuing their own personal interests. The directors must always remember that they are appointed merely as agents to run the business on behalf of the shareholders.

2.15 This so-called **agency problem** may be addressed (in theory) by the shareholders taking a very active interest in the running of the business, effectively looking over the shoulders of the directors. In practice, this is not really possible – large companies in particular are owned by numerous shareholders who cannot feasibly act together on a day-to-day basis.

2.16 Another possible solution, much more common in practice, is to align the interests of the directors with those of the shareholders, especially by giving the directors a stake in the business (eg by means of share options). This ensures that the directors are motivated to increase shareholder value, because they are themselves shareholders.

2.17 In practice, there have been a number of high-profile failures of corporate governance, where directors have effectively run companies as their own property. To address such abuses, the Financial Reporting Council in 2006 issued a (revised) **Combined Code** of practice, regulating the corporate governance of companies quoted on the Stock Exchange. In Table 1.3 we list some of the main requirements of the Combined Code.

Table 1.3 *The Combined Code*

• There should be clear division of duties between chairman and CEO to ensure that no single individual has undue power.
• Non-executive directors (part-time and independent) should be appointed to act as a check on the executive directors.
• Appointments should be conducted formally with transparent procedures.
• All directors should submit themselves for re-election by the shareholders at an interval of no more than three years.
• Internal controls should be implemented to protect shareholders' wealth.
• There should be an audit committee of non-executive directors to oversee the internal controls and to liaise with the external auditors.

2.18 The report of the Cadbury Committee in 1992 (which eventually led to the Combined Code) referred to the role of the company secretary in corporate governance. The secretary can help to ensure that board procedures are followed and regularly reviewed, and is also a source of guidance to the board on the responsibilities laid down by the Combined Code. He can provide information to non-executive directors to enable them to carry out their function effectively.

2.19 Guidelines on corporate governance, such as the Combined Code, aim to achieve a number of objectives. For example: directors should maximise returns to shareholders; business risk should be set at a reasonable level; no director should become too dominant; remuneration of directors is not excessive. In this respect, the non-executive directors have an important role to play in corporate governance. For example, the Code requires that a committee responsible for setting director remuneration should be established from the ranks of non-executive directors.

2.20 To achieve the above objectives, the Combined Code sets out standards of good practice in board composition and development, director remuneration, accountability and audit, and relations with shareholders. In the UK, companies are required to report on how they have applied the principles of the Code. If they have not complied with specific provisions, they must explain why.

3 *Corporate social responsibility (CSR)*

Ethical issues in business

3.1 Ethical issues may affect businesses (and public sector organisations) at three levels.

- At the macro level, there are issues concerning the role of business and capitalism in society.
- At the other extreme – the individual level – there are the issues which face individuals as they act and interact within the organisation and supply chain. This is the sphere which is often covered in Professional Codes of Ethics, for example.
- In between, at the corporate level, there are the issues which face an individual organisation as it formulates strategies and policies about how it interacts with its various stakeholders.

3.2 Some of these matters will be covered by legislative and regulatory requirements, and an organisation may have a 'compliance based' approach to ethics which strives merely to uphold these minimal requirements. However, the sphere generally referred to as corporate social responsibility covers policies which the organisation adopts for the good and wellbeing of stakeholders, taking a more proactive 'integrity based' approach and perhaps going well beyond the minimum requirements laid down by the regulators.

3.3 The term 'social responsibility' is used to describe a wide range of obligations that an organisation may feel it has towards the society in which it operates: its 'secondary' stakeholders (ie those not directly connected with the organisation, but affected by its operations). This is sometimes expressed in terms of 'externalities': the costs of business activities which are not absorbed in a product/service or paid for by consumers, but which are borne by the wider community – such as the costs of pollution, including associated costs of illness, environmental degradation and so on.

3.4 Corporate objectives may primarily be financial, particularly in the private business sector, but many firms now also set social responsibility objectives, in relation to matters such as:

- Sustainability issues: the conservation and perpetuation of the world's limited natural resources (eg by limiting greenhouse gas emissions or logging)
- Environmental issues: the reduction of environment pollution, waste management, the avoidance of environmental disfigurement, land reclamation, promoting recycling, energy conservation and so on
- Ethical trading, business relationships and development: consumer protection, improvement of working (and social) conditions for employees and sub-contractors (particularly in developing nations), avoidance of exploitation, debt minimisation, contribution to local communities and so on.

Why should an organisation set CSR objectives?

3.5 Milton Friedman and Elaine Sternberg took the view that 'the social responsibility of business is profit maximisation': to give a return on shareholders' investment. Spending funds on objectives not related to shareholder expectations is irresponsible: regard for shareholder wealth is a healthy discipline for management, providing accountability for decisions. The public interest is served by profit maximisation, because the State levies taxes.

3.6 'Consequently,' argued Friedman, 'the only justification for social responsibility is enlightened self interest' on the part of a business organisation. So how does CSR serve the interest of the firm?

- Law, regulation and Codes of Practice impose certain social responsibilities on organisations (eg in relation to health and safety, employment protection, consumer rights and environmental care). There are financial and operational penalties for failure to comply (eg 'polluter pays' taxes).
- Voluntary measures (which may in any case only pre-empt legal and regulatory requirements) may enhance corporate image and build a positive brand.
- Above-statutory provisions for employees and suppliers may be necessary to attract, retain and motivate them to provide quality service and commitment – particularly in competition with other employers/purchasers.
- Increasing consumer awareness of social responsibility issues creates a market demand for CSR (and the threat of boycott for irresponsible firms).

3.7   However, business also needs to remember the 'enlightened' part of the equation! Profit maximisation does not, by itself, always lead to ethical behaviour – as examples of environmental and human exploitation show. (High-profile past examples include: environmental degradation caused by Shell oil refineries in Nigeria; child labour used by Nike and other Western clothing manufacturers; fraudulent reporting by Enron...)

3.8   In addition, Henry Mintzberg notes that a business's relationship with society is not purely economic: a business is an open social system which makes a variety of non-economic exchanges with the society in which it operates (people, information/knowledge, image), and creates a variety of non-economic impacts. Social responsibility helps to create a social climate and infrastructure in which the business can prosper in the long term.

The CIPS commitment to corporate social responsibility (CSR)

3.9   The CIPS president for 2005, Ian Taylor, made CSR the theme of his year of office. The importance of the topic for CIPS members is underlined by the amount of material published by the Institute on its website. In particular, the Institute has published a comprehensive White Paper, *Corporate Social Responsibility*. The discussion below is a summarised version of the White Paper.

3.10   According to CIPS, CSR is important to all organisations for the following reasons.

- Enhancing stakeholder value
- Helping to increase reputation
- Ensuring increased knowledge of supply, enabling minimum risks from suppliers

3.11   The White Paper highlights concerns such as the use of child labour and sweatshops in the supply chains of many organisations. These are argued to have had an adverse impact on share prices, brand equity, staff morale and media profiles.

3.12   The Institute specifically encourages members to consider the long-term implications of their actions and to question objectives that may unintentionally have negative socioeconomic consequences.

Definitions of CSR

3.13   The White Paper cites a number of definitions of CSR.

- CSR places a company's social and environmental impacts in the context of its obligations to society. It promotes the integration of stakeholder issues into business operations. CSR makes company values come alive – values such as: accountability, transparency, ethics, respect, integrity and humanity.
- CSR is concerned with treating the stakeholders of the firm ethically or in a responsible manner.
- CSR is about how companies manage the business processes to produce an overall positive impact on society.
- The commitment of business to contribute to sustainable economic development, working with their employees, the local community and society at large to improve their quality of life, in ways that are good for business and good for development.

Key areas of CSR for purchasing professionals

3.14   The White Paper identifies the following key areas of CSR.

- Environmental responsibility
- Human rights
- Equal opportunities
- Diversity
- Corporate governance
- Sustainability
- Impact on society
- Ethics and ethical trading
- Biodiversity

3.15   **Environmental responsibility** is not just desirable for moral and ethical reasons, but is also increasingly addressed by legal regulations (for example, the EU Environment Liability Directive).

3.16   **Human rights** refers to such issues as child labour, working conditions, wages and exploitation. Organisations are increasingly aware that they can influence such issues, not just in their home countries but also in areas of the world from which they source supplies.

3.17   **Equal opportunities** have been the subject of legislation in the UK since at least 1976, and the Race Relations (Amendment) Act 2000 outlaws discrimination in all business functions. Purchasing professionals must be aware of the need for equal opportunities both in terms of the products and services produced, and in terms of the supply base (the issue of diversity, see next paragraph).

3.18   **Diversity** of suppliers means the structuring of the supply base in such a way as not to discriminate against minorities. Many organisations in both the public and private sectors are adopting supplier diversity programmes, which foster economic growth.

3.19   **Corporate governance** has come to prominence in the wake of some well publicised company failures. Terms and conditions agreed with suppliers may cover such areas as limiting the organisation's exposure to unnecessary risk, putting in place measures to control the circumstances under which risk will be borne, and positioning the organisation with regard to ethical matters such as CSR.

3.20   **Sustainability** means living in ways that do not compromise the wellbeing of future generations. Purchasing professionals can help in this area by ensuring appropriate policies both within their own organisations, and by encouraging similar practices among their suppliers. This has become a hot topic in recent years and we provide further coverage of the issue later in this section.

3.21   **Impact on society** is an increasingly important area of concern for purchasing professionals and for top corporate management. The White Paper distinguishes between the forward linkages and backward linkages that can affect an organisation's impact on society.

- In its backward linkages an organisation should be concerned about the conditions and wages provided by their suppliers, particularly those in third world countries.

- In its forward linkages an organisation should be concerned about how, further down the supply chain, their products are disposed of or recycled.

3.22 **Biodiversity** has been defined as 'the total variety of life on Earth'. In principle, most people support the idea of preserving diversity of habitats, genetic profiles and species. It is a responsibility of organisations to minimise any adverse impact on these areas.

Four categories of corporate social responsibility

3.23 It is common to identify four areas in which CSR principles may be followed: community relations; care of the environment; customers and suppliers; the workforce.

3.24 CSR in relation to **community relations** means that organisations should seek to be 'good neighbours'. Actions that some organisations have taken include support of local charities, sponsorship of local educational or sporting initiatives etc.

3.25 CSR in relation to **the environment** means that organisations should control actions that might be damaging to the environment and encourage actions that preserve the environment. Actions that some organisations have taken include reduction of harmful emissions, waste management, recycling, and sponsorship of local civic amenities (such as parks).

3.26 CSR in relation to **customers and suppliers** means that organisations should behave fairly and ethically in their business dealings. Actions that some organisations have taken include checking on the CSR profile of their suppliers (and in many cases insisting on minimum CSR standards), and ensuring the highest level of safety in the products they sell to customers.

3.27 CSR in relation to **the workforce** means that organisations have an obligation to care for and develop the people they employ. This includes all of the health and safety activities adopted by organisations, and also staff training and development initiatives.

The business case for sustainable procurement

3.28 The public sector has clear reasons for demanding greater levels of sustainability from its supply chain. It must ensure that the €150 billion of public money spent on goods and services every year is used responsibly and in a way that maximises its benefit to society. Sustainable procurement within the UK is government driven and at its current stage of development often viewed as a public sector initiative.

3.29 Private companies and organisations often remain to be convinced about the sustainable development agenda. This view is slowly changing as legal and environmental issues are making the private sector more aware. Many large organisations have adopted some aspects of good sustainable procurement practices. This is borne out by the Corporate Responsibility Index, developed by Business in the Community and now a leading benchmark of responsible business in the UK. The index was developed in 2002 and participants include FTSE 350 companies, sector leaders from the Dow Jones Sustainability Index, together with non-quoted Business in the Community member companies with a significant economic presence in the UK.

3.30 The conclusions of the 2006/2007 report state that 'supply chain management remains a challenge for companies, although there has been a significant increase in the number of companies working with suppliers to help them improve their social and environmental management and performance'.

3.31 There is greater awareness of sustainable development issues in small to medium sized enterprises as they come into contact with the public sector, or if they are in one of the sectors (eg construction) where the profile of sustainability is increasing.

3.32 Legislation has become a main driver for changing behaviour, and for making private and public sector organisations recognise that addressing environmental issues makes good business sense, and is the responsible thing to do. Examples of legislation on environmental and sustainability issues include the Climate Change Bill, the WEEE Directive (recycling of electrical goods), F Gas regulations (greenhouse gases) to name just a few. Many organisations are affected by this and in consequence have a higher level of awareness than might have been the case a few years ago.

3.33 However being legally obliged to do something does not ensure that companies will embrace it. There is a greater need for awareness of the issues in a way that engenders the active support of business rather than minimal compliance. For some companies this has happened already. The concept of sustainable development is one that enhances the CSR concept and many companies and organisations are well placed to position sustainable development issues at the heart of their CSR strategy.

3.34 A sustainable product is one with the following features.

- Fit for purpose and providing value for money
- Energy efficient and resource efficient
- Made with minimum use of virgin materials
- Made with maximum use of post-consumer materials
- Non-polluting (or at least, causing less pollution)
- Durable, easily upgraded, and repairable
- Re-usable and recyclable
- Ethically sourced

The commercial benefits of sustainable procurement

3.35 Sustainability in purchasing need not necessarily cost more; there is now a much wider choice of environmentally friendly products. 'Green goods' are not necessarily more expensive. Indeed, if the 'whole life cost' of a product is considered an apparently cheaper product is more expensive in the long run. (Whole life costing means taking into account the total cost of an item over its lifetime such as raw materials sourcing, running costs, transportation, admin costs and disposal costs.)

3.36 There are two main cost benefits in adopting a sustainable stance.

- By focusing on a whole life costing approach long-term benefits accrue to the organisation that would not arise if a more adversarial or short-term approach was followed.
- Many categories of cost can be reduced immediately, particularly the costs of energy, materials, stock and waste disposal.

3.37 A further benefit is the enhancement of commercial image. Organisations that embrace CSR and sustainability issues improve and help safeguard their reputation, thereby reducing risks to the company.

3.38 The global move toward sustainability presents new opportunities and new markets to companies. The effective use of technology applied to sustainable thinking will allow for the development of new products and services that will initially attract consumers who are early adopters and command a premium price while enhancing reputation in the marketplace.

3.39 This approach also enables companies to keep ahead of new national and international laws or environmental taxes. Both ISO 14001 and BS 8555 (its small business cousin) call for a legal register that serves to highlight all the environmental legal influences on the business. This must be updated regularly and provides the company with a clear and relevant document with which to ensure all legal and environmental obligations are being met.

3.40 A sustainable stance positions an organisation in a favourable light with its stakeholders. This should lead to better and closer engagement and interest with a direct payback in terms of understanding the present and future needs of these groups.

3.41 Businesses are seeing their competitors using sustainable solutions in order to differentiate themselves and their offering. Price, delivery and quality are no longer enough. As buyers demand more sustainable goods and services the competition will supply them if you don't.

4 Accounting regulations

Legal rules

4.1 We have already mentioned that the preparation of financial accounts is to some extent regulated. (Note that we are discussing **financial accounts**; regulation does not apply to **management accounts**, which managers are free to prepare in any way that they find helpful to themselves.)

4.2 The two main sources of regulation are legal rules embodied in Acts of Parliament and best practice embodied in statements issued by the accountancy profession.

4.3 The main source of legal rules affects the accounts of limited companies. Although other types of organisation are also affected by legal regulations on accounts, it is limited companies that you will mainly be dealing with in your professional work and in the examination.

4.4 The accounts of limited companies are very tightly regulated by the Companies Acts, and in particular by the Companies Act 2006. Requirements of the Act include the following.

- The information must be prepared following certain accounting principles.
- Prescribed formats must normally be adopted for the financial statements.
- Detailed disclosures of information are required. For example, amounts paid to directors as remuneration must be disclosed.
- The financial statements must show a 'true and fair view'.
- The accounts must be audited by a qualified expert from outside the company. (This requirement does not apply to small companies.)

Financial reporting and accounting standards

4.5   The requirements of the Companies Act 2006 (and similar legislation relating to the accounts of other organisations) of course have legal force. However, in addition to these legal rules, the accountancy profession has laid down guidelines for the preparation of accounts. The main aim has been to standardise practice in areas where a variety of accounting methods would be theoretically possible.

4.6   From the early 1970s the Accounting Standards Committee (representing the principal accountancy bodies in the UK and Ireland) issued a series of **statements of standard accounting practice** (SSAPs) which have covered many important areas. SSAPs are applicable to all financial statements intended to give a true and fair view, and in particular to the accounts of limited companies.

4.7   In 1990 the functions of the Accounting Standards Committee were taken over by the Accounting Standards Board, which was given wider powers than the Committee. The ASB issues **Financial Reporting Standards** (FRSs) which will eventually replace the SSAPs. Both FRSs and SSAPs are often referred to as 'accounting standards'. They are supplemented by **Statements of Recommended Practice** (SORPs) relating to the specialised accounting requirements of particular sectors.

4.8   Although accounting standards do not have direct legal force, the members of most UK accountancy bodies are required to comply with them, which means in practice that most limited companies will invariably follow the rules. If a company insists on preparing accounts that violate the rules of an accounting standard, then the independent auditor (if there is one) will comment on the fact in his report (unless the matter is a trivial one).

4.9   Regulation does not apply to all financial accounts. For example, the accounts of John Smith the plumber need not follow these regulations at all, and in practice would probably not do so, although HM Revenue & Customs would expect a degree of compliance. However, in this text we will normally display accounts that do follow the regulations so that you can become accustomed to best practice.

International accounting standards and convergence

4.10   In the paragraphs above we have described the accounting standards published in the UK by the ASC and the ASB. Until recently, these have applied to UK companies, whereas other countries have established their own accounting standards. In many cases, this has led to a lack of comparability between accounts prepared under different regulatory regimes. For those involved in purchasing (and particularly international purchasing), this gives rise to problems.

• It is difficult to make valid comparisons between different companies on the basis of their published accounts.

• Anyone wishing to interpret accounts must become familiar with different sets of rules and regulations.

4.11   In an age when international trading is increasingly the norm, standard setters have tried to address these problems. An international body – the International Accounting Standards Board, or IASB – publishes **international financial reporting standards** (IFRSs) that are intended to apply worldwide. As the result of an EU regulation, many large European companies are now required to prepare their financial statements in line with the IFRSs rather than their own national standards.

4.12   This is the culmination of a long period during which regulators have sought **convergence** between the standards applying in different countries. The new regime took effect in 2005. At the same time, US regulators have introduced stringent new requirements (the Sarbanes-Oxley Act) on financial and accounting disclosure which have a major impact on any company with US links.

4.13   The differences between IFRSs and national standards are in many cases very significant. Adoption of the new uniform regime has therefore led to major changes in the way that European companies report their financial transactions. The advantage of this is the increasing ability to perform valid comparisons between the accounts of companies in different countries.

4.14   Outside the EU, many other countries are currently in the process of adopting IFRSs or converging their national standards with IFRSs. These countries include Australia, Canada, China and Japan. Until very recently it looked as if only US companies would resist convergence and continue to operate under a different accounting regime. However, both the IASB and the US standard setter have made significant efforts to reduce the differences between the two sets of standards. The US regulatory authorities have now proposed that US companies should also eventually move to IFRSs.

The ASB *Statement of Principles*

4.15   One potential obstacle to international convergence of accounting standards arises from the different approaches to standard setting in different countries. The United States is the leading proponent of a rules-based approach, in which detailed rules are laid down to cover specific types of transaction. Organisations preparing accounts under US standards are required to follow these rules without deviation.

4.16   By contrast, the ASB (and the IASB) follow a principles-based approach. The idea here is to define certain underlying principles of accounting. New standards are developed in line with the underlying principles. When in doubt as to the correct accounting treatment of a transaction, organisations should ensure that the treatment they adopt complies with the principles. The whole regulatory framework, including accounting standards, is often referred to as **generally accepted accounting principles** or GAAP.

4.17   To put this into practice, the IASB published a *Framework for the Preparation and Presentation of Financial Statements*. Influenced by this, the UK ASB published its own *Statement of Principles for Financial Reporting*. This document is not an accounting standard; instead, it is a framework within which accounting standards may be developed. It is organised in eight chapters and is broadly similar to the IASB *Framework*.

4.18   Chapter 1 (*The Objective of Financial Statements*) states that financial statements are designed to provide information about the reporting entity's financial performance and financial position that is useful to a wide range of users for assessing the stewardship of the entity's management and for making economic decisions.

4.19   Chapter 2 (*The Reporting Entity*) distinguishes between single entities and entities that are parts of a group. In the case of group entities, financial statements should consolidate information from all the constituent entities.

4.20   Chapter 3 (*The Qualitative Characteristics of Financial Information*) requires that financial information should be relevant, reliable, comparable and understandable.

4.21   Chapter 4 (*The Elements of Financial Statements*) specifies five main categories of items that are included in financial statements: assets; liabilities; ownership interest; gains; losses. We will be looking at these items in later chapters.

4.22   Chapter 5 (*Recognition in Financial Statements*) provides principles as to how and when items should be recognised in the financial statements.

4.23   Chapter 6 (*Measurement in Financial Statements*) states that the monetary value assigned to an item in the financial statements should be based either on its historical cost or on its current value.

4.24   Chapter 7 (*Presentation of Financial Information*) states that financial statements should be as simple, straightforward and brief as is possible while retaining their relevance and reliability.

4.25   Chapter 8 (*Accounting for Interests in Other Entities*) states that a reporting entity in its financial statements must consolidate information relating to any other entity that it controls.

4.26   The IASB and the US standard setting body are currently working together to develop a revised conceptual framework (a framework of principles) that both bodies can apply in developing new and revised standards. This is intended to promote convergence of IFRSs and US accounting standards.

5   EU procurement directives

The objective of the directives

5.1   The need for a simplified legal framework adapted to modern procurement methods and best practice was highlighted in the response to the European Commission's 1996 Green Paper. The subsequent consultation process culminated in the publication of the new public procurement directives in the *Official Journal of the European Union* (OJEU) on 30 April 2004. Provisions of the new directives were transposed into UK national legislation on 31 January 2006 and were implemented by regulations made under s2(2) of the European Communities Act 1972.

5.2   The principal objective of the directives is to promote free, open and non-discriminatory competition within the EU.

Public Sector Directive

5.3 The new Public Sector Directive (2004/18/EC) simplifies and consolidates the three existing directives for public works, supplies and services into a single text. Many of the basic provisions remain the same as in the existing directives. The Directive was implemented into UK law by virtue of the Public Contracts Regulations 2006 on 31 January 2006.

Financial thresholds

5.4 Once a buyer has specified the goods, services or works he requires, and if he is purchasing on behalf of a public body, he must ensure compliance with the Regulations. The Regulations do not apply to the private sector unless, for example, a private sector company is purchasing on behalf of a public body (perhaps as result of outsourcing). The Regulations apply to all purchases above certain financial thresholds that are reviewed every two years. The current thresholds apply from 1 January 2010 until 31 December 2011 and are set out below.

Supplies – £101,323
Services – £101,323
Works – £3,927,260

For non-central government bodies (eg local authorities, education) the thresholds are as follows.

Supplies – £156,442
Services – £156,442
Works – £3,927,260

All figures exclude VAT.

Advertising the requirement

5.5 Subject to certain exceptions, the Regulations require public bodies to use open tendering procedures. They must **advertise** the invitation to tender according to certain rules designed to secure maximum publicity across member states. The contract notice advertising the requirement must be published in the Supplement to the European Journal (available in electronic form only) before it may be published in any other media.

Procedures and time limits

5.6 Contracting authorities now have the choice of four contract award procedures: open, restricted, negotiated (with or without contract notice) and competitive dialogue.

5.7 For the **open procedure** there is no requirement for pre-qualification of suppliers. Tenders must be issued within six days of request by a prospective bidder. The contracting authority must set the closing date for receipt of tenders no less than 52 days from the publication of the contract notice.

5.8 For the **restricted procedure**, pre-qualification of suppliers is permitted but the contracting authority must indicate in the contract notice a pre-determined range of suppliers to whom tenders will be sent. This must be not less than 5 and no more than 20. The contract notice must allow a minimum of 37 days for prospective bidders to register an interest and submit the required information for pre-qualification. Those suppliers who are pre-qualified must be allowed a minimum of 40 days to submit their tenders in response to the invitation issued by the contracting authority.

5.9 The **negotiated procedure** takes two forms: with publication of a contract notice, and without publication. In the latter case other formalities are dispensed with as well. The procedure without publication may be used for a number of reasons including when:

- the open or restricted procedure was discontinued, but only if the contracting authority invites to negotiate the contract every supplier who submitted a tender (not being an excluded tender) under the other procedures;

- there were inappropriate or no tenders under the other procedures;

- for technical or artistic reasons, or because of exclusive rights;

- because of urgency the time limits in the other procedures cannot be met;

- additional and/or repetitive goods/services/works are required.

5.10 Under the negotiated procedure where a contract notice is required, prospective bidders must be given a minimum of 37 days to register their interest to negotiate. Where there is a sufficient number of persons who are suitable to be selected to negotiate, the number selected must not be less than three.

5.11 Where contract notices are drawn up and transmitted by electronic means in accordance with the format and modes of transmission stipulated, the Regulations allow for the time limits for the receipt of tenders in open procedures, and the time limit for the receipt of requests to participate in restricted and negotiated procedures and competitive dialogue, to be shortened by seven days.

5.12 The time limit for receipt of tenders may be reduced by a further five days where the contracting authority offers unrestricted and full direct access by electronic means to the contract documents and any supplementary documents from the date of publication of the notice, by specifying in the text of the notice the internet address at which this documentation is accessible.

5.13 Where contracting authorities seek to take advantage of the above opportunity to shorten the time limits for the receipt of tenders on the basis of the electronic availability of their contract documents, they must publish the specifications and the additional documents in their entirety on the internet.

5.14 In general, buyers are obliged to award the contract on the basis of the lowest quoted price, or on the basis of the economically most advantageous tender. If they choose the latter alternative, they must make the fact known to candidates, and must explain by what criteria, and their relative importance, they mean to assess 'economically advantageous'. The buyer is allowed, in certain circumstances, to exclude bidders if they fail to meet defined criteria relating to general suitability, financial and economic standing and technical competence. This is discussed in more detail later in this section.

5.15 This regime of compulsory tendering has certain disadvantages. All bidders are aware that a large number of bids is likely to be made, and this may deter some suitable applicants. Moreover, since very little pre–qualification of bidders is allowed under the directive, it is likely that some will take risks in attempting to undercut potential rivals. The result may be a contract awarded at a price that gives no incentive to quality of performance. There is also a great administrative burden on the buyer who may be faced with a large number of tenders to evaluate.

Debriefing

5.16 The results of the tendering procedure must be notified to the Office of Official Publications of the European Communities, and these are then published. Unsuccessful bidders have the right to a **debrief**, if they so request. This must be undertaken within 48 days of the unsuccessful bidder's request. The practice of debriefing unsuccessful tenderers might usefully be adopted by the private sector as it supports the procurement principle of promoting open and effective competition.

New provisions

5.17 New provisions have been added to take account of modern procurement methods and developments in best practice. These include specific provisions on **framework agreements, central purchasing bodies** (eg consortia purchasing), **dynamic purchasing systems** (eg electronic frameworks, electronic auctions), and **electronic auctions**.

5.18 In another major new change, the Regulations give effect to the European Court of Justice judgement in the **Alcatel** case, which decided that an unsuccessful tenderer should have a real chance of being awarded a contract if there have been procedural irregularities. The regulations provide for a 10 day 'standstill' period between contract award and execution, in order to allow for a legal challenge. The contracting authority must notify unsuccessful tenderers promptly, and provide a 'debrief' if requested. Should a challenge emerge, the contract will be suspended for court proceedings.

Competitive dialogue

5.19 A new procedure, the **competitive dialogue**, has been introduced to complement the existing open, restricted and negotiated procedures. It is intended to be used for large complex projects in circumstances where, currently, the use of the negotiated procedure might be considered. The Commission's view of the negotiated procedure (as a fallback in circumstances where other procedures are not workable) remains unchanged.

5.20 In the competitive dialogue (and with the negotiated procedure with contract notice), in view of the flexibility which may be required and the high level of costs associated with such methods of procurement, contracting authorities are entitled to make provision for the procedure to be conducted in successive stages to gradually reduce, on the basis of the previously indicated contract award criteria, the number of tenders which they will go on to discuss or negotiate. This reduction should, in so far as the number of appropriate solutions or candidates allows, ensure that there is a genuine competition.

Environmental and social considerations

5.21 Awareness of the need to take account of **environmental and social impacts** in the procurement process has grown substantially since the publication of the existing directives. The new directive makes explicit provision for sustainability issues. Areas affected are technical specifications, selection of tenderers and **award criteria**.

5.22 Contracts should be let on the basis of objective **award criteria** which ensure compliance with the principles of transparency, non discrimination and equal treatment and which guarantee that tenders are assessed in conditions of effective competition. As a result, it is appropriate to allow the application of two award criteria only: 'lowest price' and 'most economically advantageous tender'.

5.23 To guarantee equal treatment, the criteria for the award of the contract should enable tenders to be compared and assessed objectively. If these conditions are fulfilled, economic and qualitative criteria for the award of the contract, such as meeting environmental requirements, may enable the contracting authority to meet the needs of the public concerned, as expressed in the specifications of the contract.

5.24 Under the same conditions, a contracting authority may use criteria aiming to meet social requirements, or in response to particular needs as defined in the specifications of the contract, or relating to particularly disadvantaged groups of people to which those receiving/using the works, supplies or services which are the object of the contract belong.

5.25 Examples of procurement requirements where environmental and social issues might be considered are given below.

- Inclusion of recognised environmental and social performance standards and systems, eg Fairtrade or EMAS (the Eco-Management and Audit Scheme)
- Inclusion of any new or evolving legislation concerning environmental standards or social initiatives
- Taking account of stakeholders, including any environmental managers, potential suppliers and consultants who can advise on objectives, constraints and new initiatives that could be applicable to the procurement
- Requiring bidders, as part of their plans, to explain how they will comply with the environmental and social requirements. This might involve preparation of an environmental and/or social impact assessment by bidders of their proposed work
- The EU Eco label scheme assists consumers to identify products which are up to the standard of formally approved criteria, based on lifecycle environmental impact.

5.26 For procurements where the award criterion is the most economically advantageous tender, environmental and social factors may be incorporated as part of the award criteria that determine selection of the most advantageous tender.

Utilities Directive

5.27   Changes introduced by the new Utilities Directive (2004/17/EC) are much less extensive, mainly because arrangements such as framework agreements are addressed by the existing Utilities Directive and these have not changed. The Directive was implemented into UK law by virtue of the Public Utilities Regulations 2006 on 31 January 2006. New provisions concerning electronic auctions and dynamic purchasing systems are identical to those contained in the new Public Sector Directive, as are the provisions concerning sustainability issues. The financial threshold for Utilities is £313,694 for supplies and for services contracts, and £3,927,260 in respect of works contracts (all effective from 1 January 2010).

5.28   A competitive dialogue procedure has not been included in the Utilities Directive because utilities already have greater scope to make use of the negotiated procedure than is allowable under the Public Services Directive.

5.29   The major change which is unique to the Utilities Directive is the opportunity to take advantage of an exemption mechanism (Article 30). This enables removal of the need to comply with the directive for utility activity which is subject to competition in this sector in recent years.

Enforcement of the directives

5.30   On 12 November 2009, the UK Government adopted the Public Contracts (Amendment) Regulations 2009, which introduce important new remedies for breach of the EU public procurement rules. The most significant change is the introduction of a new remedy of **contract ineffectiveness**. To date, the general rule has been that, once a contract has been entered into, it cannot be set aside pursuant to a challenge under the procurement regulations. Under the new Regulations, which came into force on 20 December 2009, the High Court may declare ineffective a contract awarded without prior competition and, if it does so, must also impose a civil fine on the authority.

5.31   In the UK, before a contract is concluded, interested third parties who allege a breach may apply to the High Court for an order to set aside or suspend the contract award procedure in question. However, if the contract has already been entered into, the Regulations provide that the contract cannot be disturbed and the complainant's potential remedy is confined to financial damages (which can be hard to establish). This makes it difficult for interested parties to challenge a contract once it has been signed, even if that contract was awarded without any prior publicity or competition, in flagrant breach of the procurement Regulations. The problem was only partly addressed by the introduction of the so-called standstill period in 2006.

5.32   The new Regulations implement an EC directive which amends the Remedies Directives. They will maintain in force all of the existing remedies provisions described above. However, alongside the existing provisions, they add a new remedy under which a claimant may ask the High Court to declare a contract to be ineffective. A claim for contract ineffectiveness may be brought where a public authority:

•   awards a contract directly to its preferred supplier, without prior publication of a contract notice in the *Official Journal of the European Union*, in circumstances where this omission was not permitted by a derogation; or

- enters into the contract after an action to suspend the award procedure has been lodged, or before expiry of the 10-day standstill period, in circumstances where the authority has also committed a breach of the substantive rules which affected the complainant's chances of obtaining the contract; or

- has breached the rules regarding call-offs under a framework agreement or dynamic purchasing system and has not allowed for the 10-day standstill period before concluding the called-off contract.

5.33   Any claim for a declaration of contract ineffectiveness must be brought within six months of the day following the conclusion of the contract. Where the awarding authority has published a contract award notice in the OJEU (after contract signature), or sent a standstill notice to the losing bidders, the deadline for any challenge is reduced to 30 calendar days from the notice in question, instead of the usual six months.

5.34   Where a declaration of ineffectiveness is made, the High Court must also order the contracting authority to pay a civil financial penalty (fine) in an amount to be decided by the Court in the case. The Regulations do not give any guidance figures or ranges for the amount of the fine. They simply state that the penalty must be 'effective, proportionate and dissuasive', taking into account the seriousness of the breach and the authority's conduct.

5.35   The new Regulations greatly raise the stakes regarding any breach of the procurement rules. They are bound to make public authorities and utilities, as well as their private sector developers, contractors, subcontractors and financiers, even more cautious regarding compliance with the procurement rules.

Chapter summary

- It requires effort and time to perform the accounting function, but this is justified by both external and internal reasons for preparing accounting statements.

- Accounts prepared for external use are called financial accounts. The form and content of financial accounts is closely regulated.

- Accounts prepared for internal use, especially by managers, are called management accounts. Management accounts may be prepared in any form that is useful to the managers concerned. One part of management accounts will be concerned with the analysis of costs (cost accounts).

- Buyers are interested in accounts primarily for the light they may throw on a supplier's financial stability, but also in connection with effective management of the purchasing department itself.

- The company secretary is an official with responsibility for ensuring that the company complies with its duties under the Companies Acts, and also with a role in corporate governance.

- Organisations are increasingly concerned with issues of corporate social responsibility (CSR), including environmental responsibility, human rights, equal opportunities, diversity, corporate governance, sustainability, impact on society, ethics and ethical trading, and biodiversity.

- Sustainable procurement can provide tangible commercial benefits to organisations.

- The preparation of financial accounts (but not management accounts) is regulated by company law and accounting standards. Increasingly, there is a move towards harmonised international financial reporting standards.

- The ASB and IASB adopt a principles-based approach to the development of accounting standards. The ASB's *Statement of Principles for Financial Reporting* is a framework for this.

- EU procurement directives make competitive tendering compulsory in the public sector. These directives are designed to ensure that public bodies advertise for tenders as widely as possible.

Self-test questions

Numbers in brackets refer to the paragraphs where you can check your answers.

1   Distinguish between external and internal reasons for preparing accounts. (1.5)

2   What is meant by an audit of a company's accounts? (1.13)

3   Why are published financial accounts inadequate for the needs of managers? (1.15)

4   List as many differences as you can between financial accounting and management accounting. (Table 1.2)

5   List responsibilities of a company secretary. (2.13)

6   What is meant by the agency problem in corporate governance? (2.14)

7   Explain the three levels at which ethical issues may impact on organisations. (3.1)

8   List the three reasons, according to CIPS, why CSR is important to organisations. (3.10)

9   Which key areas of CSR are identified in the CIPS White Paper? (3.14)

10   List tangible commercial benefits of sustainable procurement. (3.35ff)

11   What requirements relating to financial accounts are contained in the UK Companies Acts? (4.4)

12   In the context of accounting standards, what is meant by convergence? (4.12)

13   What topics are covered by the ASB's Statement of Principles? (4.18–4.25)

14   What is the principal objective of the EU procurement directives? (5.2)

15   List the four contract award procedures available under the EU directives. (5.6)

16   What are the disadvantages of compulsory competitive tendering? (5.15)

CHAPTER 2

The Key Financial Statements of an Organisation

Learning objectives and indicative content

1.4   Identify which goods and services can be categorised as capital and which will be expense items

- Capital items – plant and equipment, buildings, vehicles, high value office equipment, construction
- Expense items – cleaning materials, stationery, office supplies, consumables, cleaning services, services contracts

2.1   Analyse key financial statements to inform decisions:

- Profit and loss accounts/income statements
- Balance sheet
- Cash flow statement
- Five-year summary

Chapter headings

1   Assets and liabilities

2   Income and expenditure

3   The balance sheet

4   The profit and loss account

5   Other financial statements

6   The legal framework of limited companies

Introduction

In this chapter we identify and explain the key features of a limited company's published annual accounts (often referred to as financial statements). These documents are lodged with the Registrar of Companies and are available for inspection by interested parties for a small fee. They are an important aid for buyers in assessing the financial viability of a supplier or potential supplier.

To begin with we explain the meaning of some basic terms: assets and liabilities, income and expenditure. We then move on to look in turn at each of the main financial statements listed in your syllabus: the balance sheet (or statement of financial position), the profit and loss account (or income statement), the cashflow statement, and the five-year summary.

Once we have gained familiarity with these and other concepts we will examine how such financial statements can be analysed to provide useful information to buyers. This is the subject of the final chapter of this text.

1 Assets and liabilities

Types of asset

1.1 For simplicity, we will refer in this chapter to trading organisations which exist to sell products or services to customers and earn a profit by doing so. It is this kind of organisation that you will normally be dealing with in your professional work. However, you should be aware that the principles discussed here apply equally to other organisations – such as a local government authority, a school or university, or a charity.

1.2 An asset is something which is owned by the business and used in achieving the business objectives.

1.3 Some examples of business assets are given in Table 2.1.

Table 2.1 *Examples of business assets*

• A factory building
• An office building
• An item of production machinery
• A delivery van used to take the business's products to customers
• A motor car used by a salesman in visiting customers
• A computer used in running the business
• Office furniture and equipment, such as desks, filing cabinets and photocopiers
• Cash held in the form of notes and coins or in the form of a bank balance
• Sums of money owed to the business by customers
• Stocks of goods that have been purchased or manufactured by the business

1.4 This looks fairly simple, but there are some complications to look out for. To begin with, the items listed in Table 2.1 only rank as assets of the business if they actually belong to the business. For example, an office building is an asset if it belongs to the business, but would not count as an asset if the business merely rents it from a landlord. Similarly, if the business salesmen visit customers in their own cars, then these would not count as an asset of the business.

1.5 Another point is that the term 'asset' is used more precisely in accounting than it is in everyday speech. In everyday speech a business manager might refer to the quality of his employees as a great asset to the business. However, the value of the employees is not an asset in accounting terms. The main reason for this is that it would be almost impossible to place an objective value on such an asset.

1.6 Contrast this with the case of an office building or a delivery vehicle. Although the valuation of these assets is not completely straightforward, as we will see later, there is at least a good starting point for the valuation: namely, the amount that the business paid to acquire them. All such valuations of assets must be computed on the basis of certain important assumptions that underpin financial accounting:

- Going concern – the enterprise will continue in operation, and at its current level of activity, for the foreseeable future
- Accruals – revenues and costs are recognised (and matched against each other) as they occur (we will return to this concept of **accruals accounting** later)
- Consistency (or comparability) – there is consistent treatment of like items, both within a period and from period to period

Classifying assets

1.7 It should occur to you that there is a great variety in the items listed as assets in Table 2.1. In practice, organisations find it helpful to divide their total assets into certain categories depending on their nature. The main categories are shown in Figure 2.1.

Figure 2.1 *Classifying assets*

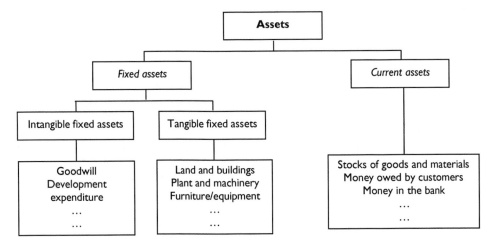

1.8 Figure 2.1 divides assets into two major groups: fixed assets and current assets.

- Fixed assets are those which will be used in running the business for a long period of time – at least, for more than a single accounting year. Fixed assets are sometimes called non-current assets.
- Current assets are those which move into and out of the business quite quickly. For example, stocks of raw materials are a current asset: they will quickly be converted into finished goods and sold to customers.

1.9 The next distinction in Figure 2.1 is between two classes of fixed assets: intangible fixed assets and tangible fixed assets.

1.10 We will have little to say in this text about intangible fixed assets. It is enough to be aware that some organisations attempt to place a monetary value on assets of an intangible nature. One example is the brands owned by a business, which reflect the fact that a customer is likely to prefer a well known brand name ahead of an (almost) identical product that does not have an equal reputation. Clearly, it is very difficult to place an objective value on such factors (rather like the value of the workforce mentioned previously). Even so, accounting regulations permit this practice in certain (strictly defined) circumstances, and you may come across references to it in your reading.

1.11 More important for our purposes is the class of tangible fixed assets, of which some examples are given in Figure 2.1. As mentioned already, the main criterion that distinguishes a fixed from a current asset is the length of the fixed asset's useful life in the business. However, another distinction is that tangible fixed assets tend to be expensive: an office building clearly costs more to acquire than a component included in manufacturing stock. In general, if an item is very cheap to acquire it will not be classed as a fixed asset, even if its useful life is long. For example, few organisations would classify a stapler as a fixed asset even though it may be used by office staff for many years. In a later chapter we will look at some of the particular issues relating to capital assets.

The valuation of assets

1.12 Accounts deal only with items to which some monetary value can be attached. In the case of assets, the relevant value is the cost of acquiring or manufacturing the asset. Thus the value attached to a stock of finished goods ready for sale to a customer would be the price paid by the business to acquire or manufacture those goods. It would be quite wrong to value the goods at selling price – the amount expected to be paid by the customer.

1.13 With fixed assets, the valuation problem is more difficult. The price paid to acquire the asset is still the starting point for valuation, but some amendment is needed to reflect the fact that several accounting periods will benefit from use of the asset.

1.14 To take a simple example, suppose that a business buys an item of manufacturing equipment for £100,000. It expects to use the equipment for about five years, and to scrap it at the end of that period. The asset will appear in the accounts of the business for the next five years, but it would be usual to reduce its value gradually over that period. For example, after one year the asset might appear in the accounts at a value of £80,000; after two years its value might be shown as £60,000; and so on, until after five years its value in the accounts has fallen to zero.

1.15 This process of gradually reducing the value of fixed assets is called **depreciation**.

Liabilities

1.16 Liabilities can be regarded as the opposite of assets. The more assets a business has, the more valuable the business is. With liabilities, the opposite is true: the more liabilities the business has, the less valuable the business is.

1.17 Liabilities are sums of money owed by the business to outsiders.

- A business may buy goods on credit terms from its suppliers. Until the goods are paid for, the business has a liability to its suppliers.
- A business may have an overdraft or loan from its bank. Until this is repaid, the business has a liability to its bank.
- A business may owe tax to the government. Until the tax is paid, the business has a liability to the tax authorities.

1.18 Valuation of liabilities will rarely pose any problems. It is usually quite clear how much a business owes to its suppliers, how large the overdraft is, and how much tax is due to the government. Other liabilities are equally straightforward to value.

2   *Income and expenditure*

Income

2.1   All organisations receive income and incur expenditure. Ideally, the amount of income will exceed the amount of expenditure. In this case, a business is said to earn a profit. (A non-trading organisation such as a school would not use the term profit. Instead, its accounts might refer to a 'surplus' or some similar term.)

2.2   In the opposite case – where the amount of expenditure exceeds the amount of income – a business is said to incur a loss. Again, the terminology would differ for a non-trading organisation. A school, for example, might refer to a 'deficit'.

2.3   Another term used for income is 'revenue'. Both of these terms are quite neutral and may therefore be used in referring to any organisation. The amounts earned by a **trading** organisation in selling goods or services to its customers are referred to as 'sales revenue'; other terms in common use are 'sales' or 'turnover'. These terms all refer quite explicitly to the activity of selling and are therefore not used in connection with non-trading organisations.

2.4   Apart from amounts earned from sales to customers, an organisation may have other sources of income. For example, the organisation may have money on deposit with a bank, and will then receive interest. Or an organisation may own investments, such as shares in a company. In this case, the organisation will receive dividend income. All of this counts as part of the total income of the organisation.

2.5   In preparing accounts, it is usual to include income in the period when it is earned. This may be different from the period in which the income is actually received. For example, consider a business that sells goods on credit to a customer in December 20X7. The customer may not pay for the goods until, say, February 20X8. Now if the organisation is preparing accounts for the twelve months from January to December 20X7, the sales revenue earned from this customer must be included. The point is that the revenue has been earned in 20X7 even though it will not be received until 20X8.

2.6   This principle is known as **accruals accounting**. The main alternative is **cash accounting**. Under a system of cash accounting, the sales revenue mentioned in the previous paragraph would be included in the accounts for 20X8, not in the accounts for 20X7, because in cash accounting the critical matter is when the money is actually received. Cash accounting is used only in certain very specialised situations, and you can usually assume that accruals accounting applies.

Expenditure

2.7   While sources of income are relatively few, there is a wide variety of items on which expenditure is incurred. For example, a manufacturing business must purchase raw materials for conversion into finished goods. A retailer must purchase goods for resale to his customers. All organisations must pay wages to their employees, and will incur many other expenses in addition, such as stationery, telephone and fax charges, business rates and so on.

2.8   As we will see later, organisations must keep records of all these expenses and total them at the end of the accounting period for comparison with total revenue.

2.9   Following the principle of accruals accounting, expenditure is included in the accounts as soon as it is incurred, even though actual payment may take place later. This can be illustrated with the mirror image of the case we have already discussed. Suppose a business purchases goods in December 20X7, but does not pay the supplier until February 20X8. The cost of the goods must be included in the 20X7 accounts.

Capital expenditure and operating expenditure

2.10   The life of a business extends over a long period of time. The problem is that reports on the profitability of the business are needed at fairly regular intervals, usually of twelve months. This requirement gives rise to certain problems. For example, how should one treat £100,000 expenditure on an item of plant which is expected to be useful to the business for the next five years (as discussed earlier)? This expenditure is referred to as capital expenditure because of the long-term nature of the benefits which are expected to be received.

2.11   The distinction between capital expenditure and operating expenditure derives from the fact that, by convention, financial statements are produced on an annual basis. Some examples of capital and operating expenditure are listed in Table 2.2. (Normal practice is to refer to non-capital expenditure as revenue expenditure, but this term is so confusing that we have chosen to adopt the term operating expenditure instead.)

Table 2.2 *Capital and operating expenditure*

Category	Types of expenditure included
Capital expenditure	Expenditure on the acquisition of fixed assets required for use in the business and not for resale
	Expenditure on existing fixed assets aimed at increasing their earning capacity (eg a major overhaul of an item of production machinery)
Operating expenditure	Expenditure on current assets (eg stock)
	Expenditure relating to running the business (administration expenses, selling expenses).
	Expenditure on maintaining the earning capacity of fixed assets (repairs and renewals).

2.12   When operating expenditure is incurred, its effect is an immediate reduction in profits. For example, if we receive an invoice from a supplier of raw materials for £2,000 we 'expense' the cost immediately, and our profits are £2,000 less than they would otherwise have been. This is appropriate because the raw materials will be used up in production very soon if not immediately.

2.13   With a large item of capital expenditure the situation is different. Such an asset is expected to benefit the business over an extended period, not just the current accounting period. For example, the £100,000 item of plant we referred to earlier is deducted from profits over the five-year period we expect it to be in use. In the meantime, the undepreciated cost of the asset – ie the amount of the cost that has not so far been charged against profits – remains as an asset in the balance sheet.

2.14 It is useful to learn some terminology associated with these differing accounting treatments.

- In the case of operating expenditure, we **expense** the costs immediately (ie in this year's profit and loss account). An equivalent term is to say that we **write off** the costs immediately.

- In the case of capital expenditure, we **capitalise** the costs (ie we classify the expenditure as an asset in the balance sheet, rather than as an expense in the profit and loss account). Gradually, over the years, we write off the capital costs by means of a depreciation charge in each year's profit and loss account. Each year we reduce the value of the asset in the balance sheet by the amount we charge as depreciation in that year. Note that depreciation is **not** an expenditure of cash. We paid the cash when we first bought the asset. In later years we gradually re-classify that original cost as operating rather than capital expenditure.

2.15 In some cases it may be difficult to decide what expenditure should be expensed and what should be capitalised. Here are some examples where the decision is not completely clear cut.

- Finance costs, such as loan interest. Usually, such costs are expensed immediately. However, interest on a loan taken out specifically to finance purchase of a capital asset ranks as part of the cost of the capital asset. In such a case the cost can be capitalised.

- Expenditure on research and development will arguably benefit the organisation for years to come. This is an argument for capitalising such expenditure, but there would then be scope for manipulating an organisation's profitability. To minimise this risk, accounting rules insist that expenditure on research must be expensed immediately, while expenditure on development may be capitalised, but only if strict criteria are met.

- In some cases, expenditure on marketing initiatives is claimed to have a long-term beneficial effect on organisations. This is similar to the argument on development expenditure. However, the accounting rules in this case are stricter: such expenditure must be expensed immediately.

2.16 The above examples show that the decision on how to account for expenditure involves the use of judgement. In view of the different effects on reported profit, managers might be tempted to manipulate the classification of capital and operating expenditure in order to show profits in a more favourable light. This is the kind of issue that auditors should be alert to.

2.17 In addition to auditors, the tax authorities also take an interest in capital expenditure.

- To encourage investment, there is a range of tax incentives attaching to capital expenditure. For certain classes of capital assets, companies are able to gain accelerated tax relief on the amounts they invest.

- On the other side of the coin, the tax authorities wish to prevent the abuse that can arise from manipulating capital expenditure. In particular, any amounts charged in the profit and loss account for depreciation are not allowed as a deduction against taxable profits. Instead, the tax authorities impose their own system of **capital allowances** as a substitute for depreciation. This means that tax relief will be given according to rules laid down by the tax man, not according to the judgement of directors.

Profit and cash

2.18 In order for a business to prosper it must make profits and also have sufficient cash to carry out its activities. The making of profits does not necessarily mean that the business has sufficient cash to pay its debts. Failure to understand the importance of cash has caused severe difficulties, and even eventual ruin, to many businesses.

2.19 A profit is made when an item is sold for more than the costs incurred by the business in making the sale. However, if the sale is on credit terms then the business has not actually received any cash. Even when cash is received, it may be invested in buying assets such as new computer equipment. This illustrates an important point: making profits does not in itself guarantee that cash resources will increase.

3 *The balance sheet*

The main financial statements

3.1 There are two main financial accounting statements.

- The balance sheet is a statement of assets and liabilities at a point in time (the end of the accounting period or the 'balance sheet date'). The balance sheet is sometimes called the **statement of financial position**. We will look at balance sheets in this section of the chapter.

- The profit and loss account summarises income earned and expenditure incurred over a period of time. If income exceeds expenditure there is a profit for the accounting period; if expenditure exceeds income there is a loss. The profit and loss account is sometimes called the **income statement** or the **statement of comprehensive income**. We will look at profit and loss accounts in Section 4 of this chapter.

3.2 Note that the balance sheet is a 'position' statement. It describes the financial position of the organisation at a point in time (hence its alternative name). On the other hand, the profit and loss account is a 'period statement', summarising what has happened during the accounting period.

3.3 In the UK and elsewhere in the EU many large companies now follow IFRSs when preparing their financial statements. Other UK companies still follow UK accounting regulations, but this is expected to change over the next few years. The ASB has proposed that small companies should continue to use a specially adapted version of the UK regulations but that other companies should move either to standard IFRSs or to a simplified form of the IFRS regime.

3.4 There are two obvious differences between UK financial statements and standard IFRS statements.

- IFRSs use different terminology from UK accounting standards. The main differences are set out in Table 2.3. In practice, use of the terminology is not compulsory, so financial statements prepared under IFRSs may use UK terms (for example, some companies continue to prepare a 'balance sheet').

- The formats of the main statements may be different. Because most UK companies are still using UK regulations, we will use UK formats to illustrate the way that the main statements work, but we will also show some typical IFRS financial statements. Unlike UK regulations, IFRSs do not prescribe the formats in detail, so some companies have continued to use the normal UK presentation.

Table 2.3 *UK and IFRS terminology*

UK	IFRS
Balance sheet	Statement of financial position
Profit and loss account	Income statement or statement of comprehensive income
Fixed assets	Non-current assets
Tangible fixed assets	Property, plant and equipment
Stock	Inventory
Debtors	Receivables
Creditors	Payables
Turnover	Revenue

An example of a balance sheet

3.5 We begin by giving an example of a balance sheet. Rainbow Limited is a retailer, buying goods from wholesalers for resale to its own customers: see next page.

3.6 This illustration is not as difficult as it looks. First of all, consider what information the balance sheet conveys. And note that all figures in the balance sheet are expressed in thousands of pounds (£000).

3.7 The assets used in the business amount to £48,390,000. This consists of fixed assets (£12,400,000) plus current assets (£35,990,000).

3.8 As regards the listing of assets in the balance sheet, the least liquid assets are dealt with first, followed by the more liquid assets. The term 'liquid assets' refers to cash and those assets which will soon be converted into cash.

- The freehold premises and plant/equipment come first and are classified as fixed assets. A fixed asset is any asset acquired for retention by an entity for the purpose of providing a service to the business, and not held for resale in the normal course of trading. It is not the intention of the company to convert these assets into cash by selling them, so these are the least liquid of the assets.

- Stock comes next, in this case consisting of goods held for resale. When the goods are eventually sold, the business will receive cash in exchange.

- If the goods are not paid for immediately (ie if the company grants credit to its customers) there will be an asset described as debtors. This term describes amounts owing from customers which will eventually result in the receipt of cash.

- Cash at bank refers to the balance on the company's current account at the bank.

- Cash in hand refers to actual notes and coins.

RAINBOW LIMITED – BALANCE SHEET AS AT 31 DECEMBER 20X6

	£000	£000
Fixed assets		
Freehold premises		10,000
Plant and equipment		2,400
		12,400
Current assets		
Stock	12,390	
Debtors	11,840	
Cash at bank	11,704	
Cash in hand	56	
	35,990	
Current liabilities		
Trade creditors	12,700	
Net current assets		23,290
Net assets		35,690
Share capital and reserves		
Share capital		25,200
Retained profits		10,490
Total		35,690

3.9 Liabilities are claims on the business by outsiders. Current liabilities are those liabilities which are payable within twelve months of the balance sheet date. Some businesses might also have long-term liabilities, ie liabilities payable more than one year after the balance sheet date. For example, a business might borrow money from its bank repayable over a period of five years.

3.10 Rainbow Limited does not have any long-term liabilities. The current liabilities consist of trade creditors. These are amounts owing to suppliers in respect of goods and services previously received. Notice that the amount of current liabilities is deducted from the amount of current assets to arrive at a subtotal referred to as **net current assets**. It is important that current assets exceed current liabilities. This means that the company has sufficient liquid assets to pay its creditors. If current liabilities exceeded current assets (a position of **net current liabilities**) the company might be in difficulties: it would not have enough liquid assets to pay its bills.

3.11 The link between the various forms of current assets, and the current liabilities, is sometimes shown in diagrammatic form: see Figure 2.2.

Figure 2.2 *The working capital cycle*

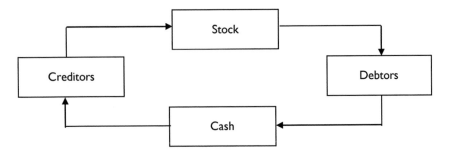

3.12 What this means is that stock is sold to customers, who then owe the company money (ie they are debtors of the company). Eventually they pay what they owe, so the debtors are converted into cash. Cash can be used to pay off creditors, who in turn supply more goods into stock. The cycle then repeats. A company's net total of stock, debtors and cash, less creditors, is often referred to as its **working capital**.

3.13 The top half of the balance sheet shows the net assets of the company, ie its total assets (fixed and current), less its liabilities. In this case the net assets total £35,690,000. This is the balance sheet value of the business to the shareholders.

3.14 The shareholders provide the finance that pays for these net assets, ie they provide an investment of £35,690,000. The way in which they provide this finance is shown in the bottom half of the balance sheet.

3.15 This indicates that the shareholders have injected £25,200,000 into the company as payment for the shares they own. The remaining finance (£10,490,000) is provided by retained profits. This means the accumulated profits that the company has earned over the years and which have been ploughed back into the business. Of course, not all profits earned by the business are reinvested in this way. Some profits are paid out to the shareholders in the form of dividend. The balance sheet figure of retained profit measures only the profits that have been retained within the business.

3.16 In summary, the balance sheet shows the position of the business at one point in time – in this case at close of business on 31 December 20X6. At that point, the shareholders' investment in the company stands at £35,690,000, and this investment is represented by the net assets listed in the top half of the balance sheet.

A further example: IFRS

3.17 Below is a typical statement of financial position prepared under IFRS. Arc plc is also a retailer, but is a much larger organisation than Rainbow.

ARC PLC
STATEMENT OF FINANCIAL POSITION AS AT 31 DECEMBER 20X6

	£m	£m
ASSETS		
Non-current assets		
Property, plant and equipment		3,500
Intangible assets		400
		3,900
Current assets		
Inventories	1,037	
Trade and other receivables	1,223	
Cash and other equivalents	198	
		2,458
		6,358
EQUITY AND LIABILITIES		
Equity		
Share capital		2,000
Retained earnings		1,258
		3,258
Liabilities		
Non-current liabilities		
Long-term borrowings		1,500
Current liabilities		
Trade and other payables	1,090	
Tax payable	510	
		1,600
		6,358

3.18 The statement looks a little different from the balance sheet of Rainbow Limited, but basically it provides the same information.

3.19 The top half of the statement of financial position shows the assets of the company and the bottom half shows the equity and the liabilities. Equity means the shareholders' interest in the company (sometimes called ownership interest). As with Rainbow, this consists of share capital plus retained profits (here called retained earnings). Arc plc also has another source of finance: the long-term borrowings (possibly a bank loan) shown under non-current liabilities.

3.20 As before, the statement of financial position shows the position of the business at one point in time. The shareholders' investment in the company stands at £3,258m. This is represented by total assets of £6,358m less total liabilities of £3,100m.

4 *The profit and loss account*

4.1 Unlike the balance sheet, the profit and loss account summarises the trading activities of a business over a period of time, usually 12 months. Once again, for Rainbow Limited all figures are expressed in thousands of pounds (£000).

RAINBOW LIMITED
PROFIT AND LOSS ACCOUNT FOR THE YEAR ENDED 31 DECEMBER 20X6

	£000	£000
Sales		93,700
Cost of goods sold		35,300
Gross profit		58,400
Sales and distribution costs	11,200	
Administrative expenses	13,385	
		24,585
Operating profit		33,815
Interest payable		365
Profit for the financial year before tax		33,450
Taxation		12,500
Profit for the financial year after tax		20,950

4.2 The figure of £93,700,000 for sales (ie sales revenue, or turnover) relates to goods sold during the year, whether or not the cash was actually received during the year.

4.3 Having arrived at a figure for sales, one must deduct the cost of buying the goods sold. In this case the cost of goods sold (often called the **cost of sales**) is £35,300,000. This means that the gross profit – the difference between the sales value of the goods and their cost to Rainbow Limited – amounts to £58,400,000.

4.4 We have already calculated the company's gross profit as £58,400,000. We next deduct the various expenses incurred by the business, in this case grouped under the two headings of sales and distribution costs, and administration expenses. This leaves us with a figure for 'operating profit' of £33,815,000. Interest payable (often called finance costs or finance expenses) is then deducted to give 'profit for the financial year after tax'.

4.5 A company has to pay tax (known as corporation tax) on its profits. In this case the tax bill amounts to £12,500,000, leaving a profit after tax of £20,950,000.

4.6 The income statement for Arc plc, which prepares its financial statements under IFRS, is shown below. As you will see, this is very similar to the profit and loss account of Rainbow Limited.

ARC PLC
INCOME STATEMENT FOR THE YEAR ENDED 31 DECEMBER 20X6

	£m	£m
Revenue		4,200
Cost of sales		2,450
Gross profit		1,750
Distribution costs	90	
Administrative expenses	250	
Finance costs	75	
		415
Profit before tax		1,335
Income tax expense		510
Profit for the year		825
Earnings per share		41.2p

4.7 An important performance indicator is **earnings per share** (EPS). This measures the amount of profit generated in the year for the benefit of ordinary shareholders, divided by the number of ordinary shares in issue. Arc plc has earned 41.2p per ordinary share in the year 20X6.

The link between balance sheet and profit and loss account

4.8 A balance sheet is a 'snapshot' of the business at a particular point in time, while a profit and loss account shows the activities of the business in between balance sheet dates. Therefore the link between the financial accounting statements can be represented as in Figure 2.3.

4.9 Thus, the balance sheets are not merely isolated statements; they are linked over time by the profit (or loss) as analysed in the profit and loss account, plus movements of cash with the owners of the business (the shareholders).

4.10 We can illustrate this using the financial statements of Rainbow Limited. We have stated that Rainbow Limited has earned retained profits over the years of £10,490,000. Some of this will have arisen in the current year, while the remainder will have been accumulated and brought forward from earlier years. The movements in the company's retained profits are shown below. This information would be provided in notes to the main financial statements.

	£000
Retained profits brought forward	5,140
Profit for the financial year	20,950
	26,090
Dividends	15,600
Retained profit carried forward	10,490

4.11 Profit for the financial year is £20,950,000. This amount can theoretically be paid out to the shareholders, since all expenses have now been covered. In practice, the directors of the company have decided to retain some of the year's profit within the business, and the amount paid out to shareholders in the form of dividends is just £15,600,000. That leaves £5,350,000 that can be ploughed back into the business just from the current year's profits. Added to retained profits from previous years (£5,140,000) that means the company has a total figure of retained profits at 31 December 20X6 of £10,490,000. This ties in with the balance sheet presented earlier. The total amount of retained profits is sometimes known as the **profit and loss reserve**; later we mention some other reserves forming part of shareholders' funds in the balance sheet.

Figure 2.3 *The link between balance sheets and profit and loss account*

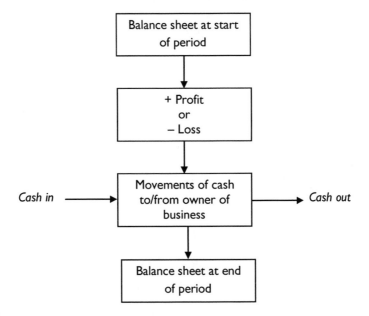

5   *Other financial statements*

The cashflow statement

5.1 We have already remarked on the fact that earning profits does not necessarily guarantee a healthy cash position. This is a limitation of the profit and loss account: a business showing a healthy profit may still be financially unstable if the cash position is weak.

5.2 To overcome this shortcoming in the profit and loss account, company accounts include a further statement: the cashflow statement. This is designed to identify the sources of cash coming into the business and the ways in which it has been spent. The statement ends by showing the overall cash surplus or deficit at the beginning of the year, during the year, and at the end of the year.

5.3 Here is an example.

SENTINI LIMITED
CASHFLOW STATEMENT FOR THE YEAR ENDED 31 DECEMBER 20X6

	£000	£000
Net cash flows from operating activities		540
Returns on investment and servicing of finance		
Interest paid		(28)
Taxation		
Corporation tax paid		(108)
Capital expenditure		
Payments to acquire tangible fixed assets	(90)	
Receipts from sales of tangible fixed assets	12	
Net cash outflow from capital expenditure		(78)
		326
Equity dividends paid		(66)
		260
Financing		
Issues of share capital	32	
Long-term loans repaid	(300)	
Net cash outflow from financing		(268)
Decrease in cash		(8)

Reconciliation of operating profit to net cash inflow

	£000
Operating profit	420
Depreciation charges	136
Increase in stocks	(4)
Increase in debtors	(18)
Increase in creditors	6
Net cash inflow from operating activities	540
Cash at beginning of the year	92
Cash at end of the year	84

5.4   What does this statement tell us about Sentini Limited?

5.5   Firstly, the company's ordinary operating activities – ie its day-to-day trading – is a healthy generator of cash. The first item in the statement tells us that operating activities during the year generated a cash surplus of £540,000. This figure would not be apparent from the profit and loss account, and to make a link between the two statements a note following the cashflow statement explains where the figure of £540,000 comes from.

5.6   The note states that the company's operating profit for the year was £420,000 (this is the link to the profit and loss account – this figure would appear as the profit for the year before interest). However, this understates the amount of cash generated from trading because the profit figure is presented after deduction of £136,000 in depreciation. Since this is not an actual cash outgoing, the true cash generated by operating activities is much greater than the profit and loss account reveals. (There are also some other, smaller, adjustments to the profit and loss account total, which do not concern us here.)

5.7   Next, the cashflow statement reveals three substantial cash outgoings: £28,000 has been spent on interest payments, £108,000 has been paid in taxation, and net expenditure on new fixed assets has amounted to £78,000. All of this reduces our cash surplus to £326,000.

5.8   Of this disposable surplus the company has elected to pay out £66,000 in the form of dividends to its shareholders, leaving a surplus of £260,000.

5.9   By issuing new share capital the company has raised further cash of £32,000, but this is more than offset by the company's repayment of a £300,000 long-term loan. Both of these are movements in the company's long-term capital funding, which is why they are shown together.

5.10   The net effect of all this is that over the year the company's cash position has worsened by £8,000 (from £92,000 in the black at the beginning of the year, to £84,000 in the black at the end of the year).

An IFRS cashflow statement

5.11   If Sentini were following IFRSs rather than UK regulations the statement of cashflows would appear as on the next page. At first sight it appears very different from the UK version, but it provides exactly the same information.

SENTINI LIMITED
STATEMENT OF CASHFLOWS FOR THE YEAR ENDED 31 DECEMBER 20X6

	£000	£000
Cashflows from operating activities		
Profit from operations		420
Adjustments for depreciation		136
		556
Increase in inventories		(4)
Increase in trade and other receivables		(18)
Increase in trade payables		6
Cash generated from operations		540
Interest paid		(28)
Tax paid		(108)
Net cash from operating activities		404
Cashflows from investing activities		
Purchase of property, plant and equipment	(90)	
Proceeds from sale of property, plant and equipment	12	
Net cash used in investing activities		(78)
Cashflows from financing activities		
Proceeds from issue of share capital	32	
Long-term loans repaid	(300)	
Dividends paid	(66)	
Net cash used in financing activities		(334)
Net decrease in cash		(8)
Cash at the beginning of the year		92
Cash at the end of the year		84

The five-year summary

5.12 One final statement that may be useful to buyers is the five-year statement of financial trends published by listed companies as part of their annual accounts. This is a round-up of key financial statistics from the current year and the four immediately preceding years.

5.13 The importance of this is that we can trace long-term trends in the business. (We look at this kind of analysis in more detail in the final chapter of this text.)

5.14 As an example, here is the five-year summary appearing in the 2005 accounts of Charles Stanley Group plc, an independently owned stockbrokers.

Five Year Summary

PROFIT AND LOSS ACCOUNT	2005	2004	2003	2002	2001
Turnover	78,021	68,164	51,064	54,613	70,443
Operating expenses	(71,773)	(62,701)	(51,058)	(48,919)	(56,153)
Operating profit	6,248	5,463	6	5,694	14,290
Profit/Loss on sale of investments	257	74	(50)	581	–
Income from fixed asset investment	438	–	–	–	–
Interest receivable	1,605	1,100	1,142	1,560	1,565
Interest payable	(118)	(55)	(120)	(123)	(384)
Profit on ordinary activities before taxation	8,430	6,582	978	7,712	15,471
Tax on profit on ordinary activities	(3,723)	(2,773)	(534)	(2,445)	(4,447)
Profit on ordinary activities after taxation	4,707	3,809	444	5,267	11,024
Minority interests	(9)	–	–	–	–
Profit attributable to shareholders	4,698	3,809	444	5,267	11,024
Dividends	(2,213)	(2,002)	(1,897)	(1,897)	(1,686)
Profit retained for the year	2,485	1,807	(1,453)	3,370	9,338
Earnings per share	11.15	9.04	1.05	12.50	26.55
Earnings per share diluted	10.66	8.64	1.02	12.26	26.19
Dividends per share	5.25	4.75	4.50	4.50	4.000
Operating profit	8.01%	8.01%	0.01%	10.43%	20.28%
Profit before tax	10.81%	9.67%	1.92%	14.12%	21.96%

BALANCE SHEET	2005	2004	2003	2002	2001
Fixed Assets					
Intangible	13,518	11,846	8,191	7,516	2,533
Tangible	5,995	5,493	5,227	6,212	6,814
Investments	4,787	3,670	2,732	3,987	3,667
	24,300	21,009	16,150	17,715	13,014
Current assets					
Debtors	232,055	171,489	178,896	144,120	173,914
Listed investments	1,108	908	322	152	624
Cash at bank and in hand	44,234	33,993	26,948	26,148	31,489
	277,397	206,390	206,166	170,420	206,027
Creditors within one year	(254,348)	(185,165)	(182,931)	(146,934)	(181,160)
Net current assets	23,049	21,225	23,235	23,486	24,867
Total assets less current liabilities	47,349	42,234	39,385	41,201	37,881
Creditors after one year	(1,679)	(1,418)	(1,155)	(277)	(1,402)
Minority interests	(203)	(244)	(44)	(44)	(44)
Net assets	45,467	40,572	38,186	40,880	36,435

Capital and reserves					
Called up share capital	10,538	10,537	10,537	10,537	10,537
Share premium account	3	–	–	–	–
Revaluation reserve	4,089	2,675	2,096	3,337	3,069
Profit and loss account	30,837	27,360	25,553	27,006	22,829
Equity shareholders' funds	45,467	40,572	38,186	40,880	36,435
Net asset value per share	107.87	96.26	90.60	96.99	86.44
Return on capital	18.54%	16.22%	2.56%	18.86%	42.46%

5.15 Notice that the summary includes key statistics from both profit and loss accounts and balance sheets, together with statistics that would not normally appear in either of these (eg at the bottom of the table, the percentage return on capital employed).

5.16 There are other items found in a company's financial statements such as a chairman's statement and notes to the accounts.

- The chairman's statement usually contains a narrative review of the company's performance and prospects.

- The operating and financial review (sometimes called a business review or a management commentary) explains the main risks and uncertainties facing the company and the main trends and factors likely to affect its future performance and position. It may also contain information about environmental matters, employees and social and community issues.

- The notes to the financial statements provide further detail and breakdown of amounts appearing in the main accounting statements. They also include a note of the company's accounting policies – the particular methods chosen by the company to compute accounting figures in areas where alternative valuations are permissible.

6 The legal framework of limited companies

Limited liability

6.1 In this section of the chapter we round up a few points concerning the legal framework which will help you to better understand the accounts of limited companies. We begin by explaining the concept of limited liability.

6.2 In the UK, and in many other developed economies, the predominant form of business enterprise is the limited company. That is why we have concentrated on the accounts of limited companies. The term 'limited' means that the liability of shareholders in the company is limited to the amount of capital they have invested. Thus, if a company's assets are insufficient to pay off its debts, the debts will remain unpaid: creditors are not allowed to call on the private assets of the shareholders.

6.3 This is an important legal difference between limited companies and sole traders. The law does not distinguish between the individual 'John Smith' and his unincorporated business 'John Smith Plumbing Services'. If John orders plumbing supplies for his business, and there is not enough cash in the business bank account to pay for them, he will be obliged to pay his supplier from his own personal bank account. The law forbids him from claiming that the debt belongs to the business and not to himself.

6.4   However, if John incorporates his business – ie converts it into a limited company 'John Smith Limited' or 'John Smith Plumbing Services Limited' – the situation is different. John Smith the individual, and John Smith Limited the company, are two different persons in law. John Smith the individual cannot be held responsible for debts incurred by John Smith Limited. This is a comfortable position for John, and a rather worrying one for suppliers granting credit to John Smith Limited.

6.5   Forming a limited company is very simple. It is sufficient to file certain documents with an official called the Registrar of Companies and to pay a modest fee. The Registrar then issues a certificate bearing the name of the new company and a unique company number. The company will be divided into 'shares' and these shares may be divided among several different owners, or may be held by a single person. If John Smith formed a company, he would probably hold all the shares himself, or perhaps allocate some of them to his wife, Joan.

6.6   John and Joan are now the shareholders (ie the owners) of John Smith Limited. They will already have set up a bank account in the name of the company and will have paid in a nominal amount to cover the price of the shares they hold. This money will form the initial capital of the company.

6.7   If the company now incurs debts (eg by purchasing goods on credit) its liability to pay those debts is unlimited. However, the assets it owns are of course not unlimited, and if there is a shortfall, so that the company assets are insufficient to pay the debts, the supplier will suffer the loss. John and Joan are not obliged to pay the debt out of their own resources: their liability is limited to the (usually very nominal) amount they paid to acquire their shares. This is what is meant by limited liability: although the company's liability for its debts is unlimited, that of its owners is limited.

6.8   John Smith Limited would be a very small company, and this illustrates the fact that size is not an essential (or even usual) difference between unincorporated and incorporated businesses.

6.9   In the case of John Smith Limited the owners of the business are also the managers. This is the usual situation in small companies. However, there is no reason in a limited company why this needs to be the case, and indeed in larger companies it never is the case. The shareholders in a large company take no part in the day-to-day running of the business. Instead, they appoint managers (called directors) to do this for them.

6.10   In principle, managers and shareholders are completely distinct. However, in practice it is sometimes found that the same people perform both roles, and this is particularly the case in very small businesses such as John Smith Limited. Such businesses are sometimes referred to as 'owner-managed companies'.

Public and private companies

6.11   Limited companies can be subdivided into private and public companies.

- In simplified terms, a public company is a company which must have a minimum share capital of £50,000. Such a company has a name ending with the letters plc (or the Welsh equivalent): these stand for 'public limited company'.

- A private company is a company that is not a public company. Private companies have names ending in the word 'Limited' or its abbreviation 'Ltd' (or the Welsh equivalents).

6.12 Some public companies have their shares 'listed' (or 'quoted') on the Stock Exchange. This means that investors may sell and purchase shares in the company through Stock Exchange dealers. Companies of this sort are called listed or quoted companies; they tend to be very large and to be owned by a large number of shareholders. Private companies are never listed, and even among public companies only a minority are listed.

Share capital

6.13 The way in which the assets of a company (fixed assets, stock, debtors and cash) are financed will vary from one company to another. Part of the finance may be provided by the owners of the company (referred to as shareholders, or sometimes as members of the company), while part may be provided by outsiders including trade creditors, banks and other lenders of funds.

6.14 Each share has a stated nominal (or par) value. For example, John Smith Limited may be divided into 100 shares, each with a par value of £1. When setting up John Smith Limited, John and Joan between them would have paid £100 into the company's bank account to acquire these shares. It is important to appreciate that the market value of a share (ie the amount which some future buyer might be prepared to pay John for a share) has no direct relationship to the nominal value.

6.15 The share capital of a company may be divided into various classes. In practice it is usually only larger companies which have different classes of share capital.

6.16 The most usual class of shares, as the name suggests, are **ordinary shares**. The normal rights of ordinary shareholders are to vote at company meetings and to receive dividends paid from the profits earned by the company. Ordinary shares are often referred to as **equity shares**.

6.17 Another common class of shares is **preference shares**. Preference shareholders are entitled to receive dividends, but only at a fixed percentage. This is different from the rights of ordinary shareholders, who are entitled to dividends without limit, except of course that the company cannot pay out more in dividends than it has earned in profits. Another difference between preference shares and ordinary shares is that preference shares do not usually carry voting rights, ie preference shareholders do not have the right to vote at company meetings. Nowadays preference shares are often regarded as a type of long-term liability.

6.18 Dividends are paid to shareholders, who are owners of the business. We discuss dividends in more detail later in this chapter.

6.19 A company may retain a proportion of its profits within the business. For example, the company may make a profit of £200,000 in a particular year, and may decide to pay dividends to shareholders of £120,000. The remainder of the profits – £80,000 – is retained. Over the years retained profits will accumulate and may form an important source of finance. Retained profits of a company are called **reserves**. They belong to the shareholders, and may be paid out as dividends whenever the company so decides.

6.20 The rights and advantages of the different classes of shares will be specified in the Articles of Association, which is one of the documents submitted to the Registrar when a company is being formed. The Articles contain the internal regulations of the company – in effect, its constitution.

Debentures (loan capital of a limited company)

6.21 A debenture is a term used to describe certain types of loan capital raised by a limited company. A debenture is a written acknowledgement of a loan, given under the company's seal. The loan carries a fixed rate of interest. Debentures may sometimes be called loan notes or loan stock.

6.22 A debenture may be a loan from one person. Debenture stock, on the other hand, rather like shares, may be held by a large number of individuals. The conditions and regulations are set out in a document called a **debenture trust deed**.

6.23 Debentures are not part of a company's share capital – they are a liability to 'outsiders'. Interest on a debenture loan must be paid just like any other liability of the company, even if the company is not making profits.

6.24 In many cases, though not always, a debenture loan will be **secured**. This means that the company assigns certain rights over its assets to the lender. If the company is unable to meet the interest payments as they fall due, or if the company cannot repay the loan, the lender may then take action such as selling the company assets in order to recover the amount owed.

The issue of shares

6.25 The terminology relating to share capital is somewhat confusing. You need to understand the following terms.

- **Authorised share capital** is the maximum amount of shares a company may issue. This is an amount specified in the company's Memorandum of Association, another of the documents submitted to the Registrar on registration. It may be changed later if the shareholders think it appropriate to do so. Companies registered after 1 October 2009 are no longer required to have an authorised share capital; they can simply issue new shares as needed.

- **Issued share capital** is the amount of shares that have actually been issued to shareholders. Not all of the authorised share capital need be in issue at a given moment.

- Only the issued share capital appears on a company's balance sheet in the section devoted to shareholders' capital. It is valued in the balance sheet at its nominal value, regardless of how much the shareholders actually paid to acquire it. (Strictly speaking the balance sheet figure is referred to as 'called up share capital', but you may ignore the distinction between issued and called up share capital.)

6.26 When a company issues shares it may do so at nominal value. In this case the shareholders are required to pay only the nominal value of the shares. This is the normal situation when a company is first being established.

6.27 However, a company may also issue shares at a premium, ie at a price above the shares' nominal value. For example, after trading successfully for some years John Smith's business might be worth much more than the nominal value of his shares. If he needs to raise new finance he might find a willing investor and issue 50 shares to him at a price of, say, £100 each, raising £5,000 for the company.

6.28 When this happens the company's share capital increases only by the nominal value of the new shares, namely £50. What happens to the other £4,950? Clearly this is an asset of the company – it boosts the bank balance. The £4,950 is called **share premium reserve**, which is included as part of shareholders' capital in the company's balance sheet.

6.29 Company law prohibits the issue of shares at a discount – in other words at a value less than their nominal value.

6.30 Another example of a reserve that may appear as part of shareholders' funds in a balance sheet is a **revaluation reserve**. This measures the amount by which tangible fixed assets (such as freehold premises) may have increased in value compared to their original value.

Rights issue

6.31 A rights issue is a relatively inexpensive method of raising further finance from existing shareholders. In a rights issue the company offers existing shareholders the right to buy new shares in proportion to their existing shareholding. For example, a '1-for-4' rights issue would mean that for each four shares held, an investor would have the right to buy one of the new shares being issued. The new shares are often offered at a price lower than the current market value, in order to make the offer attractive to shareholders.

6.32 Shareholders who do not wish to buy the shares can sell their rights to other potential investors. Thus the rights, as well as the shares themselves, have a market value.

Dividends

6.33 The amount of a dividend can be stated as a percentage based on the nominal value of the share or alternatively as an amount per share. For example, one may refer to a dividend of 8p per share. A holder of 2,000 shares would receive £160. If the shares have a nominal value of 50p one could alternatively describe the same dividend as a dividend of 16%.

6.34 Modern practice tends to state dividends on a pence per share basis and not as a percentage.

6.35 The directors of a company recommend the amount of dividend to be paid and this is usually ratified by the shareholders. Sometimes the total dividend for a year is paid in two instalments: an interim dividend during the year, and a final dividend once the final profit for the year is known.

Chapter summary

- Fixed assets will be used for a long time in the business, and typically cost a lot of money. Current assets will quickly be sold on to generate cash, or incorporated into products that will be sold on.

- Liabilities are sums of money owed by the business to outsiders, such as suppliers, lenders, or the government (for taxation).

- Income and expenditure are normally included in financial accounts in the period when they are earned/incurred, regardless of when the actual cash movement takes place. This is known as accruals accounting.

- There is an important distinction between profitability and good cashflow. Even a profitable organisation may be in danger if its cashflow is weak.

- A balance sheet is a statement of assets and liabilities at a point in time. A profit and loss account is a summary of income earned and expenditure incurred over a period of time.

- The working capital cycle shows how stock is sold to customers, who become debtors, whose balances are eventually converted into cash, which can be used to pay off creditors, who in turn supply more goods into stock.

- Gross profit is the difference between sales revenue and the cost of goods sold to customers. By deducting expenses, we arrive at net profit before tax. From this tax must be paid, leaving profits available to shareholders. Some of this will be paid out in the form of dividends; the balance will be retained in the business.

- The cashflow statement provides information on how cash was generated and what it was spent on during the period.

- The five-year summary is a good indicator of historical trends.

- Limited liability means that the liability of the shareholders is limited to the amounts they have contributed in share capital. The liability of a company for its own debts is unlimited.

- Major sources of finance for a limited company include share capital and debentures.

- Shareholders are rewarded for their investment by payments in the form of dividends.

Self-test questions

Numbers in brackets refer to the paragraphs where you can check your answers.

1   List examples of assets that a business might own, distinguishing between those that are fixed and those that are current. (Table 2.1, and 1.8)

2   What is meant by depreciation? (1.15)

3   What is a liability? (1.17)

4   Explain the basic principle of accruals accounting. (2.5)

5   Distinguish between capital expenditure and operating expenditure. (2.10, 2.11)

6   What is meant by saying that a balance sheet is a position statement? (3.2)

7   In what order are assets listed in a balance sheet? (3.8)

8   What is meant by gross profit? (4.3)

9   What is the primary purpose of the cashflow statement? (5.2)

10   What information is included in a five-year statement? (5.12)

11   Distinguish between shareholders and directors. (6.9)

12   Distinguish between ordinary shares and preference shares. (6.16, 6.17)

13   What is a debenture? (6.21)

14   What is a rights issue? (6.31)

CHAPTER 3

The Use of Statistics

Chapter learning objectives

2.2   Use descriptive and inferential statistics

- Definitions
- How and when to use them
- Assess the outcomes of analysis

Chapter headings

1   Tabular and diagrammatic presentation

2   Averages and measures of dispersion

3   Index numbers

4   Rules of probability

5   Probability distributions

6   Statistical sampling

Introduction

The statistical methods you are required to study are grouped under two headings: descriptive statistics and inferential statistics.

Broadly speaking, the distinction is as follows.

- **Descriptive statistics** means the presentation of statistical information in an understandable form. This is covered in Sections 1 and 2 of this chapter.

- **Inferential statistics** refers to methods of analysing statistical data so that we can draw conclusions relevant to the problem under investigation. Aspects of inferential statistics are covered in Sections 3–5 of this chapter.

Naturally, much of this material has a mathematical flavour, which some students will find intimidating. Before being deterred by this, however, there are two things you should bear in mind.

- Personal computers, using off-the-shelf or bespoke software programs, handle virtually all of the calculations. Rarely (or never) will a buyer have to carry out a statistical analysis by hand. Even the presentation of information by means of charts, graphs and other diagrammatic techniques is primarily the task of a computer.

- The emphasis of the syllabus is primarily on the interpretation of results presented by others, not on the generation of statistical analysis by the exam candidate himself.

1 Tabular and diagrammatic presentation

1.1 Descriptive statistics is a highly relevant area from the buyer's perspective. Typically, a buyer is swamped with information: production schedules, financial data relating to the purchasing department, details of suppliers' products and prices, general economic trends, and much more. He needs to be aware of methods for improving the presentation of such information for his own use, and also to be aware of features and shortcomings in the presentation he observes in trade journals, course handouts, internal documents, and other sources.

1.2 In this first section of the chapter we look at such methods. We then continue in Section 2 of the chapter by looking at averages and measures of dispersion. These too can be considered as aspects of descriptive statistics, though it is worth noting that the boundary with inferential statistics is by no means definite. For example, we regularly use averages in such forecasting techniques as exponential smoothing, and measures of dispersion in such decision making techniques as statistical process control. Once we reach Sections 3–5 we are definitely dealing with inferential statistics.

Pros and cons of tables and diagrams

1.3 There are several advantages of presenting a mass of data in tabular form. The figures can easily be located, comparisons between classes can be made at a glance, patterns of figures are highlighted and tables are easily understood by non-statisticians.

1.4 However, charts, diagrams and graphs are more popular ways of displaying data simply. Such visual representation of facts plays an important part in everyday life since diagrams can be seen daily in newspapers, advertisements and on television. These can be misleading and give entirely the wrong impression. It is, therefore, important to adhere to certain basic principles of construction.

(a) **Simplicity**: the material must be classified and detail kept to a minimum.

(b) **Title**: the diagram must have a comprehensive and self-explanatory title.

(c) **Source**: the source of the material used in drawing up the diagram should always be stated (usually by way of a footnote).

(d) **Units**: the units of measurement used must be stated. This can be done in the title, to keep the number of figures to a minimum.

(e) **Headings**: all headings should be concise and unambiguous.

1.5 If these principles are followed then a diagram will have several advantages over a table, as follows.

(a) It is easier to understand than the mass of figures from a table.

(b) Relationships between figures are shown more clearly.

(c) A quick, lasting and accurate impression is given of the significant and pertinent facts.

1.6 When information is of a quantitative form, it is often represented by a **bar chart**. Bars of equal width, either vertical or horizontal, are constructed with their lengths proportional to the value of the variable. Figure 3.1 represents the production of wheat in the UK for the years 20X1 to 20X3.

Figure 3.1 *Wheat production UK, 20X1–X3*

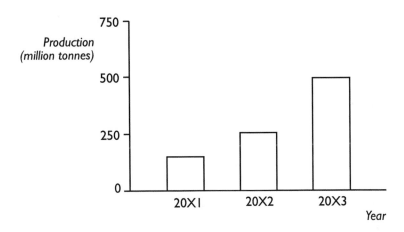

Source: government statistics

1.7 **Pie charts** are usually drawn when the **proportion** of each class to the whole is important rather than the absolute value of each class. A circle is drawn, and divided into sectors such that the area of each sector is proportionate to the size of the figure represented. Figure 3.2 represents the proportion of each type of grain produced in Disney Land in the year 20X5.

Figure 3.2 *Grain production, Disney Land, 20X5*

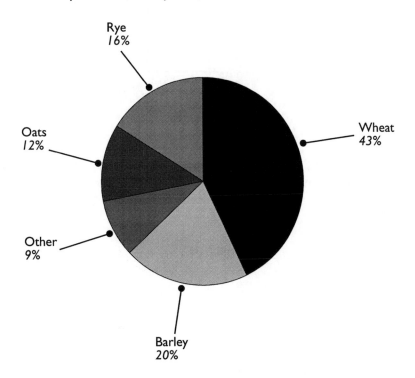

1.8 A **histogram** is a special form of bar chart that is used to represent data given in the form of a grouped frequency distribution, such as that in Table 3.1.

Table 3.1 *Distribution of ages in a sample*

Class interval Age (years)	Range of class	Frequency No of people
11 and less than 16	5	9
16 and less than 21	5	17
21 and less than 26	5	22
26 and less than 31	5	18
31 and less than 36	5	10

1.9 The standard width of a class interval in this example is five years.

Figure 3.3 *Histogram with equal class intervals*

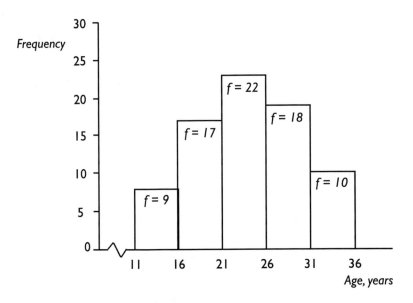

Source: Table 3.1

1.10 If the mid-points of the tops of the rectangles in the histogram are joined by straight lines, the figure is known as a **frequency polygon**. The lines at each end of the diagram must be taken to the base line at the centres of the adjoining corresponding class intervals. This is because these two class intervals have, in effect, a zero frequency since they contain no items. Figure 3.4 is a frequency polygon based on the data in Table 3.1.

Figure 3.4 *Frequency polygon*

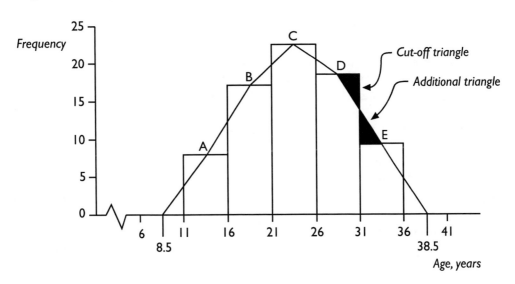

Source: Table 3.1

1.11 Information about two variables that are considered to be related in some way can be plotted on a **scatter diagram**, each axis representing one variable. For example, the amount of rainfall and the crop yield per acre could be plotted against each other, or the level of advertising expenditure against sales revenue of a product.

1.12 The values of the two variables are plotted together so that the diagram consists of a number of points. The way in which these are scattered or dispersed indicates whether any link is likely to exist between the variables. This is illustrated below. In this case there appears to be a positive correlation between the two variables; roughly speaking, higher advertising expenditure appears to lead to higher sales revenue.

Figure 3.5 *A scatter diagram*

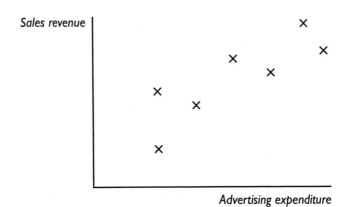

2   *Averages and measures of dispersion*

Introduction

2.1   One of the major objectives of statistics is to summarise unwieldy masses of data in such a way that their important features become apparent. One technique is to represent and summarise data in terms of its mid-values by using **measures of central location**. In speech we usually refer to these as **averages**. There are several ways of defining the midpoint of a dataset, and each has its advantages and disadvantages.

2.2   However, by itself the midpoint may not convey a good picture of the distribution. The values in a distribution may be clustered closely together around the midpoint, or they may range widely. This aspect of a distribution is called its **spread** or **dispersion**. We review various statistics used to summarise how widely spread are the individual values of a distribution. Using a measure of average together with a measure of dispersion – in particular a combination of the mean and standard deviation – provides us with a powerful predictive tool.

Averages

2.3   We will look at three ways of representing the mid-value, or average, of a set of data: the arithmetic mean, the median, and the mode.

2.4   The **arithmetic mean** is the best known type of average. It is defined as the total **value** of the items divided by the total **number** of items. Assuming a set of data consists of n items, x_1, x_2, ... x_n, then the arithmetic mean (denoted by $\overline{x}$) is given by the formula:

$$\overline{x} = \frac{x_1 + x_2 + x_3 + ... + x_n}{n}$$

2.5   For example, the arithmetic mean of 3, 6, 10, 14, 17, 19 and 22 is calculated as follows:

$$\overline{x} = \frac{3 + 6 + 10 + 14 + 17 + 19 + 22}{7} = \frac{91}{7} = 13$$

2.6   Below are summarised the advantages and disadvantages of the mean as a measure of central location.

Advantages

(a)   It is easy to understand and calculate.

(b)   All the data in the distribution is used, and so it can be determined with arithmetical precision, and is representative of the whole set of data.

(c)   It can be calculated when nothing more than the total value or quantity of items and the number of items are known.

(d)   It can be used in more advanced mathematical statistics.

Disadvantages

(a)   It may give undue weight to or be influenced by extreme items, ie high or low values. For example, the mean life of a sample of 100 electric light bulbs might be 2,000 hours, but it would only require one additional 'dud' bulb with a life of zero to reduce the mean to 1,980 hours, a drop of 20 hours.

(b)   The value of the average may not correspond to any item in the distribution. For example, the average number of children per family is approximately 1.8, but there is no family with that number of children.

2.7   The **median** is the value of the **middle item** in a distribution **once all the items have been arranged in order of magnitude**. Once the items have been arranged in order, starting with either the largest or smallest, then:

(a)   if the number of items is odd, the median is simply the value of the middle item

(b)   however, if the number of items is even, the median is the arithmetic mean of the two middle items.

2.8   For example, the set of values 3, 6, 10, 14, 17, 19 and 22 has seven members. The median is 14 since this is the value of the middle item (the items having been arranged in order of size). If another value is added to the set, say 25, it now has eight values. There is thus no one middle value. In these circumstances the median is not any value found in the dataset; it is the arithmetic mean of the two 'middle values'. Therefore:

$$\text{Median} = \frac{14+17}{2} = 15.5$$

2.9   Below are summarised the advantages and disadvantages of the median as a measure of location.

Advantages

(a)   It is simple to understand.

(b)   It is not affected by extreme values of the variable. For example, changing the last item from 22 to, say, 50 would have no effect on the median.

(c)   It can be obtained even when the values of the extreme items are not known. It is unaffected by unequal class intervals or open-ended classes.

(d)   It may be the value of an actual item in the distribution.

Disadvantages

(a)   If there are only a few items, it may not be truly representative.

(b)   It is unsuitable for use in mathematical statistics.

(c)   Data has to be arranged in order of size which is a tedious operation.

2.10   The **mode** is the value that occurs most frequently among all the items in the distribution. The mode can usually be determined by observation and no real calculation is necessary. However, it is possible for a distribution to have more than one mode or, indeed, no mode at all.

2.11 For example, eleven boys were asked what size shoes they were wearing. The following distribution resulted:

5, 7 ½ , 6, 6, 7, 5 ½ , 6, 5, 6, 5, 5

2.12 5 ½ , 7 and 7 ½ occur once, 5 occurs four times and 6 occurs four times. The modal values are therefore 5 and 6.

2.13 Below are summarised the advantages and disadvantages of the mode as a measure of location.

Advantages

(a)   It is easy to understand.

(b)   It is not affected by extreme values.

(c)   It can be calculated even if not all the values in the distribution are known.

(d)   It may be the value of an actual item in the distribution.

Disadvantages

(a)   There may be no modal value or more than one may exist.

(b)   Data has to be arranged to ascertain which value occurs most frequently and this can be tedious.

(c)   It is not suitable for mathematical statistics.

Measures of dispersion

2.14 There are three commonly used measures of dispersion that can be calculated for a set of data. They are: the range; the quartile deviation; the standard deviation.

2.15 Each is a different method of choosing a single number to measure the spread of the items. Of these, the standard deviation is by far the most important, but is the most complicated. The first two, however, are very useful for presenting information to non-statisticians.

2.16 The **range** is by far the simplest measure of dispersion, being the difference between the extreme values of the distribution. The calculation of the range is very straightforward:

Range = highest value – lowest value

2.17 For example, the range of values 3, 5, 8, 11 and 13 is simply 10, since the highest and lowest values are 13 and 3 respectively, and 13 – 3 = 10.

2.18 Since this measure yields no information about the dispersion of items lying in the interval between the highest and lowest values, it is of very little practical use except in elementary quality control, where a measure is required that can be calculated very quickly.

Advantages

(a)   It is very simple and quick to calculate.

(b)   It is very simple to understand.

(c)   It is used as a measure of dispersion in quality control work, where rapid results are essential.

Disadvantages

(a)   It can be very misleading if the data contains one extremely high or low value.

(b)   Only two values are used from the distribution, and it is not therefore representative of the whole data.

(c)   It cannot be used precisely in mathematical statistics.

2.19   The median divides a distribution into two equal parts since it is the value of the middle item. Similarly, the **quartiles** divide the distribution into four equal parts. Once the data has been arranged in order of magnitude, the lower quartile (Q_1) is the value at one-quarter of the total frequency and the upper quartile (Q_3) is the value at the three-quarters mark.

2.20   The **quartile deviation** (also called the **semi-interquartile range**) is half the difference between the upper and lower quartiles. Note that there are only three quartiles, Q_1, Q_2 and Q_3, the middle one (Q_2) being the median.

2.21   If the data consists of **n** items, the quartile deviation is calculated as follows.

Q_1 is the value of the $\frac{1}{4}$ **(n + 1)**th item

Q_3 is the value of the $\frac{3}{4}$ **(n + 1)**th item

Quartile deviation $= (Q_3 - Q_1) \div 2$

2.22   Below are summarised the advantages and disadvantages of the quartile deviation as a measure of spread.

Advantages

(a)   It is simple to understand.

(b)   It is not affected by extreme values.

(c)   It can be obtained even when the values of the extreme items are not known.

Disadvantages

(a)   It does not take all the values into account.

(b)   Data may have to be arranged in order of size.

(c)   It cannot be used in mathematical statistics.

2.23 The **standard deviation** is the most valuable and widely used measure of dispersion. However, it is also the most complex to calculate and the most difficult to understand. In essence, it is calculating the average distance of items from their mean. So, if all the items in a distribution are clustered closely around the mean (arithmetic average), their average distance from the mean, and so standard deviation, is small. Conversely, if the individual values are well spread, their average distance from the mean, and standard deviation, is large.

2.24 Below are summarised the advantages and disadvantages of the standard deviation as a measure of dispersion.

Advantages

(a) It is the most commonly used measure of dispersion in statistical work.

(b) The value of every item of data is used.

(c) It is the only measure that can be used in mathematical statistics.

Disadvantages

(a) The calculation is complex.

(b) It is difficult for the layman to understand.

(c) It can give more than a proportional weight to extreme values because of squaring the deviations.

3 Index numbers

Introduction

3.1 Index numbers are a quantitative technique used so much in every day life that we tend to overlook them altogether. Every reader in the UK will have come across the Retail Price Index (RPI), which is a prime example.

3.2 The technique for constructing index numbers – indexing – compares the value of a property of an item (or group of items) over a period of time, normally a number of years. It standardises any movement in the property over that period by expressing it as a percentage of some earlier year, a base year. The most commonly constructed indices are price indices, of which the RPI is one. But the technique is equally applicable to other properties, such as quantity.

Price and quantity percentage relatives

3.3 These are also called 'percentage relatives' and are based on a single item. There are two types.

- Price relatives
- Quantity relatives

3.4   The formulae for calculating them are as follows.

Simple price or price relative index: $\dfrac{p_1}{p_0} \times 100$

Simple quantity or quantity relative index: $\dfrac{q_1}{q_0} \times 100$

where p_0 is the price at time 0 (eg now); p_1 is the price at time 1 (eg one month or one year from now); q_0 is the quantity at time 0; q_1 is the quantity at time 1.

3.5   For example, if a commodity costs £2.60 in 20X4 and £3.68 in 20X5, calculate the simple price index for 20X5, using 20X4 as base year (ie time 0).

3.6   Simple price index:

$$\frac{p_1}{p_0} \times 100 = \frac{3.68}{2.60} \times 100 = 141.5$$

This means that the price has increased by 41.5 per cent of its base-year value, ie its 20X4 value.

3.7   Some care must be taken in deciding which year to use as the base year. In particular, it must not be a year in which any dramatic changes took place in the variable being considered. For example, you would not use the year in which there was a miners' strike as the base for an index on coal production. Additionally it is usual to bring forward the base year from time to time so that comparisons with the base year continue to be relevant.

3.8   Usually, an index number is required to show the variation in a number of items at once rather than just one as in the examples above. The Retail Price Index (RPI) is such an index and consists of a list of items as diverse as the price of bread, the cost of car repairs and cinema tickets. By using appropriate weights, price relatives can be combined to give a multi-item price index.

Limitations of indices for the purchasing professional

3.9   Many purchasing professionals find indices less than helpful because they are too general, ie they do not relate closely enough to the area of their particular interest. They can also present problems as a basis for forecasting future events, since they are historical data only. However, in conjunction with other forms of forecasting they can add useful weight to a decision.

3.10   In his comments on the November 2009 exam, the Senior Assessor outlined some specific limitations of indices. To some extent they are arbitrary (eg how do we choose a base year?) Often they relate to a group of items, in which case we must pay careful attention to the weighting given to each. They may not be sufficiently specific to the item being purchased.

3.11 This last point is particularly relevant in the case of items subject to price volatility (eg commodities). The idea of an index is to measure steady variation over time, but the determinants of a commodity's price may be too volatile for this. Often, the price movements are related to geo-political considerations which cannot be captured in a price index.

Cost-of-living indices

3.12 **Cost-of-living indices** are used to measure changes in the prices of goods and services. They exist in most countries and are widely used in negotiations about wages and pensions. They also enable governments to monitor to some extent the success of their anti-inflation policies.

3.13 In Britain, the Retail Price Index (RPI) measures the changes in the prices of some 600 goods and services which are intended to be as representative as possible of what the typical household in Britain spends its money on. The information necessary to decide which items to include and how to weight them is obtained from an extensive Government survey called the Family Expenditure Survey. The prices are obtained from a representative sample of retail outlets in all parts of the country.

Calculations using the RPI

3.14 If the RPI rises from 349 to 387, by what percentage must an index linked pension be increased?

Solution. The RPI has increased by 387 − 349 = 38 points. As a percentage, this is an increase of $100 \times {}^{38}\!/_{349}$ = 10.9 per cent. This is the percentage by which the pension must be increased.

Other indices in use

3.15 While the RPI is of use in many ways, there are a great many other indices that can be useful in specific contexts. *Supply Management* regularly lists different indices, especially in relation to production. Every night on the news you will here reference to the 'Footsie' – actually the FTSE-100, which is an index of the prices of the UK's top 100 shares (there are many other, more extensive, stock market indices, which you will find in the *Financial Times*). Finally if you visit the government's National Statistics Online website (www.statistics.gov.uk) you will find plenty more consumer indices listed under 'Consumer Price Indices' (CPI).

4 *Rules of probability*

Introduction

4.1 The general concept of probability is an everyday one and is used regularly by everyone; we speak in general terms of whether it is **likely** to rain today and how **unlikely** we are to win the lottery. We even use an approximate scale of measurement in everyday speech, describing our estimates with expressions such as unlikely, likely and very likely.

4.2   Our objective now is to refine the usual descriptions into something more accurate with a numerical scale of measurement. By convention the measurement scale ranges from 0 (impossibility) to 1 (certainty). The purpose of wishing to refine our ideas on probability is so that we can take business decisions for which there are numerical raw data on the basis of a calculated risk rather than pure guesswork.

The 'classical' definition of probability

4.3   If there are **m** equally likely outcomes to a trial, **n** of which result in a given outcome, then the probability of that outcome is n/m. For example, if an unbiased die is thrown in an unbiased way, each of the scores 1 to 6 is equally likely. Three of these scores would result in an even number (2, 4 or 6), hence the probability of scoring an even number is $\frac{3}{6}$ or $\frac{1}{2}$.

4.4   One of the main applications of probability theory is in the interpretation of results from random samples. As, by definition, all members of the population are equally likely to be included in a random sample, the above definition of probability is applicable to random sampling theory, and is the one that will be used here.

Measurement of probability

4.5   Probability is measured on a scale from 0 to 1, where 0 represents impossibility and 1 represents certainty.

Figure 3.6 *The scale of probability*

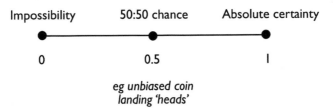

4.6   When an unbiased die is thrown, each of the numbers 1 to 6 has an equal chance of falling uppermost. Using this information, the following will be calculated; the probability that the outcome of a single throw is:

Example

(a)   the number 4;

(b)   an even number;

(c)   a number less than 3;

(d)   a number greater than 6; and

(e)   a number less than 7.

When an unbiased die is thrown, there are six equally likely outcomes: 1, 2, 3, 4, 5, 6.

4.7   For each answer, (a) to (e) above, the number of 'favourable' outcomes must be determined, and this is expressed as a proportion of the total number of possible outcomes. The probability of event 'A' occurring is represented by the symbol P(A) (some authors use Pr(A)).

(a)   P(number 4): P(4) = $\frac{1}{6}$, because one of the six possible outcomes is the number 4.

(b)   P(even) = $\frac{3}{6}$ (or $\frac{1}{2}$), because three of the six outcomes are even numbers (2, 4 and 6).

(c)   P(a number less than 3): P(<3) = $\frac{2}{6}$ (or $\frac{1}{3}$), because two of the six outcomes are less than 3, ie 1 and 2.

(d)   P(a number greater than 6): P(>6) = $\frac{0}{6}$ (or 0), because none of the six outcomes is greater than 6. This is an impossible situation.

(e)   P(a number less than 7): P(<7) = $\frac{6}{6}$ (or 1), because all six outcomes are less than 7. It is therefore certain that the result will be a number less than 7.

Mutually exclusive events

4.8   Two or more events are said to be mutually exclusive if the occurrence of any one of them precludes the occurrences of all the others, ie only one can happen. For example, when a die is thrown once, it can only show one score. If that score is 6 (say), then all the other possible outcomes (1, 2, 3, 4 or 5) will not have occurred. Hence the six possible outcomes are all mutually exclusive. On the other hand, the outcomes 'score 6', and 'score an even number' are not mutually exclusive because both outcomes could result from one throw.

4.9   Mutually exclusive events may be described in symbols as:

P (A and B) = 0

4.10   If A and B are two mutually exclusive events, then the probability that either A or B occurs in a given experiment is equal to the sum of the separate probabilities of A and B occurring, ie you add the two together:

P (A or B) = P (A) + P (B)

4.11   This rule can cover any number of events, as long as they are mutually exclusive:

P (A or B or C or D or ...) = P (A) + P (B) + P (C) + P (D) +...

Independent events

4.12   Two or more events are said to be independent if the occurrence or non-occurrence of one event does not affect the occurrence or non-occurrence of the other. For example, consider the events:

A   'I will be successful in the examination.'

B   'I will undergo a course of study for the examination.'

C   'I have blue eyes.'

4.13   We assume that A will have a higher probability if B occurs than if it does not. A is therefore dependent on B. But the colour of one's eyes has no known effect on the ability to pass examinations or *vice versa*, hence A and C are independent.

4.14   If any two events, A and B, are independent, then the probability of both A and B occurring is the product of the separate probabilities.

P (A and B) = P (A) × P (B)

Example

4.15   A case contains twelve valves of which four are defective and the rest are non-defective. The probability of drawing two non-defective valves, the first valve being replaced before the second one is selected, is calculated as follows.

4.16   Since four are defective then the remaining eight must be non-defective. So P(defective) = $\frac{4}{12}$, P(non-defective) = $\frac{8}{12}$

P(valve 1 non-defective) = $\frac{8}{12}$ = $\frac{2}{3}$; P(valve 2 non-defective) = $\frac{8}{12}$ = $\frac{2}{3}$
P(valves 1 and 2 non-defective) = P(valve 1 non-defective) × P(valve 2 non-defective)
= $\frac{2}{3}$ × $\frac{2}{3}$ = $\frac{4}{9}$ (or 0.44)

Expected values

4.17   Where there is more than one possible outcome, each with a probability attached, the expected monetary value (EMV) of the outcome (E(**x**)) will be the sum of the expected values of the individual possible outcomes.

4.18   This general formula may be simplified in the case of a single outcome. If the probability of winning £**x** is **p** then the expected value is £**px**. As with much of probability work, the principle is most easily seen through examples.

Example

4.19   A company plans to introduce a new product to the market. There is a 0.4 probability that the profit from the product will be £1m and a 0.6 probability that the profit will be £2m. What is the expected monetary value of the product?

	£
Probability of £1m = 0.4. Expected value = £1m × 0.4 =	400,000
Probability of £2m = 0.6. Expected value = £2m × 0.6 =	1,200,000
Expected monetary value of product	1,600,000

4.20   Going back to the general formula, one can see that the numerical calculation has used the formula by taking each probability in turn (first 0.4, then 0.6), multiplied it by the value associated with that probability (first £1million, then £2million), and then added the two results together.

4.21   You can see that there are no circumstances in which the new product will earn a profit of £1.6 million (it will earn either £1 million or £2 million), so what is the meaning of the 'expected monetary value'? It is not the expected outcome of any one event; rather it is the average outcome, based on many trials.

5   *Probability distributions*

Introduction

5.1   In this section our concern is to introduce three of the main, highly practical statistical distributions.

5.2   The first two, the binomial and Poisson distributions, have a common theme; their application is in problems that can be described in terms of something happening or not (success or failure). The **binomial distribution** is concerned with discrete events, such as the inspection of manufacturing output during a quality control procedure. It is accepted (success) or rejected (failure).

5.3   The **Poisson distribution** is linked to the binomial. It deals with events that occur within a continuous stream rather than as discrete success/failure occurrences. So, for example, it is applied in looking at the distribution of emergency telephone calls to the emergency services (the events being the calls, the continuous stream being time).

5.4   Of all the distributions, the **normal distribution** is probably the most widely used in practice. Unlike the binomial and Poisson distributions, which deal with events happening or not happening, the normal distribution is concerned with ranges of possibilities and how likely an event is to occur.

The binomial distribution

5.5   The binomial distribution applies to the situation where the items under investigation are classified as either possessing or not possessing a given attribute. Typical examples are as follows.

(a)   Quality control – items are either defective or non-defective.

(b)   Public opinion polls – electors are either for or against a given candidate or party.

(c)   Consumer research – households buying or not buying a particular brand of product.

5.6   Samples are often taken from populations split in this way to estimate the proportion of the population possessing or not possessing the attribute. If, as is usually the case, the population is so large compared with the sample that the taking of the sample leaves the population virtually unchanged in composition, the composition of the sample is described by a binomial distribution.

Features of the binomial distribution

5.7   An event can have only two recognisable outcomes (eg success and failure or possessing and not possessing an attribute). Examples include:

(i)   In tossing a coin, the outcomes, are 'heads' and 'tails'.

(ii)   In rolling a die, the outcomes could be 'a 6' and 'not a 6'.

(iii)   In a consumer research survey the outcomes could be, 'prefer product X' and 'do not prefer product X'.

5.8   The values of **p** and **q** can be calculated, eg for the examples above:

   (i)   If the coin is fair, $p = \frac{1}{2}$; $q = 1 - \frac{1}{2} = \frac{1}{2}$.

   (ii)   If the die is unbiased, $p = \frac{1}{6}$; $q = 1 - \frac{1}{6} = \frac{5}{6}$.

   (iii)   I household in 10 prefers product X, $\therefore p = \frac{1}{10}$; $q = 1 - \frac{1}{10} = \frac{9}{10}$.

5.9   The distribution is applicable to discrete variables, ie the number of items in the sample can be 0, 1, 2, ... but not 1.247 or any other fraction.

Applications of the binomial distribution

5.10   The binomial distribution can be used to solve problems similar to the following example.

5.11   In the manufacture of 'tweeters' by a certain process, it was found that 8 per cent were rejected. We might be interested in the probability that, in n boxes, a box of ten tweeters contained:

   (a)   exactly two rejects (the probability of two failures); and

   (b)   not more than two rejects (the probability of two failures or **fewer**).

5.12   You will not be expected to do the mathematics in a problem such as this, but it can be calculated that the chance of finding exactly two rejects is 0.148 (ie 14.8 per cent), while the chance of finding not more than two rejects is 0.96 (ie 96 per cent).

5.13   In practice, if you wish to calculate probabilities for a binomial distribution you would invariably use a computerised statistical package.

The Poisson distribution

5.14   A given length of chain consists of a discrete number of links, each of which can be either defective or non-defective. The probability of a given number of links being defective is obtained from a binomial distribution.

5.15   Now imagine that the links in this chain are made smaller and smaller, the number of links being correspondingly increased to preserve the same total length of chain. In the limit, when the links become infinitesimally small, the chain becomes a continuous length of cable or wire. It is still possible for this cable to have defects, but it no longer makes sense to talk about the number of non-defects because the continuous nature of the cable means this number is, in effect, infinite.

5.16   Similarly, if, in the binomial distribution, the value of **n** is increased and the value of **p** decreased, in the limit, as **n** approaches infinity and **p** approaches zero, the binomial distribution approaches the Poisson distribution. The Poisson distribution (named after a French mathematician) therefore describes the probability of discrete events (eg defects) occurring in a continuous medium (eg the length of cable). Another example would be the number of cars passing a census point in a given length of time. The number of cars is discrete, but time is continuous.

Applications of the Poisson distribution

5.17　The principal use of the Poisson distribution occurs where a series of rare events occur at independent random times – eg earthquakes, telephone calls, radioactive emissions, etc. If the observed frequencies follow a Poisson distribution, then it is a strong indication that the events are occurring randomly.

5.18　To identify a problem as requiring a Poisson approach it should either have a very small probability (**p**) of an event occurring in a single test and a very large number of tests (**n**) for that event.

The normal distribution

5.19　The binomial distribution is a discrete probability distribution. The values it can take are all integers. We now wish to consider how to solve problems involving continuous variables, for example: 'if the length of metal bars is normally distributed, calculate the probability that a metal bar is between 2.63 and 2.74 cm long'. The **normal distribution** can be used to answer such questions as this.

5.20　When continuous data has been collected and a frequency distribution formed, it is often shown diagrammatically in a histogram, where the total frequency of the distribution is represented by the total area of the rectangles. When **comparing** histograms based on different sample sizes it is necessary to make the total area of each diagram the same or comparison is impossible. This is quite simply achieved by letting the area of each rectangle be equal to the **relative frequency** rather than the **absolute frequency** of the class.

5.21　A particular type of histogram that is commonly met is the bell-shaped diagram, ie the highest column is in the centre of the histogram with decreasing columns spread symmetrically on either side of this peak. If the class intervals are very small, the histogram (Figure 3.7) becomes a frequency curve (Figure 3.8).

Figure 3.7 *Bell-shaped histogram*

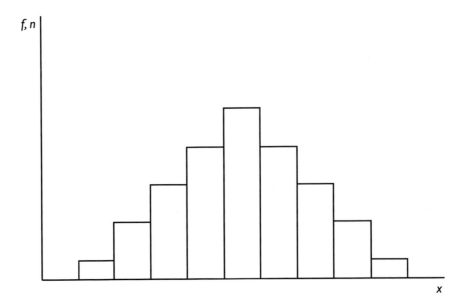

Figure 3.8 *Bell curve*

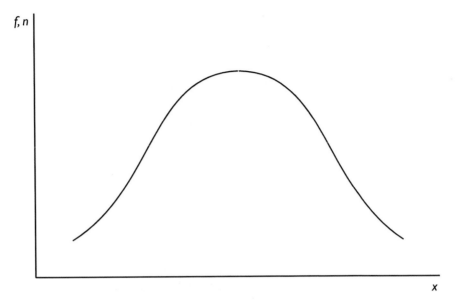

It is mathematically convenient to fix the total area under a histogram as one unit of area.

5.22 Since the area of the original histogram was one unit, the area under the curve will also be equal to unity. The **normal distribution curve** is a theoretical relative frequency curve which has a shape as in Figure 3.8. Its actual shape can be defined mathematically, and therefore the area under any particular part of the curve can be computed, albeit with some difficulty.

Mathematical formula

5.23 Since the total area under the curve is one unit, the probability that a value of the variable lies between certain limits will be the corresponding proportion of the total area.

Figure 3.9 *Bell curve*

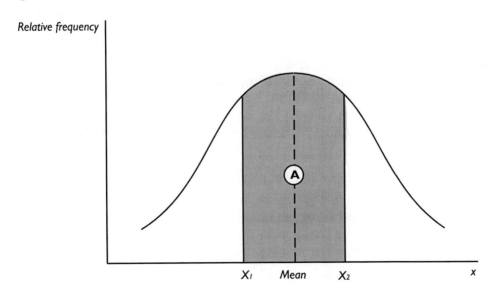

5.24 So the probability that x lies between X_1 and X_2 is the area A (shaded), or

$$P(X_1 < x < X_2) = A$$

This area can be found by using normal distribution tables, or a computerised package.

5.25 First, though, it is necessary to know the mean (μ) and the standard deviation (σ) of the distribution being studied. Knowing these, the values (X_1 and X_2) of the variable can be standardised, ie they can be expressed in terms of the number of standard deviations by which they differ from the mean.

Application of the normal distribution

5.26 As an example, suppose that the curve in Figure 3.9 represents the variability in a supplier's production process for a steel rod that we are interested in buying. We wish to buy rods with a diameter of 80mm, and we can tolerate a 2mm variance in either direction. The supplier finds that his production process outputs rods with varying diameters, the mean being 80mm, and the standard deviation being 1.5mm. How likely is it that the rods output from this process are within our tolerances?

5.27 In terms of Figure 3.9, we are interested in the range from X_1 = 78mm to X_2 = 82mm. As usual, we would normally do the analysis by means of computer, but it is also possible to use printed tables. By reference to such tables it is easy to establish that approximately 82% of the manufacturer's output will fall within our tolerance. We must use this information to discuss with the supplier how he can achieve improvements.

6 Statistical sampling

The meaning of sampling

6.1 Statistical sampling is an easily understood concept. In many cases, the total 'population' we are interested in may be vast. It would be impractical to examine every member of the population individually. Instead, we may select a carefully structured sample for testing. Provided our sample is representative, statistical techniques then enable us to draw conclusions about the wider population. (In sampling, the 'population' does not necessarily refer to people. It means the entire collection of all the items we are interested in.)

6.2 As an example, we may be interested in the likelihood of a new product being regarded favourably in the consumer market. Clearly we cannot approach every individual in the world, or even in the UK, to ask them their reaction to our new product. But we can carry out market research among a sample of consumers and from the results we can estimate the future popularity of the product nationwide or even worldwide.

6.3 We used the term 'carefully structured sample' earlier on. This reflects the fact that selecting a sample is itself a statistical technique. The sample must be of sufficient size; otherwise, it is not valid to draw statistical conclusions from the results. And similarly the sample must be representative of the wider population. For example, it might not be valid to select a sample of consumers from a particular geographical region, because that region might not be typical of the entire country in its reaction to our proposed new product.

6.4 Other possible applications of sampling are as follows (the list could be extended indefinitely).

- Quality control: inspection staff might select a sample of components delivered by a supplier. If they are all free from defect, it may be safe to conclude that the 'population' (ie all the items in the delivery) is free from defect.

- Auditing: we have already mentioned that an external auditor is needed to sign off the accounts of limited companies. In forming his opinion on the accounts the auditor will not be able to check every accounting transaction. He will check just a sample.

Methods of sampling

6.5 In some cases it may be sufficient to use **judgement sampling**. The sampler decides in advance on the factors that will determine whether or not a member of the population is included in the sample. This is not very scientific and would be unsuitable in most applications of sampling.

6.6 Instead, it is normal to use **probability sampling**. This means that every member of the population is capable of being chosen as part of the sample. Only probability sampling enables us to draw statistical conclusions.

6.7 Assuming we are using probability sampling, there are various methods by which we may select our sample.

- Simple random sampling. The sampler uses random number tables (or, nowadays, more likely a random number generator on a computer). For example, if we have 1,000 items in our population, and the first random number generated is 0175, we select the 175th item as part of our sample.

- Systematic sampling. We select every *n*th item from the total population. For example, if we have 1,000 items in the population and we seek a sample of 40 items, we would choose every 25th item: item no 25, no 50, no 75 and so on.

- Stratified sampling. We break down our population into various categories (male/female, under 30/over 30 etc – any classification that seems relevant to the object of our investigation). From each category we select a defined number of items, adding up to our total sample. By this means we seek to make the sample representative of the whole population. A variation of this is quota sampling.

- Cluster sampling. We choose clusters of items instead of individual items. For example, suppose our population consists of the residents of a particular town. We could divide the town into, say, 1,000 areas of 10 houses each. We then select a number of these groups of 10 as our sample, which is much quicker than selecting individual houses.

- Multistage sampling. If our population is every individual in the UK we could select a number of representative counties (say, Berkshire, Devon and Yorkshire). We subdivide each of these into smaller areas (say East Berkshire, South Berkshire, West Berkshire etc). We then employ cluster sampling in each of the subdivisions to generate our sample.

Chapter summary

- Tables and diagrams are useful ways of clarifying statistical data. Commonly used diagrams include bar charts, pie charts, histograms, frequency polygons and scatter diagrams.

- When summarising data, it is useful to describe the data set by reference to a measure of its central location (ie an average) and a measure of its spread or dispersion.

- Types of average include the arithmetic mean, the median and the mode.

- Measures of dispersion include the range, the quartile deviation and the standard deviation.

- Index numbers are typically used to express the values of a data set in terms of a reference point, such as a particular period at which the base value was set as 100.

- Probability is measured on a scale from 0 (impossibility) to 1 (certainty).

- When two events A and B are mutually exclusive, the probability of at least one of the events occurring is given by P (A or B) = P(A) + P(B).

- When two events A and B are independent, the probability of both occurring is given by P (A and B) = P(A) × P(B).

- The expected value of a monetary outcome £x which has a probability of p is given by £px.

- The binomial distribution measures probabilities of discrete events. The Poisson distribution is similar to the Poisson distribution but applies to cases where the number of events is huge and the probability of any of them is very small.

- The normal distribution relates to continuous variables and measures the probability that the value of the variable falls within a given range.

- There are many areas where sampling may be necessary: market research, quality control, auditing etc.

- It is normal to use techniques of probability sampling (eg simple random sampling).

Self-test questions

Numbers in brackets refer to the paragraphs where you can check your answers.

1   List some of the principles of constructing a chart or diagram. (1.4)

2   What is a frequency polygon? (1.10)

3   How is the arithmetic mean calculated? (2.4)

4   Name three measures of dispersion. (2.14)

5   What are the advantages and disadvantages of the standard deviation? (2.24)

6   What limitations does the use of indices present to the purchasing professional? (3.9–3.11)

7   Define what is meant by the probability of an event. (4.3)

8   How do we calculate the probability P(A or B), where A and B are mutually exclusive events? (4.10)

9   How do we calculate the expected monetary value of a project that has various possible financial outcomes? (4.19)

10   Give examples of situations in which the binomial distribution might be used. (5.5)

11   What kind of problems is the normal distribution used for? (5.19, 5.26)

12   Distinguish between judgement sampling and probability sampling. (6.5, 6.6)

13   What is meant by 'stratified sampling'? (6.7)

CHAPTER 4

Pricing Strategies

Learning objectives and indicative content

2.3 Determine alternative pricing strategies and assess their impact upon transfer pricing within an organisation:

- Market price
- Total cost
- Transfer pricing
- Variable cost
- Negotiated price

Chapter headings

1 Cost-based approaches to pricing

2 Marketing-based approaches to pricing

3 Other approaches to pricing

4 Transfer pricing

Introduction

The topic of pricing is relevant both in so far as it concerns sales to external customers, and in relation to prices charged by one division to another within the same organisation. In this chapter we look firstly at the various bases that can be used to set prices, particularly in the context of external sales. We then look at the principles relevant to the setting of transfer prices.

1 Cost-based approaches to pricing

The importance of the pricing decision

1.1 The primary objective of a commercial organisation is usually assumed to be profit maximisation. Businesses make profits by selling goods and services at a price higher than their cost. In most markets, the sales volumes they can achieve will be largely determined by the prices charged for the goods and services. The conclusion from this is that setting price levels is a decision of fundamental importance to most businesses.

1.2 How do businesses set prices? There are various approaches to this.

- Cost-based approaches
- Marketing-based approaches
- Other approaches

Cost-based approaches (the accountant's approach)

1.3 A much favoured traditional approach is to establish the selling price by calculating the unit cost, then adding on a mark-up or margin to provide profit. The mark-up is subjective and often reflects the risk involved in the product, competitors' mark-ups, desired profit and/or return on capital, type of product, etc.

14. Note the difference between the profit mark-up and the profit margin.

   • Profit mark-up: the profit is quoted as a **percentage of the cost**.

   • Profit margin: the profit is quoted as a **percentage of the selling price**.

1.5 For example, if a product costs £80 to manufacture, and sells for £100, we can say that the business enjoys a mark-up of 25% on cost or a margin of 20% on selling price.

1.6 Table 4.1 shows the advantages and disadvantages of cost-plus pricing.

Table 4.1 *Cost-plus pricing*

Advantages of cost-plus pricing	Disadvantages of cost-plus pricing
• It is widely used and accepted. • It is simple to calculate (provided costs are known). • The selling price decision may be delegated to junior management. • It provides a justification for price increases. • It may encourage price stability (provided all competitors have similar cost structures and use a similar mark-up).	• It ignores what customers are prepared to pay. • It involves circular reasoning – price changes affect volume which affect unit fixed costs which affect price! • Different methods of treating fixed costs give rise to different costs and hence different selling prices. • It does not guarantee that we earn a profit – if sales volumes are low fixed costs may not be covered. • We must decide whether to use full cost, manufacturing cost or marginal cost. • It fails to recognise managers' need for flexibility in pricing.

Total cost or variable cost?

1.7 In Chapter 5 we will look in detail at the nature of an organisation's costs, and in particular we will distinguish between fixed costs and variable costs.

   • Variable costs are those that increase or decrease in line with the level of activity. For example, the cost of raw materials will be higher or lower depending on how much output we manufacture.

   • Fixed costs remain the same as activity increases or decreases. For example, the cost of factory rental is unaffected by how much or how little output we manufacture.

1.8 If a company sets its selling prices by adding a mark-up to **variable costs only** it must ensure that the mark-up is relatively substantial. Otherwise, it may fail to cover all of its fixed costs, and will make a loss.

1.9 This risk is avoided if the company adds a mark-up to its **total costs**, including fixed costs. However, to do this it needs to allocate a fair share of fixed costs to each product, which is not a simple matter. We look at this again in Chapter 5.

Target costing

1.10 A radically different approach to pricing based on costs is the technique of **target costing**.

- The traditional model builds up the cost of a product by analysing its components step by step. A profit margin is then added on and the result is the selling price of the product. With luck, this will be a price that the market can stand; if it is not, the product will be unsuccessful.

- Target costing starts at the other end. The manufacturer first estimates the selling price that the market will be willing to pay for a product with specific features. He then works backward to calculate the production cost that must be achieved in order to provide a reasonable profit.

1.11 The difference between these approaches is crucial.

- The traditional approach accepts costs as given, and calculates a selling price that must be achieved. We must then hope that the market will be willing to pay.

- Target costing starts with what the customer will pay, and then attacks costs so that they are reduced to the required level.

1.12 This leads neatly into the next section of the chapter: marketing-based approaches.

2 Marketing-based approaches to pricing

Introduction

2.1 A marketing-based approach to pricing is one that recognises the attitudes of customers and potential customers. A cost-based approach may lead to us charging less or more than customers are willing to pay, both of which are likely to be unsuccessful strategies. It is preferable to see the pricing decision as being linked in to the whole range of marketing activity carried out by the business with a view to satisfying customers profitably. This allows flexibility to change prices in response to changes in market conditions.

2.2 A key issue is the degree of competition in the market. If there are many companies providing similar products or services, the prices charged by competitors will be an important influence on our own prices. The power of buyers is high when there are numerous suppliers of similar products, which means that sellers are not free to charge as much as they might like. Sellers must naturally aim for a desired level of profit, but in a competitive market this may mean attacking costs: the luxury of simply raising selling prices may not be available.

2.3 By contrast, sellers have more scope to increase their prices if they are able to differentiate their products effectively from those of competitors. If a product has distinctive features not available from other sources, buyers may be willing to pay a premium price for it.

2.4   The concept of **price elasticity** is important in this context.

- If a change in the price of a product causes a big change in the demand for that product by buyers, we say that the product is price elastic. If we increase our prices even slightly we risk losing many customers. If we reduce our prices even slightly there may be opportunities to increase sales significantly.

- If a change in the price of a product leads to little change in demand, we say that the product is price inelastic. There is little point in reducing our prices, because we will not stimulate much additional demand. We have good scope to increase our prices, because demand will probably remain steady.

2.5   For products where there are plentiful substitutes demand is likely to be elastic. If a seller puts up his prices even slightly, the customers will desert him and buy from a different supplier. On the other hand, where a product is distinctive, and/or there are no real substitutes, demand will be inelastic and even significant price rises will not stop people from buying.

2.6   This last consideration explains why increased taxes on tobacco have little effect in discouraging smoking. Demand for tobacco is very inelastic: smokers are willing to pay even if prices are high. Of course, the demand for a particular brand of cigarette may well be elastic, because there are many competing brands. If a particular manufacturer raises prices, smokers may switch to other brands. But overall demand for tobacco will not change by much.

Pricing new products

2.7   A new product pricing strategy will depend largely on whether a company's product or service is the first of its kind on the market.

2.8   If the product is the first of its kind, the business (for a time at least) will be a monopolist. Monopolists have more influence over price and are able to set a price at which they think they can maximise their profits. A monopolist's price is likely to be higher, and his profits bigger, than a company operating in a competitive market. There are two basic strategies for pricing a new product in these circumstances.

- Penetration pricing
- Market skimming

2.9   On the other hand, if the new product being launched by a company is following a competitor's product on to the market, the pricing strategy will be constrained by what the competitor is already doing. The strategies available here include the following.

- Premium pricing
- Penetration pricing
- Market skimming

Penetration pricing

2.10   Penetration pricing is the charging of low prices when a product is initially launched in order to gain rapid acceptance of the product.

2.11 A penetration policy may be chosen in any of the following circumstances.

- The firm wishes to discourage new entrants into the market.
- The firm wishes to shorten the initial period of the product's lifecycle in order to enter the growth and maturity stages as quickly as possible.
- There are significant economies of scale to be achieved from high-volume output, and so a quick penetration into the market is desirable in order to gain unit cost reductions.
- Demand is highly elastic and so would respond well to low prices.

2.12 For penetration pricing to be effective, the total market in which the firm is operating must be substantial, and the anticipated market share significant.

Premium pricing

2.13 In most situations, the new product will either differ, or be made to appear different, in a way which will justify a premium over competing products thereby covering the additional production or marketing costs.

2.14 A number of factors can contribute towards successful premium pricing.

- **High price prestige** – market research constantly confirms the existence of a section of the buying public that blindly equates higher prices with better quality products.
- **Brand loyalty** – an extensive advertising campaign could seek to establish the brand on the market, and build up a loyal consumer following.
- **Quality** – if the supplier can convince the customer that his product is of better quality than its rivals, then a higher price can be charged.
- **Reliability** – most customers are willing to pay more for goods which are perceived to be of above-average quality.
- **Durability** – if a particular good is likely to have a longer physical life than similar items on the market, then it can justify a premium price.
- **After-sale service**.
- **Extended warranties**.
- **Geographical location**.

Market skimming

2.15 Market skimming is an attempt to exploit those sections of the market which are relatively insensitive to price changes. Initially high prices may be charged to take advantage of the novelty appeal of a new product when demand is inelastic.

2.16 A market skimming policy may be chosen in any of the following circumstances.

- The product is new and different, and customers are prepared to pay high prices so as to be 'one-up' on other people who do not own one.
- The strength of demand and the sensitivity of demand to price are unknown. It is much easier to lower prices than to increase them. From a psychological point of view it is far better to begin with a high price, which can then be lowered if the demand for the product appears to be more price sensitive than at first thought.

- High prices in the early stages of a product's life might generate high initial cashflows. A firm with a liquidity problem may prefer market skimming for this reason.

- Products have a short lifecycle, and so need to recover their development costs and make a profit quickly.

- Barriers to entering the market deter potential competitors. With high prices being charged potential competitors will be tempted to enter the market. For skimming to be sustained, one or more significant barriers to entry must be present to deter these potential competitors. Examples include patent protection, prohibitively high capital investment, or unusually strong brand loyalty.

2.17 A skimming policy offers a safeguard against unexpected future increases in costs, or a large fall in demand after the novelty appeal has declined. Once the market becomes saturated the price can be reduced to attract that part of the market that has not been exploited.

3 Other approaches to pricing

Demand-based approaches (the economist's approach)

3.1 Most firms recognise that there is a relationship between the selling price of their product or service and the demand for it. This relationship can often be described with reasonable accuracy by an inverse linear relationship. In other words, a high selling price probably leads to a relatively low level of demand, whereas if the selling price is reduced, demand may well increase. This relationship is illustrated in Figure 4.1.

Figure 4.1 *Price and demand*

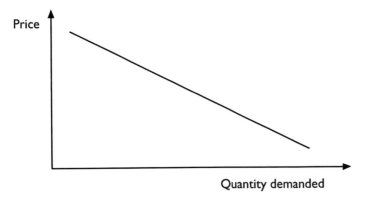

3.2 By investigating and analysing this relationship it is possible (in theory) to establish an optimum price, ie a price that will maximise profits.

3.3 There are two methods of solving problems about the relationship between price and demand.

- The tabular approach
- The algebraic approach

3.4 The tabular approach is essentially based on trial and error. A range of possible prices is tabulated. For each price the resulting expected sales volume (and hence production volume) is tabulated. From this data, we can calculate total revenue and total costs at each choice of unit price. We then produce (and hope to sell) the quantity leading to the highest profit.

3.5 The algebraic approach is based on application of the economic principle that the optimum price to charge occurs where marginal revenue equals marginal cost. You do not need to know the details of this.

Negotiated prices

3.6 As a professional buyer, you will already be completely familiar with the idea that a selling price is based upon agreement between a willing buyer and a willing seller, often after a process of negotiation. Naturally, there are situations where this does not apply. For example, an organisation selling direct to consumers will not want to enter into negotiations with every potential purchaser.

3.7 However, in business-to-business trading this method of pricing is of course very common. It also has an important place in the process of setting prices for **intra-organisational sales**. This leads us into the subject of **transfer pricing**.

4 Transfer pricing

Introduction

4.1 A transfer price is an amount charged by one division to another within a single organisation. For example, in a very simple case a company might consist of just two divisions: a manufacturing division and a sales division. The manufacturing division produces output which it transfers to the sales division at an agreed transfer price. This price represents revenue to the manufacturing division and a cost to the sales division.

4.2 Why bother to do this? After all, the transfer price is purely an internal mechanism which has no effect on how much the business can charge its external customers.

4.3 One reason for bothering is so that each division can be regarded as a profit centre. This may help to stimulate improved performance, particularly if divisional managers are appraised on the basis of the profits earned by their divisions. The level of transfer price may have a significant effect on the profitability of both the transferring division and the receiving division. If the transfer price is very high, the transferring division will appear very profitable, whereas the high cost of 'purchase' in the receiving division will depress its profits. A low transfer price of course has the opposite effect.

4.4 Historically, this situation has led to a possibility of profit manipulation within multinational groups. Such companies have been able to set transfer prices not so much with the idea of achieving fairness between their respective divisions, as to achieve tax advantages. The basic idea is to set transfer prices in such a way that group companies operating in countries with low rates of corporate tax should enjoy high profits; while group companies operating in countries with high rates of corporate tax should have low profits. Nowadays, such abuse is subject to tough regulation and policing by tax authorities, but no doubt still occurs in practice.

4.5 When one division transfers goods to another division we refer to the goods transferred as an **intermediate product**. The idea is that the final product is what the receiving division sells externally. This may or may not be identical with the intermediate product, depending on whether or not the receiving division further processes the goods.

Objectives of transfer pricing

4.6 There are three main considerations for a firm when setting the transfer price for goods.

- **Goal congruence.** Within a divisionalised company, divisional managers will have responsibility for and will be judged on their division's performance. It is the task of the management accounting system in general and the transfer pricing policy in particular to ensure that what is good for an individual division is good for the company as a whole.
- **Performance measurement.** The transfer pricing system should result in a report of divisional profits that is a reasonable measure of the managerial performance.
- **Maintaining divisional autonomy.** One of the purposes of decentralisation is to allow managers to exercise greater autonomy. There is little point in granting additional autonomy and then imposing transfer prices that will affect the profitability of the division.

Establishing the optimum transfer price

4.7 The general rule for decision making is that all goods and services should be transferred at the relevant cost. The correct transfer price for decision making will ensure that goal congruence is achieved within the firm. Possible transfer prices include market price, cost price and negotiated price, all of which are discussed below.

4.8 We shall consider two key objectives.

- Setting a transfer price to achieve goal congruence, ie to bring about the correct decisions for the group
- Setting a transfer price to provide a suitable performance appraisal measure.

4.9 There are three possible situations, each of which is considered in turn below.

- There is a perfectly competitive market for the intermediate product.
- There is surplus capacity within the firm.
- There are binding production constraints.

There is a perfectly competitive market for the intermediate product

4.10 A perfect market means that there is only one price in the market, there are no buying or selling costs and the market is able to absorb the entire output of the primary division and meet all of the requirements of the secondary division. In this situation the optimum transfer price is the market price (less any savings achieved by transferring internally as compared with selling externally).

Performance evaluation

4.11 The aim is to set a transfer price that will give a fair measure of performance in each division.

4.12 When transfers are recorded at market prices divisional performance is more likely to represent the real economic contribution of the division to total company profits. If the supplying division did not exist, the intermediate product would have to be purchased on the outside market at the current market price. Alternatively, if the receiving division did not exist, the intermediate product would be sold on the outside market at the current market price. Divisional profits are therefore likely to be similar to the profits that would be calculated if the divisions were separate organisations.

There is surplus capacity within the firm

4.13 In other words, external demand (if any) can be fully satisfied, and the firm still has spare capacity. In this situation the optimum transfer price is the marginal cost incurred by the supplying division.

Performance evaluation

4.14 The problem is that transferring at marginal cost is unlikely to be 'fair' to the supplying division, because that division is not recording a profit.

4.15 A number of possible solutions are adopted in practice.

- **Two-part tariff**: the transfer is at marginal cost, but in addition a fixed sum is paid per annum or per period to the supplying division to go at least part of the way towards covering its fixed costs, and possibly even to generate a profit. This method often proves to be popular and acceptable to the divisions.

- **Cost-plus pricing**: the transfer price is the marginal cost or full cost plus mark-up. This method often causes conflict over an acceptable mark-up. The method may not encourage goal congruence.

- **Dual pricing**: dual pricing is where one transfer price is recorded by the supplying division and a different transfer price is recorded by the buying division. An adjustment account in the HQ books holds the differences between the divisions. Dual pricing can prove to be difficult to control effectively.

There are binding production constraints

4.16 The selling division has insufficient capacity to meet demand for its work. There exists a situation of scarce resources. In this situation the optimum transfer price is the marginal cost incurred by the supplying division plus the shadow price.

4.17 The shadow price is the opportunity cost of the lost contribution from the other product or it is the extra contribution that would be earned if more of the scarce resource were available.

Performance evaluation

4.18 Whether the transfer price is fair for performance evaluation purposes depends on what the shadow prices reflect.

4.19 There are two possibilities.

- Where internal demand has to be met by forgoing external sales of another product, the shadow prices reflect contribution forgone on that other product. The resulting transfer price (for decision making) is also suitable for performance evaluation.

- Where the supplying division makes only one product which is only sold internally, the shadow price must now reflect contribution from the final production. The transfer price (for decision making) builds that contribution into the supply division's revenue. Therefore all contribution will appear in the supplying division's books (and none in the buying division's).

4.20 The problem with this is that the optimum transfer price (for decision making) is unfair to the buying division. The possible solutions are as before: two-part tariff, cost-plus pricing or dual pricing.

Divisional autonomy

4.21 Should transfer prices be imposed on divisions by HQ, or should the divisions negotiate the transfer prices between themselves?

4.22 The negotiation route appears to be more consistent with divisional autonomy. There are significant disadvantages however.

- Negotiation is time-consuming.
- It leads to conflict between divisions.
- Negotiated transfer prices are unlikely to reflect rational factors.
- Negotiated transfer prices will reflect personality/status/skill.
- It requires the time of top management to oversee the negotiating process and to mediate disputes.

4.23 If an organisation really believes in divisional autonomy, divisions should be allowed to source goods externally if they can find a better price or quality outside the group. But this might mean that an internal company loses 'sales' and has to operate below maximum capacity. Many organisations would refuse to allow this and would insist on internal 'trading'.

4.24 By the same token, divisional autonomy may be compromised if a group company is forced to transfer its goods internally at a lower price than it could achieve in the external market. These are difficult issues of **goal congruence**, which (as stated earlier) is one of the key objectives of transfer pricing.

Chapter summary

- A traditional approach to setting prices is to establish the cost of producing a product, and then to add on a mark-up or margin for profit. The cost of the product may be its variable cost or its total cost.

- More commonly in modern organisations, the approach to pricing is based on marketing considerations.

- New products may be priced on the basis of penetration pricing (a low price to gain customer acceptance) or market skimming (a high price to exploit sections of the market that are not sensitive to price levels).

- Premium pricing may be used particularly to emphasise superior quality or brand prestige.

- According to the economists' view, the theoretically correct way to set prices is by analysis of supply and demand.

- Another method of price setting is by negotiation between buyer and seller.

- An organisation with more than one division may need to establish transfer prices, being the price charged by one division to another when products or services are transferred between them.

- The main objectives of transfer pricing are to achieve goal congruence, performance measurement, and divisional autonomy.

Self-test questions

Numbers in brackets refer to the paragraphs where you can check your answers.

1   A product costing £150 is sold for £300. What is the mark-up percentage? What is the margin percentage? (1.4)

2   List advantages and disadvantages of cost-plus pricing. (Table 4.1)

3   Distinguish between fixed costs and variable costs. (1.7)

4   In what circumstances might a policy of penetration pricing be appropriate? (2.11)

5   What factors might contribute towards successful premium pricing? (2.14)

6   In what circumstances might a market skimming policy be appropriate? (2.16)

7   Graph the relationship between price and demand for a product. (Figure 4.1)

8   What are the three main objectives of transfer pricing? (4.6)

9   What solutions to the transfer pricing problem may be adopted in cases where there is surplus capacity in the firm? (4.15)

10 What are the disadvantages of setting transfer prices by means of negotiations between the divisions concerned? (4.22)

CHAPTER 5

Decision-Making Situations

Learning objectives and indicative content

2.4   Use contribution analysis and marginal costing to evaluate a range of decision-making situations.

- • Cost-volume-profit and breakeven analysis
- • Make or buy decisions
- • Deciding on product range
- • The analysis, and most profitable use, of limiting factors

Chapter headings

1   Cost behaviour

2   Marginal costing and absorption costing

3   Contribution analysis

4   Limiting factors

5   Make or buy decisions

Introduction

An important part of a buyer's work is to negotiate on prices. It is difficult to do this unless you understand your supplier's cost structure. In this chapter we explain how costs behave and how this knowledge can be used by a buyer.

1   Cost behaviour

Fixed and variable costs

1.1   Cost behaviour is the way in which costs of output are affected by fluctuations in the level of activity. The level of activity usually refers to the volume of production in a period, though in some contexts another level of activity might be relevant (eg the level of sales).

1.2   To illustrate how total costs are affected as production levels vary we use a simple example. Suppose that when 10,000 widgets are produced in a period, a company's total production costs are £9,000, but when 20,000 units are produced total costs are £13,000.

1.3   Total costs have increased by less than 50 per cent although production has doubled. This is because some costs will not rise in relation to the increase in volume. For example, it may be that the production costs include simply the following two elements.

- Rental of a fully equipped factory, £5,000 for the period
- Raw materials, £0.40 per widget

1.4 When production doubles, the raw materials cost increases from £4,000 to £8,000. We say that this is a **variable cost**. However, the factory rental is unchanged at £5,000. We say that this is a **fixed cost**.

1.5 The way in which costs behave as production output changes is a key element in the way prices are set by suppliers. Consider Figure 5.1.

Figure 5.1 *Patterns of cost behaviour*

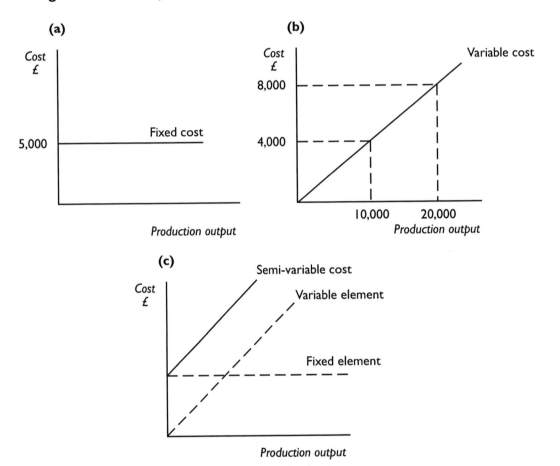

1.6 The first diagram shows the behaviour of a fixed cost. An example already cited is that of factory rental: no matter how much production output is achieved the rental remains fixed at £5,000 (per year, say).

1.7 As with many cost behaviour patterns, this assumption might break down in extreme cases. For example, if production expanded massively it might be necessary to rent a second factory and rental payments would double. But the descriptions given here are adequate for most purposes, and certainly within what is called a 'relevant range of activity'.

1.8   The second diagram shows a cost which is strictly variable with the level of production. An example might be the cost of raw materials used in producing widgets. If no widgets are produced, the cost of raw materials is zero; if 10,000 are produced, the total cost of raw materials is £4,000 (ie 40p per unit). And this unit cost remains constant: if production expands to 20,000 units, the total cost of raw materials rises to £8,000. Again, we are simplifying slightly by ignoring the possibility of bulk discounts.

1.9   Some costs comprise a mixture of fixed and variable elements (see the third diagram). An example might be the cost of machine maintenance. Even if no production is undertaken, an element of standby maintenance will be needed and must be paid for; this is the fixed element. And once production begins the need for maintenance will increase roughly in line with how hard the machines are worked. Strictly this situation is to be regarded as two separate costs, one fixed and one variable.

Contribution

1.10   Contribution is the selling price less the variable cost of sales. It is a vital concept and must be understood thoroughly.

1.11   Suppose that the unit selling price of a widget is £1. We know that its variable costs are £0.40. Its contribution is therefore £0.60. What this means is that every time we sell a widget we earn a contribution of £0.60 towards covering fixed costs and making a profit.

- If we sell only a few widgets, our total contribution will not be sufficient to cover fixed costs and we will make a loss.

- If we sell very many widgets our total contribution will more than cover fixed costs and we will make a profit.

- Somewhere in between there is a sales level such that our total contribution exactly matches our fixed costs. In this case we make neither profit nor loss: we break even. We look at how to calculate this breakeven point later in the chapter.

How to account for fixed costs?

1.12   It is fairly easy to account for variable costs. When we work out the cost of a unit of output we include all the variable costs in the total, because it is clear that an additional unit produced leads to an additional variable cost incurred. This in turn means that the variable cost is clearly part of the cost of that additional unit.

1.13   Accounting for fixed costs is different. If our factory rental is £5,000 for the period, and we produce 10,000 units in that period, we might say that the fixed cost is £0.50 per unit. What then happens in the next period if we produce 20,000 units? Do we say that the true fixed cost per unit is £0.25, or do we say that the additional 10,000 units are 'free' as far as fixed costs are concerned, or what?

1.14   The problem of accounting for fixed costs has given rise to essentially two different approaches. These are called marginal costing and absorption costing, and are discussed in the next section of this chapter.

2 *Marginal costing and absorption costing*

2.1   Marginal cost is the cost of one unit of product or service which would be avoided if that unit were not produced or provided. Under a system of marginal costing only variable costs are included in the cost of a unit of production. Fixed costs for a period are deducted in total from total contribution; we do not try to split them up so as to share them among cost units. This contrasts with absorption costing.

2.2   The following example illustrates the preparation of a profit statement under both marginal costing and absorption costing. Note how the layouts differ. Under absorption costing the fixed costs are included in cost of sales, whereas under marginal costing they are treated as a period cost and shown as a deduction from total contribution.

Example

2.3   Company A produces a single product with the following budget.

Selling price	£10
Direct materials	£3 per unit
Direct wages	£2 per unit
Variable overhead	£1 per unit
Fixed overhead	£10,000 per month
Expected production volume	5,000 units per month

2.4   For absorption costing purposes, the fixed overheads are attributed to units of production on a 'fair' basis. In our example, with expected fixed overheads of £10,000 and expected production of 5,000 units, we 'absorb' £2 into each unit of production.

2.5   The task is to show the profit statement for the month, when 5,000 units were produced and sold, under both marginal and absorption costing principles. (Assume that the actual costs incurred were as budgeted.)

Solution to the example

2.6   *Profit statement for the month – marginal costing*

	£
Sales (5,000 units)	50,000
Variable cost of sales (5,000 × £6)	30,000
Contribution	20,000
Fixed costs	10,000
Operating profit	10,000

2.7 *Profit statement for the month – absorption costing*

	£
Sales (50,000 units)	50,000
Cost of sales (5,000 × £8) (working below)	40,000
	————
Operating profit	10,000
	=====

Working: *Fully absorbed cost per unit*

The fully absorbed cost per unit represents materials (£3) + wages (£2) + variable overhead (£1) + fixed overhead absorbed (£2) = £8 per unit.

2.8 In this example operating profit is the same under both methods. That will not be so, however, when production is more or less than sales, ie stocks of finished goods are maintained.

The problem of fixed overheads

2.9 As explained already, the distinction between marginal costing and absorption costing lies in the treatment of fixed overhead costs.

- Under marginal costing, we regard the cost of a product as comprising the **variable** production costs only. We do not attempt to attribute any proportion of *fixed* overheads to individual products. Instead, we deal with such costs as a single total to be deducted at the bottom of our profit and loss account. This is illustrated in paragraph 2.6 above.

- Under absorption costing, we attempt to absorb a 'fair' proportion of the total fixed overheads into each unit we produce. This is illustrated in paragraph 2.7 above. The problem under this method is deciding on a fair method of absorption.

Traditional absorption costing

2.10 Historically, the approach to this problem has been to calculate the amount of some measurable resource consumed in a production period, and to relate the fixed overhead to this resource. For example, we might expect to require 5,000 labour hours in our assembly department during a particular production period, while expected fixed overhead costs during the same period are £4,000. We might therefore conclude that for every labour hour worked we clock up £0.80 of fixed overhead. We would refer to an **overhead absorption rate** of £0.80 per direct labour hour.

2.11 Pursuing this logic, for any unit of product that is worked on in the assembly department for 30 minutes an amount of £0.40 of fixed overhead is incurred. This would be added to the direct costs incurred by the same unit of product, and by this means we could eventually determine all the costs – both variable and fixed – relating to that unit of product.

2.12 In practice there are three main problems associated with this kind of calculation. We need to estimate total overheads to be incurred, select a measurement unit (eg labour hours, machine hours) and estimate the level of activity (eg the total labour hours that will be worked). Any one of these three could lead to a discrepancy: we could wrongly estimate the total overheads; we could select an inappropriate measurement unit; or we could wrongly estimate the level of activity. The result is that total product costs calculated under absorption costing may well be incorrect. We may either over-absorb overhead (ie include more overhead in our product costs than we have actually incurred) or under-absorb overhead (which is the opposite problem).

2.13   In earlier decades this was less important than it has recently become. In a factory 30 years ago most costs were direct variable costs of labour and materials. As a proportion of the total, fixed overheads did not amount to much, and any inaccuracy in attributing such costs to product units would not make too much difference to the overall picture.

2.14   This situation has now changed dramatically. In most industries there has been a tremendous spurt of automation. Production workforces have been reduced, leading to a decrease in direct labour costs. In their place, expensive machines have been installed, leading to a massive increase in overhead costs. Inaccuracies in attributing such costs to product units can completely distort the information provided by the costing system.

Activity-based costing

2.15   In response to this, new methods of absorption costing have been developed. One such method that has enjoyed great success in recent years is **activity based costing** (ABC).

2.16   This is not a textbook on costing techniques, and it would not be appropriate to delve too deeply into ABC. However, you may be expected to know some general principles, and these are explained below.

2.17   As the name suggests, ABC is based on the idea that activities cause costs. The first stage of setting up an ABC system is therefore to identify all the activities undertaken by the enterprise, and to analyse them into those that add value (primary activities) and those that are non-value-adding (secondary activities). All primary activities have some form of output that can be identified, and this is called the activity's **cost driver**. For example, an activity is the placing of a purchase order; the cost driver of the activity is the purchase order itself.

2.18   Another key feature of ABC is the use of **cost pools**. For example, all of the overhead costs associated with running the purchasing department might be regarded as a cost pool. The overheads associated with setting up machines for a production run might be another cost pool. When an overhead cost is incurred, it must be attributed to one or other of the available cost pools.

2.19   Once we have built up a cost pool (eg we have a total for the fixed overhead costs incurred in running the purchasing department) and determined an appropriate cost driver (eg the raising of a purchase order) we can calculate a **cost driver rate**. This is simply the total overheads divided by the number of purchase orders. It is equivalent to the overhead absorption rate used in traditional absorption costing, but the method of calculating it is believed to lead to more accurate costing information.

2.20   Remember that all of this relates just to the fixed overheads included in total cost. If we are interested in the total cost of placing a purchase order we must also include the direct variable costs.

2.21 Absorption costing and activity-based costing can give very different results. Nowadays, activity based costing is widely believed to present a more accurate picture and is regarded as more useful information for managers.

3 Contribution analysis

Costs, sales volume and profitability

3.1 Your syllabus uses the terms 'contribution analysis' and 'cost-volume-profit analysis'. Another term in even more common use is 'breakeven analysis'. For practical purposes, all of these terms mean the same thing: we are concerned with how changes in output and sales affect costs and hence profits.

3.2 To simplify matters, let us first consider a supplier (Y Limited) who produces just a single product. The normal selling price for the product is £15 per unit and the variable costs of production are £6 per unit. Again for simplicity, we will assume that all the supplier's other costs are fixed and amount to £630,000 per annum.

3.3 The table below shows the supplier's position on different assumptions regarding sales volumes.

Sales volume	50,000 units	75,000 units	100,000 units
	£000	£000	£000
Fixed costs	630	630	630
Variable costs @ £6 per unit	300	450	600
Total costs	930	1,080	1,230
Sales revenue @ £15 per unit	750	1,125	1,500
(Loss)/profit per annum	(180)	45	270

3.4 The position is fairly clear: if sales of only 50,000 units are achieved, the supplier expects to make a loss of around £180,000; at a sales volume of 75,000 units a small profit is made; and at higher sales volumes profit increases quite nicely.

3.5 This has been a very simple example to illustrate the point clearly. In practice things will be more complicated. But the example does show the importance of what is called breakeven point: the point where sales volumes enable a loss to be transformed into a profit. We look at this in more detail below.

Contribution and profit

3.6 A firm's breakeven point is where it sells sufficient product to cover its costs exactly, so that neither profit nor loss is made. Breakeven analysis is the process of computing a breakeven point. Either arithmetic or graphical methods may be used, and both are illustrated in this chapter.

3.7   A key concept in breakeven analysis is that of contribution, which we have already defined as the difference between sales revenue and the variable cost of making the sales. Another way of putting this is to say that it is the amount of selling price left over after variable costs have been paid for. It is this amount which must be sufficient to cover fixed costs and, perhaps, to make a profit. In fact, contribution is an abbreviated expression; in full, it should be **contribution to covering fixed costs and making a profit**.

3.8   Consider the example of Y Limited already given. The company sells its product at £15 per unit, but has to pay £6 per unit in variable costs. This leaves a contribution of £9 for every unit sold.

3.9   Now, for Y Limited to break even the company must earn sufficient contribution each year to cover its annual fixed costs of £630,000. This implies a target sales volume of £630,000 ÷ £9 = 70,000 units. Notice that this bears out the results in the table above. From the table it is clear that a large loss is made at a sales volume of 50,000 units, whereas at 75,000 units the company has just moved into profit. In fact, we can now see that the exact point where this happens is at a sales volume of 70,000 units.

3.10   Instead of using the monetary amount of £9, we could have expressed contribution as a percentage of selling price: £9 = 60% of £15. We could then have calculated the breakeven point (in £) as £630,000 ÷ 60% = £1,050,000. At a selling price of £15 per unit, this equates to a breakeven sales volume of 70,000 units, as in our previous calculation.

3.11   The arithmetical approach we are developing here gives us further information. It is clear that once we have covered fixed costs, any contribution earned on additional sales volumes represents clear profit. So for Y Limited, a sales volume 5,000 in excess of the breakeven point leads to a profit equal to the excess contribution, namely 5,000 × £9 = £45,000. This is borne out by the calculations in the table.

Margin of safety

3.12   The margin of safety is the difference between the planned sales level and the breakeven sales level. For example, if Y Limited plans to achieve a sales level of 100,000 units, the margin of safety is 30,000 units. This means that sales can fall short of the target by as many as 30,000 units before Y Limited begins to make losses.

Planned sales level – breakeven sales level = margin of safety
100,000 units – 70,000 units = 30,000 units

3.13   The margin of safety is often expressed as a percentage of the planned sales.

Margin of safety $= \dfrac{30,000}{100,000} = 30\%$ of planned sales

A loss will result if there is a shortfall of more than 30 per cent from the planned sales level.

A graphical approach to breakeven analysis

3.14 To show how breakeven analysis can be illustrated graphically we will again use the example of Y Limited. See Figure 5.2.

3.15 The diagram is simpler than it looks. To construct it just follow these steps.

- Mark a vertical axis for sales and costs in monetary terms, and a horizontal axis for sales volume in units.

- First draw in fixed costs. This is a horizontal line at the level of £630,000, reflecting the fact that these costs are unchanged no matter what sales volume is achieved.

- Sales revenue rises in a straight line as sales volume increases. Just pick any two levels of sales volume, mark the relevant points on the graph and join them up in a straight line.

- Total costs also increase in a straight line. For a zero sales volume, total costs consist of fixed costs of £630,000; for a sales volume of 100,000 units, fixed costs remain the same, but variable costs of £600,000 have to be added, a total of £1,230,000. Now join up the two points you have calculated.

Figure 5.2 *Y Limited – breakeven analysis*

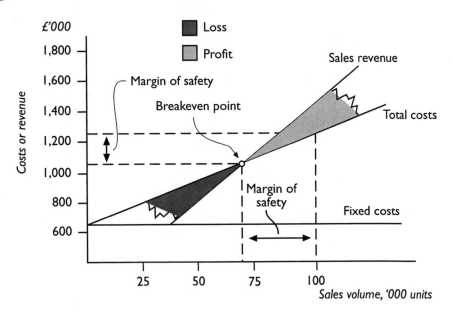

3.16 Notice how the breakeven point can simply be read off the graph: it is the intersection of the sales revenue and total costs lines. In other words, it is the point where total sales revenue is equal to total costs. In our example, this corresponds to the point on the horizontal axis representing 70,000 units of sales. This in turn corresponds to the point on the vertical axis representing £1,050,000 of sales revenue and total costs.

Implications for buyers

3.17 Of course in practice the situation is not as simple as we supposed for Y Limited. For one thing, we have assumed that the company produces only a single product. But despite its limitations, breakeven analysis has a number of important implications for buyers.

3.18 An important trend in modern manufacturing is the increased reliance of manufacturers on automated processes, and the consequent fall in use of direct labour. The use of automation has the effect of reducing variable costs (namely the cost of direct labour), while increasing fixed costs (the heavy capital costs of expensive plant).

3.19 To illustrate this, return to the example of Y Limited and suppose that the company has only recently automated its manufacturing. Before this happened its fixed costs were much lower at £250,000 per annum, while its variable costs were much higher at £10 per unit. With a contribution of £5 on every unit sold (£15 – £10) Y Limited had only to achieve sales volume of 50,000 units to break even.

3.20 Since automation, the task facing the company is much tougher. As we have seen, they will make a loss at all sales volumes below 70,000 units. This places great pressure on the sales staff of Y Limited: they must obtain substantial extra business to feed their hungry new machines. Other things being equal, they will be more prepared than previously to offer a tight selling price.

3.21 Another implication concerns the situation when the supplier has passed breakeven point. From then on his low variable costs mean high contribution and high profit. The supplier does not have to press too hard for optimum prices: even a comparatively low selling price will more than cover variable costs and so add to contribution and profit.

3.22 In the case of Y Limited, after automation and once the breakeven point of 70,000 units has been passed, any sales achieved at prices in excess of the £6 variable costs will add to profits. There is a wide gap between £6 and £15 for buyers to target in negotiations.

3.23 It is worth mentioning a further point about fixed and variable costs. Suppose that Y Limited had budgeted at the start of the year to achieve sales of 90,000 units. At that sales level the company's costs would consist of:

	£
Fixed costs	630,000
Variable costs @ £6 per unit	540,000
Total costs	1,170,000

3.24 Dividing this total costs figure by the output of 90,000 units, a Y Limited salesman might be inclined to say that the cost of producing a unit of product is £13. In effect, he is spreading the total fixed costs over the 90,000 units at the rate of £7 per unit; added to variable costs of £6 this gives the 'total cost' of £13. It might seem very unfair of a buyer to ask for a price of, say, £10 per unit.

3.25 However, as we have already seen, this analysis would be quite misleading. Once the breakeven point has been passed fixed costs drop out of the equation – they have already been paid. The true benchmark is the **variable** cost of £6 per unit.

3.26 This example shows that buyers must be wide awake to what is meant by the idea of total cost. Otherwise, they will overlook opportunities for negotiating more favourable deals for their organisations.

3.27 One final point about fixed and variable costs should have become apparent from the discussion above, but we will make it explicit here. That is that a company with a high level of fixed costs is at greater risk than a company with relatively low fixed costs if the economy takes a turn for the worse. We can illustrate this as follows.

3.28 Suppose Company A makes annual sales of £1m, variable costs amount to 20 per cent of sales, and fixed costs are £600,000. Company A therefore makes a contribution of £800,000 per year (80% × £1m) and a profit of £200,000 per year.

3.29 Now suppose that trading deteriorates and sales drop to only £700,000. Contribution (80% × £700,000 = £560,000) is insufficient to cover the high fixed costs and the company suffers a loss of £40,000.

3.30 Contrast Company B, which also makes sales of £1m per year, but whose cost structure is different: relatively high variable costs of 50 per cent, but much lower fixed costs of £300,000. With sales of £1m Company B makes the same profit – £200,000 – as Company A. But if sales fall to £700,000 Company B is much better placed. Contribution, at 50 per cent of £700,000 = £350,000, is still sufficient to cover the low fixed costs and the company remains in profit.

Price/cost analysis

3.31 In a typical negotiation, much of the debate revolves around price. Of course, this is not the only issue at stake, but price is always important and you will do better in negotiations if you can grasp how your supplier's prices are derived. This in turn depends partly on understanding your supplier's cost structure.

3.32 Any supplier will want to achieve a price for their goods or services that covers their costs and gives them a profit. However much a buyer may want to minimise costs – and therefore minimise the price charged by the supplier – the buyer should bear in mind that no supplier is going to supply for long if costs are not covered, or if costs are only just covered and there is no profit to justify continuing to trade at all.

3.33 A supplier will often seek to relate the price he charges to a buyer, and any increase in that price, to his own costs. This is where price/cost analysis by the buyer comes in. For instance, if there has been a well-publicised price increase of, say, 5 per cent for a certain raw material, and it is known that the raw material comprises 30 per cent of the cost of the finished good, then an increase in price of the finished good is not unreasonable – but how large an increase? Consider the cost structure of the supplier, who expects a 20 per cent mark-up on total costs:

	£	Increase in cost, %	£	Increase in selling price, %
Raw material	3,000	5	3,150	
Labour	2,000	0	2,000	
Overheads	5,000	0	5,000	
Total costs	10,000		10,150	
Profit (20%)	2,000		2,030	
Selling price	12,000		12,180	1.5

3.34 An overall increase of 5 per cent would seem to be unreasonable; 1.5 per cent seems more reasonable from the analysis above. However, there are quite a number of factors that we have not taken into account.

- Has the raw material cost actually risen by 5 per cent to the supplier, or is this the average rise which has not actually affected the supplier's costs as badly, perhaps due to bulk discounts?
- Are there any changes in labour costs to be taken into account (maybe the more expensive material is better quality, so lower labour costs will be incurred)?
- Is the 20 per cent profit mark-up reasonable?
- Does the supplier mark up total costs by 20 per cent or are allocated overheads ignored for this purpose?
- When will the price rise take effect, given that the supplier may have items in stock that include the raw material at the lower price?

3.35 The buyer will not always find answers during a price/cost analysis. It may or may not validate the supplier's position, but it may give rise to some interesting questions for the buyer to ask, and it will make the buyer better prepared for negotiations with the supplier.

Deciding on a product range

3.36 A particular use of contribution analysis is mentioned in your syllabus: deciding on a product range. This type of problem is well illustrated by a question in the November 2007 exam, which we summarise below.

3.37 The question concerned a manufacturing company that produces three different products: Products A, B and C. Financial results for the current year are as follows.

	A	B	C
	£	£	£
Sales	400,000	300,000	260,000
Direct materials	168,000	84,000	112,000
Direct labour	104,000	96,000	76,000
Variable overheads	48,000	40,000	20,000
Fixed overheads	60,000	50,000	90,000
Total costs	380,000	270,000	298,000
Profit/(loss)	20,000	30,000	(38,000)

3.38   The problem concerns Product C, which appears to be unprofitable to produce. In the exam question we were required to discuss whether production of Product C should be terminated.

3.39   The trap in this kind of situation is to ignore the impact of fixed costs on the calculations. The bottom line loss of £38,000 for Product C suggests that we should immediately cease its production, but notice that this loss only arises after we apportion £90,000 of fixed overheads to the product. The key thing to note is that these fixed overheads **will not disappear** if we stop producing Product C. They will simply have to be apportioned to A and B instead.

3.40   A truer way of appraising the situation is to focus on contribution. Product C generates sales of £260,000 and incurs variable costs totalling £208,000. This means that the product earns a contribution of £52,000, which will be lost if we cease production. The company's results without C would be an overall loss of £40,000: the £50,000 of profits currently earned by A and B, less the £90,000 of fixed costs which will now have to be re-apportioned to A and B. This compares with an overall profit currently of £12,000. The difference between the current profit of £12,000 and the future loss of £40,000 is caused by losing the £52,000 contribution currently earned by C.

3.41   By focusing on contribution we can see that it would be a poor decision to cease production of Product C. The profit and loss accounts presented in the question are misleading because of the apportionment of fixed costs. Remember, if we close down Product C we will lose all of the variable costs associated with it, but also the sales revenue it earns, a net loss of £52,000 in contribution. We will **not** lose the £90,000 of fixed costs: they will simply have to be borne by Products A and B, which will lead to an overall loss for the company.

3.42   It would also be relevant to consider the non-financial factors involved in a decision to cease production of C. For example, would there be an adverse reaction from customers? Would sales of A and B be affected by the absence of C? Whereabouts in the product lifecycle does C currently stand? Would the company need to lay off staff, incurring redundancy costs etc?

Limitations of contribution analysis

3.43 Contribution analysis is a useful tool for managers, but it is as well to be aware of its limitations. These are described below.

3.44 A producer will rarely be supplying only one uniform product. In practice he is likely to be offering many different products to the market, so the idea of a single selling price is inadequate.

3.45 Some products clearly cost more to produce than others, but it may not be easy to split the total costs between the total outputs. For example, how should the cost of factory rent or the cost of the managing director's salary be allocated to individual units of product? We have seen how absorption costing attempts to cope with this, both in the traditional manner and by use of activity based costing, but it is clearly not an exact science.

3.46 In practical situations, selling price can affect costs, and not just *vice versa*, which means that circular reasoning comes into force. The reason for this is that selling price affects demand ('Buyer X will purchase 10,000 units if the price is £1.10 but may look elsewhere if the price is £1.20'); and then in turn demand affects production output ('we can increase our production run if Buyer X places the order'); and finally the volume of production output affects many costs.

3.47 We have assumed that selling price is always constant. In practice, increasing selling volumes is often associated with granting discounts, so this assumption is simplistic.

3.48 Similarly, it may be simplistic to assume that variable costs per unit never vary. In practice, if we increase our purchases, we would expect to benefit from discounted prices.

3.49 Finally, it is not always easy to determine whether a cost if fully fixed or fully variable. In deed, some costs are certainly a mix of fixed and variable elements, as we saw at the beginning of this chapter.

4 *Limiting factors*

The nature of limiting factors

4.1 Marginal costing principles are widely used in decision-making by managers. Its useful distinction between variable costs (which will change under various decision alternatives) and fixed costs (which may not change) is preferable to the approach of absorption costing, in which fixed and variable costs are all aggregated in the cost of cost units.

4.2 Another way of putting this is to say that variable costs are always **relevant costs** in terms of decision making, whereas fixed costs frequently are not relevant (because they won't change anyway). Another type of cost which is not relevant in decision-making is a **sunk cost** – a cost that has already been spent or committed, whether we were wise to have spent it or not.

4.3   One type of decision in which marginal costing principles are essential is the case where a production resource is in scarce supply (a 'limiting factor'). All businesses which aim to maximise profit find that the volume of output and sales is restricted. For many, sales demand is the limiting factor – there is no point producing more than customers want to buy. In such a case the business will seek to make the maximum profit by concentrating its selling efforts on those products which yield high contributions.

4.4   Other limiting factors may prevent sales growth: shortage of building space, of machine capacity, of skilled labour, or of the necessary materials. In such cases it is important for the business to obtain maximum profit by concentrating its efforts on those products which yield high contributions relative to the amount of the limiting factor they consume.

Example

4.5   Two products – Alpha and Gamma – are given a final finish by passing them through a spraying process. There is considerable demand for both products but output is restricted by the capacity of the spraying process. The product details are as follows.

	Alpha £	Gamma £
Selling price	10.00	15.00
Variable cost	6.00	7.50
Contribution	4.00	7.50
Finishing time in spraying process	1 hour	3 hours

4.6   Without any restriction in the capacity of the spraying process, Gamma is the more profitable product and should be preferred. However, as the spraying process is the limiting factor, it is important for the business to use the capacity of the process as profitably as possible, ie to earn the maximum profit for each spraying hour.

4.7   The contributions per spraying hour are £4.00 for Alpha and £2.50 for Gamma and, therefore, it is Alpha which should be preferred. This can be proved by assuming a fixed number of spraying hours per week, say 45.

	Alpha	Gamma
Number of units to be sprayed in 45 hours	45	15
Contribution per unit	£4.00	£7.50
Total contribution	£180.00	£112.50

4.8   Where a limiting factor prevents a company from producing all the units it would like to it must decide which products to concentrate on. This example shows that the decision rule in these circumstances is as follows: give priority to the product that earns most contribution **per unit of the scarce resource**.

Other considerations regarding limiting factors

4.9 In the long run management must seek to remove the limiting factor. In the example above, management should be attempting to increase the capacity of the spraying process. Thus, any one limiting factor should only be a short-term problem. However, as soon as it is removed, it may be replaced by another limiting factor.

4.10 Even in the short run management may be able to find ways round the bottleneck. For example, overtime working or subcontracting might be solutions to the situations described.

5 Make or buy decisions

Types of make or buy decision

5.1 Occasionally a business may have the opportunity to purchase, from another company, a component part or assembly which it currently produces from its own resources.

5.2 In examining the choice, management must first consider the following questions.

- Is the alternative source of supply available only temporarily or for the foreseeable future?
- Is there spare production capacity available now and/or in the future?

Spare capacity

5.3 If the business is operating below maximum capacity, production resources will be idle if the component is purchased from outside. The fixed costs of those resources are irrelevant to the decision in the short term as they will be incurred whether the component is made or purchased. Purchase would be recommended, therefore, only if the buying price is less than the variable costs of internal manufacture.

5.4 In the long term, however, the business may dispense with or transfer some of its resources and may purchase from outside if it thereby saves more than the extra cost of purchasing.

Example

5.5 A company manufactures an assembly used in the production of one of its product lines. The department in which the assembly is produced incurs fixed costs of £24,000 per year. The variable costs of production are £2.55 per unit. The assembly could be bought outside at a cost of £2.65 per unit. The current annual requirement is for 80,000 assemblies per year. Should the company continue to manufacture the assembly, or should it be purchased from the outside suppliers?

Solution to the example

5.6 A decision to purchase outside would cost the company £(2.65 – 2.55) = 10p per unit, which for 80,000 assemblies would amount to £8,000 per year. It is worth buying the assembly from outside if internal cost savings of more than £8,000 can be achieved.

5.7 Management would need to analyse the current fixed costs of £24,000. If these costs, or at least £8,000 of them, would be saved by sourcing from outside then it is worth doing. However, if most of the fixed costs would still be incurred anyway, then the company will gain little by ceasing its own production, and will incur extra costs of £8,000 by sourcing from outside.

Other considerations affecting the decision

5.8 Management would need to consider other factors before reaching a decision. Some would be quantifiable and some not.

- Continuity and control of supply. Can the outside company be relied upon to meet the requirements in terms of quantity, quality, delivery dates and price stability?
- Alternative use of resources. Can the resources used to make this article be transferred to another activity which will save cost or increase revenue?
- Social/legal. Will the decision affect contractual or ethical obligations to employees or business connections?

Relevant costs

5.9 As in all decision making situations, we should consider only the **relevant costs**. Variable costs will almost always be relevant. Other costs directly attributable to the operation will also be relevant, if they would change as a result of the decision (eg directly attributable fixed costs that can be disposed of).

Chapter summary

- A variable cost is a cost that increases as the level of activity increases. A fixed cost is a cost that is not dependent on the level of activity

- Contribution per unit of production is the selling price per unit less the variable costs per unit. Total contribution earned from selling all units of production must be sufficient to cover fixed costs and, ideally, to make a profit.

- Using marginal costing, we calculate the cost of a unit of production simply as the total variable costs. Using absorption costing, the cost of a unit of production is the total variable costs plus a fair share of fixed costs.

- Traditional absorption costing may not be sufficiently accurate in an era where the proportion of fixed costs is very high. Many authorities now support the alternative approach of activity based costing.

- Contribution analysis (otherwise known as cost-volume-profit analysis, or breakeven analysis) is concerned with the effect of changes in output and sales levels on costs and profits.

- A firm's breakeven point can be computed (in simple cases) by either arithmetic or graphical methods.

- Buyers must be aware of their suppliers' cost structures in order to perform effectively in price negotiations.

- Contribution analysis is a useful theoretical concept, but in practice we need to be aware of its simplistic assumptions.

- Where a production resource is in short supply, the rule is to give priority to the product that earns most contribution per unit of the scarce resource.

- In a make or buy decision managers must calculate the relative costs of the two options, but must also take into account non-quantitative factors such as the likely reliability of the outside supplier.

Self-test questions

Numbers in brackets refer to the paragraphs where your answers can be checked.

1   Distinguish between a fixed cost and a variable cost, giving an example of each. (1.4)

2   Define 'contribution'. (1.10)

3   How are fixed production costs accounted for under a system of absorption costing? (2.2)

4   What is meant by a firm's breakeven point? (3.6)

5   Define 'margin of safety'. (3.12)

6   Explain the effect on costs of the modern trend towards increased automation. (3.18)

7   Explain why a company is at greater risk if a high proportion of its costs are fixed. (3.28–3.30)

8   What is meant by a limiting factor of production? (4.3)

9   What is the decision rule when a producer is faced with a limiting factor? (4.8)

10   What non-quantitative factors should a firm consider in a make or buy decision? (5.8)

CHAPTER 6

Sources of Finance

Learning objectives and indicative content

3.1   Analyse the use of the different types of expenditure

- Capital expenditure (CapEx)
- Operating expenditure (OpEx)
- Public sector expenditure

3.2   Evaluate and select a range of sources of finance to assessing funds for capital acquisitions and projects

- Retained profit
- Controlling working capital
- Sale of assets
- Factoring
- Overdrafts
- Grants
- Venture capital
- Debentures
- Share issues
- Bank loans – medium or long-term
- Leasing
- PPP/PFI
- Public borrowing for public sector (Bank of England and HM Treasury)

Chapter headings

1   Different types of expenditure

2   Sources of short-term finance

3   Sources of long-term finance

4   Finance for the public sector

5   The importance of adequate finance

Introduction

In this chapter we begin by distinguishing between various types of expenditure incurred by an organisation. This expenditure of course needs to be funded, so we continue by examining the various sources of funds available to organisations, including the funds required for public sector expenditure. We end with a brief discussion of why it is important to have adequate finance.

1 Different types of expenditure

Cashflow from operations

1.1 Every organisation needs cash to run its operations: to purchase supplies, to pay wages and salaries and so on. Obtaining the finance to pay for these items is obviously a key task of management. This requirement is quite distinct from the desirability of making profits. Even organisations that do not seek to make profits – such as charities – still need cash to pay bills.

1.2 The most obvious way in which cash comes into an organisation is through the activities carried out by the organisation. These presumably have some economic value and someone is therefore prepared to pay for them.

- A charity raises finance by collecting from donors who support the work of the charity.

- A central government department is allocated cash by the government. The cash is derived ultimately from taxpayers.

- A local government authority raises cash by charging rates to individuals and businesses in its local area. In Britain, such rates are called 'council tax' when levied on individuals, and 'business rates' when levied on non-domestic organisations.

- A health authority runs hospitals which are funded ultimately by taxpayers. The government collects taxes and passes cash on to hospitals either directly or indirectly.

- A commercial business raises finance by selling its goods or services and collecting cash from its customers in return.

1.3 It may well be that the organisation's cashflow from its basic operations is positive (ie it generates more cash than it spends). However, in most cases this will not be sufficient to keep the organisation in operation. In the short term, the amounts that must be paid out by the organisation may exceed the amounts coming in from the sources listed above. In such cases other sources of finance must be found and we will look at the various possibilities in later sections of this chapter.

1.4 To begin with, though, we will look in slightly more detail at the nature of the expenditure that needs to be funded. As usual in this text, we focus for simplicity on the characteristics of commercial businesses. However, the points we make are equally applicable to other organisations such as those already mentioned.

Operating expenditure (Opex)

1.5 For most organisations, it is useful to distinguish between **operating expenditure** and **capital expenditure**. We have touched on this topic already in Chapter 2, and you should refresh your memory at this point by referring back. In broad terms, the distinction is easily understood by anyone who has ever purchased a motor car.

- The purchase cost of the motor car is capital expenditure.
- The running costs of the car are operating expenditure (the costs of fuel, road fund licence, insurance, routine servicing etc)

1.6   Operating expenditure, as the name suggests, is the expenditure incurred in routine running of the organisation. There are numerous items on which an organisation will routinely incur costs.

- Purchase of raw materials for use in manufacture
- Purchase of goods for resale
- Payment of wages and salaries to staff
- Purchase of office supplies such as stationery
- Expenditure on utilities, such as light and heat
- Expenditure on advertising and other marketing activities

Capital expenditure (Capex)

1.7   This is money spent on items that will last in the business for a substantial period, certainly more than one year. Typically, such items will cost large sums of money. Some examples are given here.

- Purchase of freehold premises and/or land
- Purchase of large-scale manufacturing equipment
- Purchase of delivery vehicles
- Development cost of a major new computer system, whether this is spent on internal staff or on a specialist external contractor

1.8   For convenience, we reproduce below a table from Chapter 2, summarising the differences between capital and operating expenditure.

Table 6.1 *Capital and operating expenditure*

Category	Types of expenditure included
Capital expenditure	Expenditure on the acquisition of fixed assets required for use in the business and not for resale
	Expenditure on existing fixed assets aimed at increasing their earning capacity (eg a major overhaul of an item of production machinery)
Operating expenditure	Expenditure on current assets (eg stock)
	Expenditure relating to running the business (administration expenses, selling expenses).
	Expenditure on maintaining the earning capacity of fixed assets (repairs and renewals).

Planning for Capex and Opex

1.9   The major sums invested in capital assets and projects call for specialised forms of investment appraisal. These are the subject of Chapter 10. They include such discounted cashflow techniques as net present value and internal rate of return. But before this, we need to decide whether the capital investment option is preferable; often, there are ways of avoiding capital expenditure if it seems convenient to do so.

1.10   As an example, we may be considering the purchase of a large item of capital equipment to be used in a project over the next 12 months. It may make sense to purchase the item right away, which will be capital expenditure. However, alternatives could also be considered. We might, for example, decide that a better option is to rent the equipment for the period of the project only. This would be operating expenditure.

1.11   Similarly, we might be considering an upgrade of internal IT systems. One possibility would be gradual change, increasing capacity and functionality by just a small amount, and dealing with one application after another over an extended period. This would be operating expenditure. Alternatively, we might decide that a more major upgrade is essential: we need to replace our existing systems with newly designed programmes perhaps residing on an altogether different software 'platform'. At the same time this will require major upgrading of hardware. All this would be capital expenditure.

1.12   In cases such as these, an important factor in the decision is the impact on cashflows. Often, the Capex option will require a very large payment up front, with a potentially serious dent in cashflows. The Opex option will typically protect cashflows: smaller amounts are paid out in total, and over an extended period. The Opex option may prove more expensive in total, but if the organisation is not cash rich this may be a more acceptable method of raising the funds. For organisations who do not have immediate access to large liquid funds, the Capex route may not even be an option.

1.13   Another factor influencing the decision might be the useful life of the capital asset. It would not make sense to purchase an expensive asset if we plan to use it for just a small fraction of its useful life (perhaps for the duration of a short project). In such a case it would be much more sensible to rent it, returning the asset to its owner after our need for it is over.

2   *Sources of short-term finance*

2.1   Your syllabus lists a large number of sources of finance. To help you grasp the various possibilities, it is useful to categorise them in some way. There are various possible classifications, and we have chosen to distinguish between sources of short-term finance and sources of long-term finance.

Bank overdraft

2.2   Perhaps the most obvious way of solving a short-term cashflow problem is to request overdraft facilities from the bank. This procedure is familiar to most people in a personal context, and is even more common for businesses. In simple terms, the bank allows the business to spend more cash than it actually owns, the bank itself making up the shortfall. Of course, the bank requires something in return for this service. It will usually charge an arrangement fee for setting up the overdraft facility. And it will charge interest on the amount of cash that has been 'overspent' by the business.

2.3   The rates of interest charged on bank overdrafts are high, and there are other disadvantages of this form of finance. One such disadvantage is that the bank will take a close interest in the affairs of the business until the overdraft is repaid. Before even granting the overdraft the bank will probably insist that the business produces forecasts and budgets. And the bank manager will require these forecasts to be monitored and updated regularly.

2.4   Another disadvantage is that an overdraft is, technically, repayable on demand. In other words, the bank can withdraw the facility at a moment's notice and require the business to pay the amount owing. In practice, some businesses manage to run an overdraft for very long periods, but this possibility of immediate withdrawal always remains present.

2.5   A bank overdraft is an example of **debt finance** or simply **debt**. Other examples of debt finance include loans and debentures (which we discuss later). An important feature of debt finance is that any interest payable is an allowable deduction from taxable profits. This means that by paying interest we at least reduce our tax bill. The effect is that debt capital is cheaper than the quoted interest rate might suggest.

Credit from suppliers

2.6   Another short-term method of improving cashflow is simply not to pay bills. If a business purchases goods and services on credit terms there will usually be an agreed date by which payment must be made. However, many businesses fail to comply with this agreement: they pay their bills late. Their suppliers have in effect – probably unwillingly – 'loaned' goods to the business, which is equivalent to loaning money.

2.7   In the case just described, there is likely to be a very bad effect on relations with the suppliers concerned. Although suppliers are of course anxious to win business, their patience will wear thin if they find that payment is regularly late. They can take serious action against the business in default: for example, they can sue for payment of the debt, and they can refuse to supply goods on credit in the future. All of this can have a damaging effect on the business and is not recommended.

2.8   However, there are cases where suppliers agree to this situation. In other words, the business might persuade a supplier to agree on payment several months after the goods or services change hands. The supplier might assent to this if he sees a chance of doing good business into the future by showing patience now.

Controlling working capital

2.9   In most businesses, working capital consists of stock, debtors and cash/bank balances, less any creditors. We have already seen how a short-term cashflow advantage can be obtained by withholding payment from creditors. Careful management of stock and debtors can provide a similar boost.

2.10   A company that holds stock must obviously pay for it, whether it consists of goods for resale or goods manufactured. The more stock that is held, the more money is tied up. A company that holds high levels of stock will be that much less liquid in terms of cash balances, because some cash must have been expended in order to purchase or to manufacture the stock. High stock levels may be necessary to cope with customer demand, but holding more stock than necessary is a waste of cash resources. For this reason, a company should monitor its stock levels carefully and not hold more stock than it needs.

2.11   A similar pattern applies to debtors. Companies may need to offer credit terms to their customers in order to attract business. But until the customers pay up, cash resources are lower than they might be. A business should have in place efficient procedures for chasing debtors. An unduly high level of debtor balances suggests inefficient working capital management, which can lead to cash shortages. In Chapter 12 we look at financial ratios which can help us to evaluate our control of working capital.

Factoring and invoice discounting

2.12 These are methods of addressing the point made above about debtors. Suppose a company has high levels of debtor balances because its customers are slow to pay. One remedy might be to install efficient debt collection procedures, but an alternative solution is to hand the problem over to someone else: a specialist finance company.

2.13 Installing and maintaining debt collection systems may be difficult, and in any event business circumstances may make it difficult to insist on prompt payment. For example, in an industry where long credit periods are the norm, a business which refuses to grant extended credit may find it difficult to attract customers.

2.14 The basic problem is that a business wants cash immediately on selling its products, whereas commercial considerations may require the business to grant credit to its customers. Ways have been found to overcome this problem. In particular, financial institutions (such as banks) offer services such as invoice discounting and factoring.

2.15 In simple terms, invoice discounting works like this.

- A business sells goods to a customer and raises an invoice for the amount owing. The invoice is payable after, say, 30 days and is for a sum of, say, £1,000.

- The business now owns an asset, but it is not yet a cash asset. Instead, it is a legal right to receive £1,000 30 days hence.

- The bank immediately purchases this legal right from the business. The effect is that when the customer pays after 30 days the £1,000 will belong not to the business but to the bank.

- In the meantime, the business has received payment from the bank.

2.16 Naturally, the bank charges a fee for this service. What happens in practice is that the amount paid by the bank to the business is less than the amount that will eventually be received from the customer. In the example above, the bank might pay the business, say, £950 on Day 1 in exchange for the right to receive £1,000 after 30 days. This means that the bank will make a profit of £50 on the transaction, while the business is paying £50 for the benefit of receiving the cash sooner rather than later.

2.17 There are many variations on this basic theme. In particular, full **factoring** services are offered by many financial institutions. This means that the institution not only pays the business in exchange for its invoices, but also manages the entire process of raising invoices in the first place and dealing with the customers later on to chase payment. The charges for this kind of service may be quite high, but it means that the business is spared many administrative headaches.

2.18 A possible downside of using a factor's services is the loss of direct relationship with the customer. From the bank's point of view, the customer is just a source of payments, and it is possible that a fairly tough line will be adopted in ensuring that the payments keep coming in on time. By contrast, the supplier might be more sympathetic to delays in payment, because he regards the buyer as an ongoing source of business. The buyer may well be upset at having to deal with a factor rather than the supplier.

2.19 There is one final point to note before we leave the subject of invoice discounting and factoring: whether the bank provides the service with or without recourse.

- With-recourse factoring means that the bank has recourse to the supplier if the buyer fails to pay. The supplier himself bears the risk of bad debts.

- Non-recourse factoring means that the bank has no recourse to the supplier and must bear any bad debts itself. Needless to say, the bank will apply a higher charge for this service.

Sale of assets

2.20 Another way of raising funds is to sell off unwanted assets. For example, a company that has experienced a downturn in trade may find itself with factory premises surplus to requirements. Or a company may want to focus on certain core activities and divest itself of peripheral activities.

2.21 Naturally, this kind of occurrence will be infrequent. But the amounts of cash involved could well be large and businesses should be alert to the possibility of selling assets no longer required. If the long-term strategy of the business suggests that there will be no further need of such assets, then disposal is a sensible move in order to realise cash.

Sale and leaseback

2.22 Rather than simply selling off surplus assets, a company may enter into a sale and leaseback agreement. A fixed asset, often a freehold property such as office premises, is sold to a leasing company and then immediately leased back. The advantage to the business is that it can continue to occupy the premises (paying rent to the leasing company) while at the same time raising cash from the sale.

2.23 The disadvantage to the business is that it will have an ongoing commitment to make regular payments to the leasing company, under the terms of the lease agreement. Furthermore, the business will forgo any potential future gain in the value of the premises. At the end of the lease agreement the business will need to renew the lease or find alternative premises.

Bills of exchange

2.24 One final technique, common in transactions with overseas customers and suppliers, is the use of a bill of exchange. This is very much like a cheque – in fact, a cheque is (technically) a special type of bill of exchange. The main difference is that a bill is usually expressed as being payable at some time in the future – say, 90 days hence. Effectively, a firm can secure a cashflow advantage by not having to pay immediately, provided this is acceptable to the supplier.

3 Sources of long-term finance

3.1 When a business's cashflow problems are short-term in nature, then short-term solutions are adequate. But managers must also look to the long term. They must ensure that adequate finance is available to permit investment and development of the business. Addressing these long-term needs by means of short-term finance is poor management strategy. Long-term finance must be found instead.

Ordinary share capital

3.2 The simplest form of long-term finance is the capital provided by the owner(s) of a business. Normally, initial capital will have been injected into the business at its commencement. Further sums may be invested in the business at later stages by the owner(s).

3.3 Clearly there are limits on what can be provided from this source. For example, if John Smith wants to provide capital for his plumbing business he is dependent on his own private resources to do so. Unless he is a very rich man, there is not much capital he can advance.

3.4 John may see a solution in admitting a partner into the business. If the partner is able to provide some capital that will strengthen the cash resources of the business. Of course, John will then have to share any profits he makes with his partner in some agreed proportion.

3.5 Even this may not be sufficient, especially if the business is expanding. For example, more equipment and vans may be needed, and John may also wish to spend money on marketing the business (perhaps placing advertisements in the press). If the resources of himself and his partner are insufficient for this it may be necessary to attract further investors into the business.

3.6 Often in practice the business would be converted into the form of a limited company. The point about companies is that they may be owned by numerous individuals, each claiming a share in the profits and assets of the business. For that reason they are called **shareholders** of the company, and the company is said to be funded by share capital. Shareholders do not necessarily play any part in the running of a business, though in small companies the shareholders and the managers of the business may happen to be the same people, as we saw in an earlier chapter.

3.7 By opening up the business to large numbers of shareholders, John can potentially find far more capital than would be available from his own resources. The price he pays for this is that he is no longer the sole owner of the business: the assets and profits of the business are now owned by the shareholders in agreed proportions that depend on the amount that each shareholder has invested. The reward expected by shareholders is the receipt of dividends (a 'division' of the profits). Dividends are not tax-deductible.

3.8 Ordinary shareholders are not entitled to receive dividends by right. If the company is trading unprofitably, or is in cashflow difficulties, the directors may decide not to pay a dividend in a particular year. This makes ordinary shares a risky investment from the shareholder's point of view. The upside, though, is that if the company does well, the wealth it generates belongs to the shareholders. From the company's point of view, cash paid out as dividends does not count as an allowable deduction from taxable profits, ie we do not get tax relief on the cost of dividends. This contrasts with debt finance, where interest payable does attract tax relief.

3.9 The capital provided by the owner(s) of a business is long-term capital, because in the normal course of events it will not be repaid to the owner(s). Only when the business comes to an end, or in certain other exceptional circumstances, would repayment be necessary.

3.10   A company can issue shares only up to the limit set by its authorised capital in its constitution. However, if additional share capital is considered desirable it is an easy matter to amend the company's constitution so as to permit this.

3.11   In Chapter 2 we saw how a company might raise additional capital from its existing shareholders by means of a rights issue. However, it may be difficult to find sufficient shareholders privately, in which case the company could 'float' its capital on a recognised stock exchange, a process which is highly regulated. In effect, the company would be encouraging the general public to invest money in its shares and by doing so to become shareholders.

Retained profits

3.12   When a business makes profits the value of its assets increases. The owner(s) may decide to withdraw the extra assets (usually in the form of cash) and spend it on personal living expenses. However, the owner(s) may instead decide to leave the money in the business. Any profits earned by the business and not withdrawn by the owner(s) are called **retained profits**.

3.13   In practice, a business owner needs cash to fund his personal living expenses, and so some of the business profits will invariably be withdrawn for this purpose. However, if he is keen for the business to grow and expand he will certainly aim to retain at least some of the profit within the business. (The phrase 'ploughing profits back into the business' is sometimes used to describe this.)

3.14   Although profits may be retained within the business they belong to the owner(s) and may at some stage be withdrawn. Usually, though, they remain in the business for the long term.

3.15   The advantage of this form of capital is that, in effect, it is 'free'. The retained profits belong to the owners (usually the ordinary shareholders in a limited company), and provided that the owners do not actually need to withdraw the money it can simply remain in the business at no cost.

Venture capital

3.16   In some cases, a company may not be able, or may not wish, to raise additional capital from its ordinary shareholders. This may prevent adoption of a potentially attractive opportunity. For example, the company may be keen to launch a new product range, but needs cash to fund the costs of development and launch. If existing shareholders are not seen as a good source of funds, one solution may be to raise venture capital.

3.17   A number of institutions specialise in providing speculative finance in cases such as this. Often they raise funds from individuals who enjoy a surplus. They then look for attractive business opportunities in which to invest the funds. Inevitably, they sometimes back a losing venture, but over time they will expect to make more successes than failures.

3.18   Such funds are referred to as venture capital, and can be of great assistance to a business requiring additional finance and either not able or not willing to raise it from its existing owners. The structure of venture capital funding may vary from case to case, but typically there will be a large element of equity shares involved. This is good news for the business, because it means that the venture capital provider is sharing the risk: if the project is unsuccessful, at least the venture capital may not have to be repaid. This may be more attractive than raising a loan, which *always* has to be repaid.

Preference share capital

3.19 Ordinary share capital and retained profits together form the 'equity' of a limited company. This means they are the capital provided by owners of the company. If the company were to cease trading the assets represented by these sources of funds would be divided up among the ordinary shareholders.

3.20 Some companies, in addition to their ordinary (equity) shares issue 'preference shares'. A preference shareholder is in some senses an owner of the company, but his stake is limited. Typically, his right is to receive a fixed level of dividend each year. For example, the holder of 1,000 £1 6% preference shares is entitled to a dividend of £60 per year, provided the directors decide to pay a dividend at all.

3.21 If the company were to cease trading, the preference shareholders would be entitled to repayment of their original investment, but any additional wealth created by the company during the period of their investment belongs to the equity shareholders.

3.22 The distinction between an ordinary shareholder and a preference shareholder is essentially one of risk. The ordinary shareholder risks receiving no dividends and no return of his capital if the company is unsuccessful. On the other hand, he benefits potentially without limit if the company does well.

3.23 The preference shareholder can be reasonably confident of receiving a fixed level of dividend and having his capital returned eventually (unless the company is a complete failure). But if the company does very well, the preference shareholder does not benefit from the extra wealth created. In this sense, preference shares have many of the features of loan capital, which we discuss next. However, one feature which distinguishes preference shares from loan capital concerns tax relief. Payments to preference shareholders are dividends, which do not attract tax relief; whereas loans are debt capital, meaning that interest payments do attract tax relief.

Loan capital

3.24 A business may finance its long-term development by taking out a loan with a bank or other financial institution, to be repaid over a long period of time. This can be an effective way to meet large one-off expenditure (such as the purchase of a capital asset), or generally to provide a basis for long-term growth.

3.25 The terms on which the loan is agreed will vary from one case to another. The lender will take account of various factors, such as:

- the purpose of the loan
- the financial forecasts supporting the application
- the financial strength of the applicant
- the nature and value of any security for the loan (in which case it would be a loan backed by a mortgage)
- the riskiness of the venture.

3.26   On the basis of this assessment the bank will decide the terms, if any, on which it is prepared to lend. A key factor in the decision will be the existence of security for the loan. If the business has assets which can be mortgaged to the bank in the event of the loan not being repaid the bank will be much more inclined to do business. If there are no assets valuable enough to cover the loan the proposition becomes much more risky, and less attractive, for a lender.

3.27   There are two components of risk.

- Business risk, ie the risk inherent in the project. If a project is risky, a provider of finance will be less certain of recovering his investment, and will charge a higher rate of interest to compensate for that danger.

- Financial risk, ie the risk associated with the capital structure of the borrower. If the borrower is already heavily dependent on outside finance, much of his profits will be consumed by the interest and repayments. There will not be much profit left to cover any new borrowings, which means that a lender will again be inclined to increase the rate of interest in order to compensate.

3.28   If a loan is granted, the borrower will be required to pay interest on the amount owing, usually at a risk-adjusted variable rate related to the base rate. When the base rate is low, interest payments will be comparatively low. He will also be required to repay the loan according to agreed terms, whether the loan is secured by a mortgage or charge, or unsecured. This may mean a single repayment when the term of the loan has expired. Or there may be a schedule of repayment by instalments over the period of the loan.

Debentures

3.29   Another form of loan finance is a debenture. This is a loan taken out by a company and secured either on its fixed assets (a fixed charge) or on its current assets (a floating charge). Interest is payable at defined intervals, and the principal sum must be repaid on or before a specified date. Both forms of repayment are a major commitment; the firm must have the cash available to repay the capital and pay interest according to the agreed terms, otherwise it is in default. This has significant consequences, including the sale of mortgaged or charged assets.

3.30   Interest on bank loans and debentures is an allowable deduction from a company's taxable profits, so although the interest has to be paid, at least a reduction in the tax bill will partly compensate.

Leasing and hire purchase

3.31   A frequent reason for seeking long-term finance is to purchase long-term (ie fixed) assets. Leasing and hire purchase offer ways of achieving this without making a single lump-sum payment at the time of the purchase. Instead, the buyer in effect pays instalments over an agreed period, and legal ownership of the asset does not pass until the payments are complete. (On some variations of these schemes, ownership never passes to the buyer.)

3.32   There are two main ways in which these schemes operate. One involves just a buyer and a seller. The other in addition involves an intermediary – a financial institution such as a bank.

3.33 Suppose John Smith wishes to purchase a new van costing £20,000 for use in his plumbing business. He approaches a motor dealer and agrees to acquire the van under a lease agreement.

3.34 Under the first type of agreement, the dealer simply allows John the use of the van immediately and requires payment in agreed instalments over an agreed period. Until the payments are complete the dealer is in effect out of pocket, though he would compensate for this by setting the total instalments at a level higher than the actual price of the van.

3.35 Under the second scheme a financial intermediary would be used. In effect the dealer would sell the van to a bank, and would receive payment immediately. The bank would allow John immediate use of the van in return for instalment payments. This allows the motor dealer to concentrate on what he does best – selling motor vehicles – and transfers to the bank the problem of collecting payment.

3.36 From John's point of view there is no essential difference. In essence, he is acquiring an asset and at the same time assuming an obligation to make instalment payments over an agreed period.

3.37 There are many advantages to using lease or HP finance. The problem of finding a large amount of cash at once is avoided, while the agreement can also include repair and maintenance costs or even frequent options to replace the asset with a more up-to-date model. At all times the amount of expenditure in relation to the asset is known, as the regular payments are fixed, and the payments are (usually) completely tax-deductible.

3.38 However, there can be disadvantages. In many cases the asset never becomes the property of the business, and the interest rate charged can be quite high. If the entity wants to continue using the asset the payments must continue, so a lease agreement is as long-term a commitment as a loan, usually without the benefit of ownership.

3.39 In the above paragraphs we have been referring to finance leases (and HP arrangements, which are very similar to finance leases). These are adopted to finance major assets that the company prefers not to pay for up-front, usually because of cashflow considerations. It is just worth mentioning another type of lease: an operating lease. This is familiar to anyone who has ever 'rented' a hire car while on holiday, or a piece of specialist equipment for use in DIY, gardening etc. The point here is that the user only wants the asset for a relatively short time, and can avoid the high cost of purchasing it by just renting it instead for the period he requires. There is no intention to acquire the asset, or even to have use of it for an extended period.

Grants

3.40 One final source of finance is grants. Grants are available from a huge variety of sources, many of them connected with government institutions. Tracking availability of grants is so complicated that specialist consultancies exist to advise businesses whether they qualify for any kind of grant assistance. They might do so for instance if they operate in geographical regions where the government is attempting to stimulate employment. Or they might be engaged in research and development work into scientific areas which the government wishes to encourage.

3.41 Often a grant will be awarded only if the applicant is able to put up finance himself. For example, the terms of the grant might be to fund one third of a particular project. If the business wishes to proceed it will have to find finance itself for the other two thirds of the costs.

4 Finance for the public sector

Taxation and rates

4.1 In the UK, the primary funding for public sector services – schools, hospitals, the police force, the armed forces etc – comes from local government and central government. Each of these must raise funds to finance the projects and services for which it is responsible, and must account to the public for their use of funds.

4.2 By far the largest element of public finance is raised from taxation. The central government raises tax revenue from both direct taxes (income tax, national insurance contributions, corporation tax, capital gains tax, etc) and indirect taxes (such as VAT and excise duties). Local governments raise revenue from council tax charged on householders and business rates charged on non-domestic occupiers of premises. Local governments also receive revenue from central government.

4.3 Central and local government use these sources of revenue to fund the services for which they are responsible. Unlike private sector commercial organisations, they do not have an objective of maximising profit. Indeed, the whole concept of 'profit' is out of place in the context of government organisations. However, this does not mean that financial disciplines are irrelevant to such organisations. Their objective is to provide the best possible value for taxpayers' money.

Government investment products and securities

4.4 Another way in which central government raises funds is by the issue of investment products. Members of the public are encouraged to purchase such investments. In most cases the investors are entitled to recover the sums they have paid according to the terms of the investment concerned. In the meantime, the government usually pays them interest for the use of the funds.

4.5 Many types of investment product are offered to the public under the banner of National Savings. For example, it is possible to pay money into a National Savings investment account which, just like a bank account, offers interest on the sum invested. Also under this heading, investors can purchase Premium Bonds. No interest is paid on Premium Bonds, but investors can hope to win cash prizes in a monthly draw.

4.6 National Savings provides the government with a source of long-term finance via products sold to the general public such as ISAs, National Savings certificates and Children's Bonds. Another source of long-term finance is government stocks and securities. For historical reasons, these are often called 'gilt-edged securities' or simply gilts. Gilts are effectively a form of borrowing by the government, and are the most secure form of investment for the people lending the money to the government, since they are guaranteed repayment.

4.7 For example, an investor may purchase a block of £1,000 7% Treasury Stock 2015. This has the following consequences.

- The investor must pay a lump sum to acquire this investment. The lump sum may be more or less than the £1,000 face value, depending on market conditions.

- Whatever sum the investor pays is effectively a loan to the government.

- The £1,000 face value is repayable to the investor by the government in the year 2015. However, the purchaser may choose to sell the investment on the open market before that date.

- Until the investment is redeemed, the government pays the holder interest of £70 per annum (7% of £1,000). Usually the interest is payable at six-monthly intervals, which in this case would mean two payments per year of £35 each.

- The figure of 7 per cent is referred to as the 'coupon rate'. The date of 2015 is referred to as the 'redemption date'.

4.8 An advantage for the government of using gilts is that the government retains control (which it might not do if the funds came from outside investors). A disadvantage arises if the availability of government funds leads to slack budgetary procedures; this could in turn lead to overspending.

Public–private partnerships

4.9 So far we have looked at direct financing of services by government. However, this does not exhaust the possibilities. An alternative that has been explored in recent years is the financing of public services by a mixture of private and public enterprise, often involving some kind of partnership between a public sector organisation and a commercial private sector firm.

4.10 Strategic partnerships are becoming common, particularly for large infrastructure projects. Public–private partnerships (PPP, the Labour government's name for what its predecessor called the Private Finance Initiative, PFI) and design, build, finance and operate (DBFO) schemes have been – and are being – used to create national infrastructure such as the Channel Tunnel, the QEII bridge across the Thames at Dartford, and the North Birmingham Relief Road, as well as smaller projects such as hospitals, schools and barracks.

4.11 Under these schemes a private developer obtains capital, and designs and builds the facility, in exchange for which he is given exclusive rights to charge a fee for its use for a period designed to recoup the original investment plus a reasonable return. In this way the country gets the new infrastructure that it needs, but the government does not have to cover the initial cost from tax revenue.

4.12 There are also examples where this operates in reverse, ie the public authority provides the initial capital and the facility is managed and operated by a private company. In a scheme to encourage the use of rail transport on the 'Fife Circle' in Scotland, the local authority proposes to provide minibuses for a service linking Markinch station with villages in the local hinterland. The operation of these buses will be by a private company on a tender basis.

4.13 One advantage of this kind of scheme is that the public sector can tap into the expertise of the private partner. This can provide excellent value for money, especially if the private partner is able to deploy state-of-the-art technology. It can also enable the public sector body to complete the project much faster than would otherwise be possible, and possibly also to achieve significant cost savings.

4.14 On the other hand, critics of PPP argue that the public sector may in effect be surrendering control of the project, with possibly damaging effects on the level of service and a lower level of public accountability.

4.15 PPP projects may take a variety of forms.

- An operation and maintenance contract means that the private partner is required to operate and maintain a public facility (eg a waste disposal facility).

- A design-build contract means that the private partner designs and builds a facility (eg a motorway), which the government will then operate once completed.

- A turnkey operation means that the public sector provides funding and retains ownership of the facility, but the private partner designs and builds it, and also operates it for a period. This might apply, for example, to a toll road.

- A build-operate contract means that the private partner builds the facility (eg a toll road) and operates it for a period, then transfers ownership back to the public sector body.

5 *The importance of adequate finance*

5.1 We end this chapter with a brief recapitulation of the reasons why it is important for an organisation to obtain adequate finance.

5.2 A saying in common use is that 'cash is king'. Making profits does not guarantee that cash resources will improve. For one thing the profit may be invested in non-liquid assets, such as buildings or machinery. For another, profits may simply be withdrawn by the business owner(s), leaving the business short of resources.

5.3 So merely earning profits, though desirable, is not enough to ensure the survival of a business. When suppliers are clamouring for payment it is only cash that will satisfy them. When the time comes to pay monthly wages and salaries, there must be funds in the bank to satisfy the employees.

5.4 Equally, it is important to ensure that the right type of finance is obtained. We have already remarked that short-term finance is suitable only for meeting short-term cashflow problems. If the need is for investment in capital assets or general business expansion over the long term, then long-term finance is the answer.

5.5 This point may not be immediately obvious, but consider the case of a business wishing to invest £100,000 in a fixed asset with an expected useful life of five years. Clearly the business must believe that the value that the asset will create over that period will more than repay its cost.

5.6 However, it may take the full five years before that hope is realised. That is fine if the asset has been financed by a five-year loan; the funds will be available to repay the loan when required. But it could be disastrous to finance the asset with a one-year loan. At the end of a year the full £100,000 must be repaid, whereas the extra value created by the asset in that time may be only a fraction of that amount. The result is that the business is unable to meet its debt when it falls due. This explains the general principle that short-term funding is suitable to fund short-term assets, but for long-term assets the business should choose long-term finance.

Chapter summary

- The most obvious way in which organisations raise finance is by conducting their normal operations and generating a positive cashflow from them.

- You need to be familiar with the distinction between operating expenditure and capital expenditure.

- Sources of short-term finance include bank overdraft, credit from suppliers, controlling working capital, schemes of factoring or invoice discounting, and sale of assets.

- Long-term capital may be provided either by the owner(s) of a business or by external third parties. The owner(s) may pay actual cash into the business, and/or they may decline to withdraw profits from the business. Both of these possibilities rank as owner's capital, the second taking the form of retained profits.

- Other long-term possibilities include venture capital, preference share capital, loan capital, leasing and hire purchase, and grants.

- Sources of government funding include taxation and Treasury bills, rates and borrowing (eg through National Savings and gilts). Public sector bodies may also provide services through public–private partnerships.

- 'Cash is king.' Without a sufficient level of appropriate finance even profitable organisations may founder.

Self-test questions

Numbers in brackets refer to the paragraphs where your answers can be checked.

1   Describe how different types of organisation raise finance from their normal operations. (1.2)

2   Give three examples of operating expenditure and three of capital expenditure. (1.6, 1.7)

3   What are the disadvantages of overdraft finance? (2.3, 2.4)

4   Explain how control of stocks and debtors can improve liquidity. (2.9–2.11)

5   Describe how invoice discounting works. (2.15)

6   What is a sale and leaseback arrangement? (2.22)

7   What is a shareholder? (3.6)

8   What is meant by the term 'ploughing profits back into a business'? (3.13)

9   Distinguish between an ordinary shareholder and a preference shareholder. (3.22)

10   How do financial intermediaries act in relation to leasing and hire purchase schemes? (3.35)

11   How much interest is payable on a gilt-edged security with face value £10,000 and a coupon rate of 6 per cent, which cost the investor £9,500 to purchase? (4.7)

12   Why may it be disastrous to pay for a long-term asset with short-term finance? (5.5, 5.6)

CHAPTER 7

Budgeting

Learning objectives and indicative content

4.1 Explain how to develop and manage budgets to achieve target performance

- The importance of setting and controlling budgets to achieve performance targets
- The importance of setting a realistic budget
- Financial objectives
- Motivational objectives
- SMART objectives
- How to create and present a budget to support a business plan
- The importance of financial forecasting

4.2 Analyse resource requirements and their application in purchasing activities

- Time
- People
- Money
- Quality

4.3 Communicate findings and recommendations effectively

- Target audience: finance professionals and other parts of a business
- Budget presentation
- Presenting the business case

Chapter headings

1 Setting and controlling budgets

2 Assessing resource requirements

3 Budgetary control

4 Preparing the budget

5 Presenting the business case

6 Cashflow forecasts

Introduction

In this chapter we look at a vital element of managerial control: the use of budgets for planning and monitoring performance. We begin by describing the purpose of budgeting in terms of motivation, planning and control. We explain the various resource requirements that may be embodied in the budget: time, people, money etc.

We then look at the use of budgets for control of operations.

Finally we show how budgets are prepared and presented, dealing with cash budgets (or cashflow forecasts) in a separate section.

1   *Setting and controlling budgets*

The relationship of corporate plans to operational budgets

1.1   All organisations must plan. Plans vary in the level at which they are taken, the breadth of the business they cover, the detail they examine and the length of their horizon (or how far ahead they look).

- Strategic plans apply to the whole organisation. They focus on the broad, general direction of the organisation over the long term (say, 3–5 years. Note that 'long term' is no longer thought of in terms of 10-year plans, because of the pace of environmental change!)

- Tactical plans apply to particular divisions and functions (or strategic business units). They focus on the tasks and objectives required to pursue the chosen strategies in particular markets, over the medium term (say, 1–2 years).

- Operational plans apply to functions and departments. They focus on the specific detail of tasks, targets, resources and actions needed to implement the chosen tactics, over the short term (day to day and up to a year, say).

1.2   Even from this brief description, you should appreciate the need to integrate planning activity in two directions.

- **Vertical integration** ensures that individual plans are designed to support team objectives, which are designed to support functional plans, which are designed to support organisational objectives. This is essential for purposeful activity: all efforts contribute to the goal. Purchase and supply objectives, for example, are not formulated in isolation: they further the organisation's value-adding and competitive strategies by reducing costs, improving quality and lead-times and so on.

- **Horizontal integration** ensures that the objectives of different individuals, units and functions dovetail with each other. This is essential for co-ordinated effort, reduced waste (from duplicated activity, bottlenecks or gaps) and the presentation of a coherent face to the outside world. So, for example, purchasing and supply plans must be co-ordinated with the needs of customers (defined by marketing plans), the requirements of operations (defined by operations plans) and the availability of resources (eg through HR and financial planning) and so on.

Why are goals and objectives important?

1.3   Setting effective goals is important for organisational reasons. Goals promote unity of direction, aiding co-ordination and efficient organisation: they reduce overlaps and gaps in activity. They enable limited resources to be intentionally allocated to optimise corporate performance (rather than potentially sub-optimal unit performance). They provide an objective measure against which performance can be measured and   accountability maintained. They support flexibility, by focusing on end results rather than inputs (which may change).

1.4   Goal setting is also important, at an individual and team level, for behavioural reasons. Goals enable tasks to be broken down into manageable time-bounded 'chunks', while at the same time giving people a sense of their role and contribution to the whole activity of the organisation. They are important in motivation: people are motivated by the decision that it is worth expending effort to reach desired outcomes (goals), and by feedback information telling them to what extent they have achieved those goals. Goals are, for the same reason, vital in learning and change.

Achieving performance targets

1.5   Organisational goals are usually captured in budgets. A budget has been defined as 'a plan quantified in monetary terms, prepared and approved prior to a defined period of time, usually showing planned income to be generated and or expenditure to be incurred during that period and the capital to be employed to attain a given objective'.

1.6   Budgetary control is the establishment of budgets relating the responsibilities of executives to the requirements of a policy, and the continuous comparison of actual with budgeted results, either to secure by individual action the objectives of that policy or to provide a basis for its revision.

1.7   The objectives of preparing a budget are as follows.

- To motivate people to attain targets
- To measure performance
- To authorise levels of expenditure
- To co-ordinate operations
- To control activities and costs

1.8   For our present purposes the first two of these objectives are the most relevant. The budget embodies targets that we mean to achieve, and enables us to compare targeted performance with actual performance. (The later objectives – mostly to do with control – are addressed in later sections of this chapter.)

1.9   In general, budgets are set for specific periods of time in the future, for example the budget for the coming year. Sometimes budgets are constructed for specific projects that are to be undertaken, but again these can be analysed into the periods of time that the projects are expected to last. Thus, if a project is planned to last two years, the total budget for it can be split into that relating to the first year and that relating to the second year.

1.10   Budgets are plans expressed in financial and/or quantitative terms either for the whole of a business or for the various parts of a business for a specified period of time in the future. The budgets are prepared within the framework of objectives and policies that have been determined by senior management as part of its own planning activities.

The motivational effect of a budget

1.11   Who lays down the targets contained in the budgets? One possible system would be for top management to draw up the budgets in isolation from other staff. Managers lower down the chain would then be held responsible for meeting the targets.

1.12   Although this would be possible in theory, in practice most people would agree that this is a poor way of preparing a budget. The problem is that the managers responsible for implementing the budget should have some input to its creation. Otherwise, they will feel no 'ownership' and will not feel motivated to achieve the targets. They may well find the targets quite unrealistic, which is demoralising.

1.13   For this reason it is considered better practice for managers to have a big say in the budgets for which they will bear operational responsibility.

1.14   What kind of performance targets should the budget embody? One school of thought is that the budget should be a simple description of what is considered most likely to happen. The problem with this is again to do with motivation: it is too easy to set targets that do not stretch managers. The term 'forecast' would be more usual to describe this kind of budget.

1.15   At the other extreme, some people would say that the budget should embody very ambitious targets with a view to stretching managers to their utmost. Once again, though, there is a problem of motivation. With this kind of budget it is likely that managers will constantly be falling short of target. This is demotivating, and makes the manager's performance appear poor, when in reality the problem is with the over-ambitious targets.

SMART objectives

1.16   Somewhere in between these extremes, there is a consensus that budget targets should be SMART.

- **S**pecific
- **M**easurable
- **A**chievable
- **R**ealistic
- **T**ime-bound

1.17   In the context of a budget, we might aim to increase sales revenue in the coming period by 10% compared with the current period.

- This is specific, because we (presumably) know our sales revenue for the current period, and a 10% increase is therefore unambiguous.
- It is measurable, because sales revenue is one of the key figures generated by our accounting system.
- Achievable and realistic are the key terms here. Achievable suggests that there has to be an element of stretching the manager to achieve the target; while realistic suggests that the target is not foolishly ambitious. Whether a projected increase of 10% fits the bill depends on the circumstances of the firm and the market.
- Time-bound. We need to have a date by which we intend to have accomplished the target. In the context of a budget, this is given by the budget period, often a year.

Types of budget

1.18   There are various ways of establishing budget targets.

- With an **incremental budget** we begin by looking at the actual figures for the previous period. We then adjust in line with known changes to arrive at a budget for the current period.
- With a **zero-based budget** we ignore previous periods and start completely from scratch.
- With a **priority based budget** we allocate funds in line with strategic goals.

1.19 Whichever of these methods is used, it is important to keep the budget up to date. Two techniques are worth mentioning in this context.

- A **rolling budget** is usually maintained. For example, a 12-month budget may be constructed for the period January to December. At the end of January, we update this by adding figures for the following January. Our revised budget then still covers a 12-month period, from February to January inclusive.

- At intervals during the year it is common to revisit the budget and update it in line with new information. This is sometimes referred to as producing a **forecast**.

Benefits and limitations of budgeting

1.20 Benefits of budgeting include the following.

- It compels managers to think ahead and anticipate the future.
- The budget system ensures that organisational objectives are translated into operational targets.
- A budget is a systematic method of communicating targets throughout an organisation.
- A well constructed budget can improve staff motivation.
- Budgets provide a mechanism whereby managerial performance can be assessed.
- Budgets provide a method of control. By comparing actual outcomes with the budget, managers are quickly alerted to any problems. Corrective action can then be taken quickly.

1.21 Limitations of budgeting include the following.

- The whole budget system can be cumbersome to establish and maintain.
- Budgeting takes time that managers could otherwise employ in carrying out their operational responsibilities.
- Political aspects of budgeting (eg competing for funds with other functions within the organisation) can cause serious waste of managerial time.
- Budgets necessarily involve estimation, which means they will invariably be 'wrong' to a greater or lesser degree.
- Where managers are judged against departmental budgets, they are likely to take decisions that benefit their department, regardless of the impact on the organisation overall (a problem called 'dysfunctional behaviour').

2 *Assessing resource requirements*

Planning the programme of activities

2.1 Once objectives have been determined, they must be expressed as a series of stages and tasks which can be allocated to individuals and teams. This can be done using various project and performance management techniques.

2.2 A form of **management by objectives** may be used to analyse objectives in terms of: key tasks (which are directly relevant to the achievement of the objectives) and key results (which must be achieved in order for the key tasks to be successfully performed and objectives met).

2.3 This analysis can then be used as the basis of agreed individual and team plans for a defined planning period: selecting specific improvement objectives and forming action plans for each key task. Progress against the improvement plans will be monitored and reviewed at agreed intervals, and adjustments made as required.

2.4 A work breakdown structure (WBS) may be used to analyse the key elements of the task into smaller and smaller component parts, until the project consists of a series of specific activities or 'work packages' which can be individually scheduled and allocated within the project plan. This is a project management approach which is often used to estimate resource requirements for a project, since it allows a realistic picture of all the activities required.

Prioritisation and resource allocation

2.5 Once we know what tasks are required, we need to decide what order we will tackle them in! The process of prioritisation assigns relative priority to tasks, which determines their sequence in the plan. A task is likely to be high priority if:

- It has to be completed by a certain time (deadline)
- Other tasks or people depend on its completion
- Its potential consequences, impacts or value are considered important.

2.6 A range of tools and techniques for prioritising may be relevant.

- **Pareto analysis** (or '80/20 rule') is a useful technique for finding the activities or changes that will leverage your time, effort and resources to bring the biggest benefits. Which are the 'vital few' tasks or factors which will make the biggest impact or contribution to the change programme? Which are the 'trivial many' aspects that will not have a great impact, and can be addressed later, if necessary? (In its simplest form, this only requires you to list the factors/tasks being considered, and scoring them in any appropriate way: potential cost savings, say.)

- **Paired comparison analysis**: weighing the relative importance of different options/factors against each other in pairs, to decide which is the more important of the two and by how much (scored from 0 to 3). The scores for each 'winning' option are then added up to show the order of importance of all the options.

- **Critical path analysis** or **precedence network analysis**: which tasks need to be completed before others (sequential tasks), and which can be undertaken simultaneously (parallel tasks)? Which tasks need to start and finish on time in order for the project as a whole to meet its deadlines?

- **Risk analysis**: which external threats or internal weaknesses pose the greatest threat/risk to the organisation (in terms of likelihood of occurrence and severity of consequences)? These may be a priority for change intervention.

- **Screening questions** as to the suitability, feasibility and acceptability of various options.

- The **importance-performance matrix** *(Slack et al)*: what aspects of performance are important to the customer – and how does our organisation perform in those areas? Low organisational performance in areas of high customer importance urgently requires change; low performance in low-importance areas is less urgent; high performance in high-importance areas must be maintained; and high performance in low-importance areas may suggest the need to divert resources.

Time, people and money

2.7 The budget incorporates our estimates of the costs and revenues that will arise over the coming period. It is a financial document. However, the resources that will be consumed are not necessarily financial in nature. For example, we will need to estimate how many staff will be needed to achieve the targets, and of what grades. We will need to estimate how much time our staff will expend on performing the tasks required to achieve the targets. That is why the syllabus mentions the resources of time, people and money.

2.8 In fact we should go further than this, because other resources are needed as well. For example, in a manufacturing company we need physical resources such as raw materials, machinery, vehicles, computer equipment etc. All of these must be estimated and translated into monetary terms.

2.9 Some of the decisions to be made in resource planning include those displayed in Table 7.1 (most of which are standard purchasing decisions, and should be familiar to you from your other studies).

Table 7.1 *Decisions in resource planning*

Human resources	• What skills and expert input will be required to implement the programme of activities?
	• How many people, for how long?
	• Are the required skills and labour hours available within the organisation – and at what replacement, overtime or opportunity cost?
	• Will they need to be sourced from outside: if so, how?
	• What orientation, training, support and other inputs will be required to enable their contribution?
Physical resources	• What equipment and materials will be needed to implement the programme of activities (eg required for new operations, IT systems or office locations) and to manage the process (eg training/education resources for staff)?
	• Are the required resources available in the organisation?
	• If resources must be bought in, what constitutes the 'right product of the right quality at the right place at the right time at the right price'?
Financial resources	• What capital and operating expenditure will be required to finance the human and physical resources?
	• Is cash available or will some form of long- or short-term finance be required?
	• For capital items, what is the 'real' cost of the item over its useful life (including maintenance costs etc) at net present value?

Cost prediction

2.10 It is clear that the budget process will involve the prediction of future costs. To do this effectively it is important to understand the nature of the costs in question, and in particular whether the cost is fixed, variable, or a mixture of the two. Analysis of costs incurred in the past will help with this.

2.11 As a reminder, note the distinction between fixed costs (which are unaffected by changes in the level of output), and variable costs (which change in accordance with changes in the level of output). For example, the cost of raw materials is a variable cost, because the more output we produce the more we must spend on raw materials to create the output.

The impact of inflation

2.12   In the UK and in most other developed countries there is a long history of gradual price inflation. As managers try to look ahead in the budget process the problems that this causes must be addressed.

2.13   Budgets are often expressed to begin with in terms of units. The problems arise when managers attempt to convert this into monetary amounts. For example, we may know, or guess, that we will need 1,000 kilos of Material X in the forthcoming budget period, but it is unclear whether a price increase for this material will affect our calculations.

2.14   The main effect of this is that managers must be very careful in interpreting variances from budgeted expectations. If our expenditure on Material X is higher than the budget predicted this does not necessarily mean that we have been inefficient in our use of X. It may simply arise because of an inflationary increase beyond our control.

3   *Budgetary control*

Functions of budgetary control

3.1   Essentially the budgetary control process consists of two distinct elements.

- **Planning.** This involves setting the various budgets for the appropriate future period. Managers at the various levels in an organisation should be involved in the budgetary planning stage for their own areas of responsibility. In many medium and large businesses this activity can take a considerable amount of time. As we have already seen, there is a need to coordinate the budgets of the various parts of a business to ensure that they are all complementary and in line with overall company objectives and policies.

- **Control.** Once the budgets have been set and agreed for the future period under review, the formal control element of budgetary control is ready to start.

3.2   This control involves comparison of the plan in the form of the budget with the actual results achieved for the appropriate period. Significant divergences between the budgeted and the actual results should be reported to the appropriate managers so that the necessary action can be taken.

3.3   The benefits of budgetary control are numerous.

- **Planning.** Budgetary control provides a formal framework for planning, which involves making sure that problems are anticipated and that steps are taken to avoid or reduce them. The organisation develops a plan of what it will aim to achieve in terms of costs and revenues, and management has a formal set of objectives to work towards, ie management by objectives.

- **Coordination.** The system integrates budgets for the various sections of a business into a master budget for the whole business. Individual managers will, therefore, recognise the overall objectives in forming their plans.

- **Authorising and delegating.** Approval of the master budget explicitly authorises the policy represented by the budget. The responsibility for carrying out the policy is delegated to individual managers.

- **Evaluating performance.** The budget represents a target against which the performance of managers can be assessed.

- **Communicating and motivating.** Preparing budgets involves communication between top management and lower levels on how to attain the objectives. Agreement motivates managers to achieve the targets set.

- **Control.** Continuous comparison of actual against plan indicates where control is needed. Budgetary control reports can be designed to focus management attention where it is most needed, for example where there are major differences between budgeted and actual performance. Following the principles of management by exception in this way means that control attention is directed where it will be most worthwhile and those areas of the business which are proceeding according to plan are not subjected to unnecessary scrutiny.

3.4 However, there are also limitations in the use of traditional budgeting.

- **Over-reliance.** Variance analysis based on traditional budgeting is not the only technique available to managers in this area. For example, managers might make greater use of key performance indicators, service level agreements etc as a method of exercising control over operations.

- **Dysfunctional behaviour.** A traditional budget system encourages managers to focus on achieving their own, local objectives. This is usually the basis on which their performance is measured. But unless budgets have been very carefully designed, these local objectives may conflict with overall corporate objectives.

- **Conflict between departments.** The traditional budgeting systems may encourage conflict as different departments compete for scarce resources.

- **Inaccuracy.** Budgets may simply be inaccurate, either through lack of care in preparation, or through unexpected changes in circumstances, or because of 'padding' for contingencies. Managers must be prepared to recognise that budgets are not always a perfect guide to planning operations.

Budget centres

3.5 A budget centre is a section of an organisation for which control may be exercised and budgets prepared.

3.6 A budget centre is a clearly defined part of an organisation for the purposes of operating a budgetary control system. Each function within an organisation will be sub-divided into appropriate budget centres.

3.7 In determining budget centres it is important to be able to define them in terms of management responsibility. The manager responsible for a budget centre (eg the machining department within the production function) will be involved in the planning stage of setting the budget for his area of responsibility and he will be the recipient of control information in due course. This is referred to as **responsibility accounting.**

3.8 To apply responsibility accounting effectively it is important to distinguish between costs that are controllable by the manager concerned, and those that are uncontrollable. It would obviously be unfair to assess the manager's performance in relation to costs that he is unable to control (eg the costs of centralised service functions on whose services he has to rely).

The budget period

3.9   The budget period is the period for which a budget is prepared and used which may then be subdivided into control periods. The length of a budget period will depend on various factors.

- **The nature of the business.** In the ship-building or power supply industries budget periods of ten to twenty years may be appropriate. Periods of less than one year may be appropriate for firms in the clothing and fashion industries.

- **The part of the business being budgeted.** Capital expenditure will usually be budgeted for longer periods ahead than the production output.

- **The basis of control.** Many businesses use a twelve month period as their basic budget period, but at the same time it is very common to find the annual budget broken down into quarterly or monthly sub-units. Such a breakdown is usually for control purposes because actual and budgeted results need to be monitored continuously. It is not practicable to wait until the end of a twelve month budget period before making control comparisons.

The methodology of budget preparation

3.10   Preparation of the budget involves seven steps (see Figure 7.1). The sales budget is shown as the first step in Figure 7.1. This is because it is the **principal budget factor**. It is the factor which limits the activities of an organisation and stops it expanding indefinitely. For most organisations the limiting factor or principal budget factor is sales volume. However, especially in the short term, another factor – for example production capacity – may limit activities.

Figure 7.1 *The steps in budget preparation*

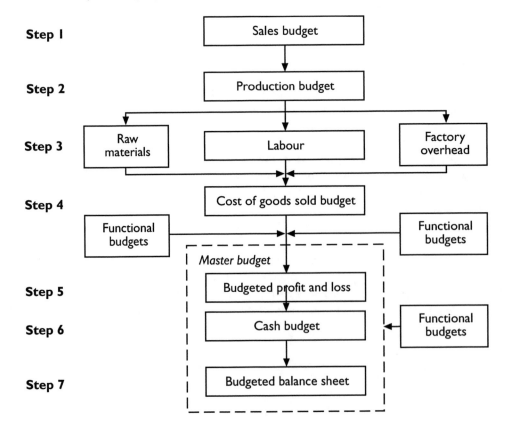

3.11 It is important to identify the principal budget factor and prepare the budget for it early in the budgetary planning process, since all other budgets must be co-ordinated to this one. For example, a budget that leads to production in excess of sales demand would obviously not make sense.

Calculation of budget variances

3.12 The following example illustrates the comparison of actual and budget results.

3.13 The differences between the budget and actual values are known as variances. Where they relate to costs (rather than revenue), if the actual cost is less than the budget cost the variance is described as favourable; if the actual cost is greater the variance is said to be adverse.

Example

3.14 Bug Ltd manufactures one uniform product only. The following statement shows the departmental overhead budget based on an average level of activity of 20,000 units of production per four week period, and the actual results for four weeks in October.

	Budget average for four week period	Actual for 1 to 28 October
	£	£
Indirect labour	20,000	19,540
Consumables	800	1,000
Depreciation	10,000	10,000
Other overheads	5,000	5,000
	35,800	35,540

3.15 You are required to produce an analysis of the variances between budget and actual.

Solution to the example

3.16 The analysis is given below.

	Average four week budget	Actual results	Variances favourable/ (adverse)
	£	£	£
Indirect labour	20,000	19,540	460
Consumables	800	1,000	(200)
Depreciation	10,000	10,000	-
Other overheads	5,000	5,000	-
	35,800	35,540	260

Fixed and flexible budgets

3.17 Some care is needed when analysing such variances. This is because some organisations make use of 'fixed budgets', which can be very misleading when used as a basis for variance analysis.

3.18 A fixed budget is based on a particular estimate of activity levels. For example, it may assume that sales volume will be 200,000 units in the coming year. The revenue and costs shown in the budget will all be based on this assumption. The problem arises when the assumption turns out to be wrong.

3.19 Suppose that an unexpected opportunity arises to increase production by 50,000 units because of a sudden surge in sales demand. This is obviously good news for the business, but it means that the fixed budget is no longer much use as a control tool.

3.20 For example, it is likely that we are going to be overspending all of our estimates of costs. While this would normally cause concern, in this case it is just an inevitable consequence of the increased production. The budget is sending the signal that we are overspending, whereas the truth is that we are doing well.

3.21 To cope with this problem most businesses use flexible budgets in preference to fixed budgets. A flexible budget is a budget which, by recognising different cost behaviour patterns, is designed to change as volume of output changes. In the example above, as soon as we know that sales are way ahead of target all of the variable costs of sales are automatically revised on the flexible budget. Fixed costs of course are not altered. That is why it is important to be able to distinguish fixed from variable costs.

4   *Preparing the budget*

Preparation of a master budget

4.1   The following data will be used to explain the technique of budget preparation.

4.2   Hash Ltd has the following opening stock and required closing stock of its two products: the PS and the TG.

	PS units	TG units
Opening stock	100	50
Required closing stock	1,100	50

4.3   You are also given the following data about the materials required to produce PS and TG and the whittling and fettling processes involved in production.

	PS	TG
Finished products		
Kilos of raw material X, per unit of finished product	12	12
Kilos of raw material Y, per unit of finished product	6	8
Direct labour hours per unit of finished product	8	12
Machine hours per unit – whittling	5	8
Machine hours per unit – fettling	3	4

	Raw material	
	X	Y
Direct materials		
Desired closing stock in kilos	6,000	1,000
Opening stock in kilos	5,000	5,000

Standard rates and prices

Direct labour	£2.20 per hour
Raw material X	£0.72 per kg
Raw material Y	£1.56 per kg

Production overheads

Variable	£1.54 per labour hour
Fixed	£0.54 per labour hour
	£2.08 per labour hour

The sales budget

4.4   The sales budget represents the plan in terms of the quantity and value of sales. In practice this is often the most difficult budget to calculate.

4.5   Hash Ltd makes two products – PS and TG. Sales for next year are budgeted at 5,000 units of PS and 1,000 units of TG. Planned selling prices are £65 and £100 respectively. The sales budget would be as follows.

	Total	PS	TG
Sales units	6,000	5,000	1,000
Sales value	£425,000	£325,000	£100,000

The production budget

4.6 The next step is to produce the production budget. This is usually expressed in quantity and represents the sales budget adjusted for opening/closing finished stocks and work in progress.

	PS units	TG units
Sales budget	5,000	1,000
Budgeted stock increase		
(1,100 – 100)	1,000	
(50 – 50)		-
Production in units	6,000	1,000

4.7 The production budget must next be translated into requirements for: raw materials; direct labour; machine utilisation; production overheads; closing stock levels. We look at each of these in turn below.

The raw materials budget

4.8 Hash Ltd is going to produce 6,000 units of PS and 1,000 units of TG.

		X Kilos		Y Kilos
For production of PS	6,000 × 12 kilos	72,000	6,000 × 6 kilos	36,000
For production of TG	1,000 × 12 kilos	12,000	1,000 × 8 kilos	8,000
		84,000		44,000
Increase/(decrease) in stock (6,000 – 5,000)		1,000	(1,000 – 5,000)	(4,000)
Raw materials required		85,000		40,000
		£		£
Budgeted value				
X £0.72 per kilo × 85,000		61,200		
Y £1.56 per kilo × 40,000				62,400

The direct labour budget

4.9 We can now prepare the direct labour budget.

	Hours		£
For PS 6,000 × 8 hrs	48,000		
For TG 1,000 ×12 hrs	12,000		
	60,000	@ £2.20	132,000

The machine utilisation budget

4.10 We can now prepare the machine utilisation budget.

	Whittling hours		Fettling hours
For PS 6,000 × 5 hrs	30,000	6,000 × 3 hrs	18,000
For TG 1,000 × 8 hrs	8,000	1,000 × 4 hrs	4,000
	38,000		22,000
Total hours			60,000

Production overheads

4.11 We can now calculate the production overheads.

		£
Variable costs	60,000 hours × £1.54	92,400
Fixed costs	60,000 hours × £0.54	32,400
		124,800

Other budgets

4.12 Depending on the requirements of management, additional budgets may be prepared for any or all of the following.

- Purchasing – consolidates purchases of raw materials, supplies and services in raw materials/expense budgets, analysed to show when the goods are received (for control of supply) and also when they are paid for (for cash budget).
- Personnel (manpower) – shows detailed requirements, month by month, for production and administration personnel.
- Stocks – itemises quantity and value, month by month, of planned stock levels for raw materials, work in progress and finished goods.
- Debtors – details time analysis of collections from sales suitably analysed by type of customer or type of product.

Using computers in budgeting

4.13 The nature of the budgeting exercise is that many of the resulting final values are dependent on the estimate made of sales volumes, together with a few policy decisions (for example stockholding policies, payment period policies).

4.14 It is also true to say that budgets are a planning device designed to assist in the achievement of an organisation's longer-term plans.

4.15 These two factors have the following consequences.

- There are likely to be a number of alterations made to the first draft of the budget to see the effects of such changes.
- The alteration of one value will cause many other values to alter.

4.16 It is these factors which have led to the preparation of budgets being computerised, using spreadsheet packages. A spreadsheet is a computer package which stores data in a matrix format where the intersection of each row and column is referred to as a cell. Columns are referenced alphabetically and rows numerically with the result that a cell reference is a combination of these.

4.17 Each cell within a spreadsheet may be used to store:

- a label (description), eg the title of the spreadsheet
- a value, or
- a formula.

4.18 The formula is used to carry out calculations on values entered in other parts of the spreadsheet. The benefit of using formulae is that if some value on the spreadsheet is changed – eg the forecast of sales volume may be amended – the computer automatically recalculates all the formulae. In an instant the effect of the new assumption is displayed in the budget without any manual recalculation.

5 Presenting the business case

Introduction

5.1 Once the budget has been prepared it is often necessary to argue for its adoption by presenting the business case for it. This is particularly the case if the budget relates to a project or a new activity.

5.2 To do this it will be important to prepare a structured justification of the budget, which will often be presented by means of a personal delivery, eg to a group of senior managers.

5.3 The presentation will typically include the following elements.

- An executive summary
- A summary of the background to the issue, including what has given rise to the need for a budget
- The business objectives that we are attempting to achieve
- An outline of the various options that might be adopted to achieve these objectives
- Identification of the preferred option with a justification for its selection
- A plan of action, including appropriate 'milestones'
- The budget itself, often including different scenarios based on different possible levels of funding that may be available
- A summary of the funds required and the likely financial outcomes
- Measures of success that can be used to control outcomes

Making the presentation

5.4 A general approach to giving effective presentations may be described as follows.

- **F**ormulate a strategy for the specific purpose and audience
- **O**rganise the presentation content for clarity and impact
- **R**einforce oral content with appropriate visual aids
- **C**larify and emphasise the content with a confident and vivid presentation style
- **E**nd the presentation with informed responses to challenges and questions

You might use the mnemonic 'FORCE' to remember this framework.

5.5 The **purpose** of a presentation should be expressed in specific, active terms. What do you want the audience to do/remember/believe/know/feel as a result of attending your presentation? What observable/measurable response will allow you to evaluate your success? Once you have stated your primary objective, you can work out the subsidiary objectives you need to achieve along the way.

5.6 Since your purpose is defined primarily in terms of audience response, it is important to take into account the needs, abilities and motivations of the **audience** you will be addressing. The purpose of the meeting may indicate something of what the participants will be expecting, what they will be interested in and what they will be able to understand.

5.7 An effective introduction is vital to the presentation. It establishes credibility, gains the audience's interest and motivates them to keep attending, and gives the audience an overview of the shape and direction of the presentation. Introductions should:

- make an initial impact: arousing curiosity, setting up a problem to be solved or a question to be answered which relates to the audience's needs;
- establish credibility and congeniality, by demonstrating authority, clear thinking and/or rapport with the audience;
- give a statement of the subject and the style in which you intend to address it, to orient the audience and manage their expectations.

5.8 The structure of the main body of the presentation is critical because it facilitates or hinders the accessibility, credibility, comprehension and recall of the message.

5.9 The conclusion is another vital element, because people tend to rally their concentration towards the end of a talk and tend in any case to remember the last thing they hear (the principle of 'recency'). A conclusion should:

- clarify and draw together the points made into a final summary of the main idea;
- state, reinforce or imply the response required of the audience;
- give the audience a satisfying sense of closure or completeness.

6   *Cashflow forecasts*

Preparing a cashflow forecast

6.1   A cashflow forecast (or cash budget) is a detailed budget of income and cash expenditure incorporating both operating and capital items. The objective of a cash budget is to anticipate cash shortages/surpluses and allow time to make plans for dealing with them.

6.2   The steps in preparing a cash budget are as follows.

- Forecast sales.
- Forecast time-lag on converting debtors to cash, and hence forecast actual cash receipts from customers.
- Determine stock levels, and hence purchase requirements.
- Forecast time-lag on paying suppliers, and hence forecast actual cash payments to suppliers.
- Incorporate other cash payments and receipts, including such items as capital expenditure and tax payments.
- Collate this information so as to find the net cashflows.

6.3   A tabular layout should be used, with columns for months and rows for receipts and payments. We will use an example to illustrate the procedures. The task is to convert the profit and loss account into a cash budget.

Example

6.4   Here is a company's profit and loss account for the three months to 30 September. We assume that all revenue and costs accrue evenly over the three months. The task is to convert the profit and loss account into a cash budget.

	£'000	£'000
Sales (cash received one month in arrear)		1,200
Purchases (paid one month in arrear)	1,044	
Depreciation	72	
	———	
		1,116
		———
Budgeted profit		84

6.5   The company's capital expenditure and receipts budget for the three month period is as follows.

	£'000
Payments for new plant	
July	12
August	25
September	13
Increase in stocks, payable August	20
Receipts: new issue of share capital (September)	30

6.6 Current assets at 1 July include debtors of £210,000 and cash of £40,000. Liabilities at 1 July include trade creditors of £160,000, dividends payable in August of £24,000 and tax payable in September of £30,000.

Solution to the example

6.7 The solution can be prepared as follows. You should work carefully through this solution to ensure you can establish where each figure comes from. The trickiest figures are those relating to payments from debtors and to suppliers, because of the one month delay.

CASH BUDGET FOR THREE MONTHS TO 30 SEPTEMBER

	July £'000	August £'000	September £'000
Cash receipts			
From debtors	210	400	400
Share capital			30
Total	210	400	430
Cash payments			
To creditors	160	348	348
Purchase of plant	12	25	13
Increase in stock		20	
Tax			30
Dividends		24	
Total	172	417	391
Surplus/(deficit)	38	(17)	39
Opening balance	40	78	61
Closing balance	78	61	100

Remedying a cash shortage

6.8 If a cashflow forecast shows a poor position, now or in the future, we need to consider how to improve matters. Possible remedies may involve either boosting cash receipts or reducing cash payments.

6.9 To boost cash receipts we could consider any of the following actions.

- Inject new capital from the owner(s).
- Raise an overdraft or bank loan.
- Increase the level of sales (eg by promotional activities).
- Reduce the period of credit allowed to customers to accelerate receipt of cash from them.
- Encourage prompt payment by customers (eg by offering discounts in return).

6.10   To reduce cash payments we could consider any of the following actions.

- Defer capital expenditure (or finance capital items by borrowing or leasing instead of payment from cash).
- Reduce purchases from suppliers, perhaps by running down stock levels.
- Negotiate discounts from suppliers to reduce purchase costs.
- Negotiate increased credit period from suppliers to defer payments to them.

Differences between the cashflow forecast and the budget

6.11   It is worth glancing briefly at the main differences between the cashflow forecast described in this section of the chapter and the budget described earlier.

- As the title suggests, the cashflow forecast deals only with cash movements. Non-cash expenses (such as depreciation of fixed assets) are ignored.
- The timing of cashflows is often different from the incurring of revenue and expenditure. For example, we may earn sales revenue by making a sale in Month 1, but we may not receive cash from our customer until Month 2 or 3.
- The cashflow forecast includes amounts that have no place in an operating budget, such as tax payments, dividends to shareholders, and capital expenditure.

Chapter summary

- A budget is a plan expressed in monetary terms. It is used for purposes of planning and control. Control is exercised in particular by comparing budgeted outcomes with actual outcomes, and if necessary investigating any differences.

- Most people are agreed that a budget should be based on SMART objectives: specific, measurable, achievable, realistic, time-bound.

- Inflation can have a distorting effect on budgetary control. Care must be taken in interpreting variances from budget.

- The budgetary control process consists of two elements: planning and control. The benefits of budgetary control relate to planning, coordination, authorising and delegating, evaluating performance, communicating and monitoring, and control.

- There are seven main steps in preparation of a budget: sales budget; production budget; budgets for materials, labour and production overhead, leading to the cost of goods sold budget; functional budgets for non-production departments; budgeted profit and loss account; cash budget; and budgeted balance sheet.

- Many companies use flexible budgets which can be automatically revised if the level of activity is different from expectations. To do this requires analysis of fixed and variable costs.

- Budgeting is typically performed by means of spreadsheet software.

- In preparing cashflow forecasts, particular attention must be paid to the timing of receipts and payments, especially when goods are supplied and received on credit terms.

Self-test questions

Numbers in brackets refer to the paragraphs where your answers can be checked.

1	What are the objectives of preparing a budget? (1.7)
2	What is meant by SMART objectives? (1.16)
3	List benefits and limitations of budgeting. (1.20, 1.21)
4	What is the potential effect of inflation on the budgetary control process? (2.12–2.14)
5	List the benefits of budgetary control. (3.3)
6	What is a budget centre? (3.5)
7	What are the seven steps in budget preparation? (3.10, Figure 7.1)
8	What is meant by the term 'principal budget factor', and why is it important in the budgetary planning process? (3.10)
9	What is a flexible budget? (3.21)
10	List elements that will typically be included in a budget presentation. (5.3)
11	What are the main steps in preparing a cash budget? (6.2)
12	What actions might we adopt to improve our cashflow position? (6.8–6.10)

CHAPTER 8

Cost Management

Learning objectives and indicative content

4.4   Develop process and plans for managing costs

- Estimating
- Controls
- Review stages
- Contingency planning
- Who should be involved
- Tools and techniques
- Procurement spend authorities

4.5   Develop a plan to manage the cost base of the purchasing function

- The principles of cost management
- Planning
- Coordination
- Control
- Reporting
- Effective programme and project management

Chapter headings

1   Estimating costs

2   Controlling costs

3   Review procedures and contingencies

4   Managing costs of the purchasing function

5   Effective programme and project management

Introduction

In this chapter we look at techniques for managing and controlling costs. Purchasers are responsible for a very large proportion of the total expenditure incurred within their organisations. Responsible and effective management of this spend is a critical factor in organisational profitability.

1 *Estimating costs*

Fixed and variable costs

1.1 The main principle involved in controlling costs is to estimate in advance what the costs are expected to be, and to compare the estimate with actual outcomes. Any material discrepancies should be investigated.

1.2 To get started on the process of estimating costs we need a good understanding of cost behaviour patterns. Specifically, we need to know which costs are variable (because the level of these costs will depend on the estimated level of activity), and which costs are fixed (these costs will be unaffected by the level of activity). We examined fixed and variable costs in Chapter 5 and you should revise this now.

1.3 We have used the phrase 'level of activity'. Often, the main activity influencing the level of costs is our sales volume, which of course has a knock-on effect on the production volume. This suggests that a critical step in forecasting costs is to estimate our sales volume for the period under consideration. We discussed the use of sales volume as a 'principal budget factor' in the previous chapter.

1.4 Once we have estimated a level of sales it should be possible to estimate the costs that depend on sales volume. Fixed costs are easier, as they will not vary in line with sales volume.

Mixed costs and the high-low method

1.5 Some costs include a mix of fixed and variable elements. These are sometimes called semi-variable costs, or mixed costs. For example, the cost of heat and light will to some extent be fixed, because the premises must be heated and lit during normal working hours. However, there may also be a variable element in this cost, perhaps because additional hours are being worked as overtime.

1.6 In these cases, it is necessary to determine the amount of the fixed element included in the mixed cost. A common technique for achieving this is the high-low method. This is based on looking at the total cost at a time when activity is at a high level and comparing it with the total cost at a time when activity is low.

1.7 As an example, suppose that a particular cost amounted to £3,100 in a month when sales volume was 300 units, while in another month the cost amounted to £2,400 and sales volume was 200 units. Clearly this cost is not fixed, but neither is it wholly variable (because if it was the cost level at 200 units would be exactly two thirds of the cost level at 300 units, and this is not the case).

1.8 So we are dealing with a mixed cost. The difference in the total amount (namely £700, ie £3,100 – £2,400) must be the variable element associated with the additional 100 units. This indicates that the variable cost per unit is £7, which means that the variable cost of 200 units is £1,400. Since the total cost of 200 units is £2,400, this means that the fixed element included in this particular cost is £1,000 per month.

1.9   We can check this by looking at the total cost for 300 units. According to our calculations this should comprise a fixed element calculated at £1,000, plus a variable element of £7 per unit or £2,100 in total. Our calculations therefore indicate a total cost at the 300 unit level of £3,100, which is indeed the case.

Simple moving average

1.10   The high-low method is an attempt to estimate future cost levels by analysing cost levels known from past periods. Another technique for doing this is simply to calculate an average based on past cost levels.

1.11   Using a simple moving average, we look at the costs in recent periods, and assume that costs for the coming period will be the average of that experienced in the past. There is no particular rule about how many past periods we should take into account. If we are trying to estimate costs during July we might, for example, look at the actual costs experienced during January to June, and take the average of those six months.

1.12   Suppose that the level of a particular cost was as follows in the months of January to June.

Month	Cost (£)
January	450
February	190
March	600
April	600
May	420
June	380
Total cost January to June	2,640

1.13   Using a simple moving average we would simply take the average of these six months: $^{2,640}/_6$ = £440. This would be our estimate of cost in July.

1.14   The reason for the term 'moving' average is that each month we move along by one step. Thus in estimating cost for August, we discard the January figure above and replace it with the figure for actual cost in July. Our estimate for August is therefore based on the six months preceding August, namely February to July.

1.15   Of course, this procedure is really a bit too simple. It is clear from the figures that this particular cost fluctuates quite markedly. The figures for January to June show a low of £190, and a high of £600. The simple average of such figures does not inspire confidence. The actual figure in July might turn out to be either of these extremes, in which case our estimate of £440 will prove wide of the mark. The next method tries to inject greater sophistication into the estimates.

Weighted average method, or exponential smoothing

1.16 The simple moving average gives equal weight to each of the figures recorded in previous periods. In the example, the figure for January contributed exactly as much to the averaging calculation as did that for June. This does not take account of a fact which is very commonly observed in practice, namely that older figures are a less reliable guide to the future than more recent figures. If there is any gradual change taking place in the level of this cost, it is more likely that the change will be reflected in our usage for June than in the figure for January six months ago.

1.17 To take account of this, the technique of exponential smoothing can be used. This is designed to give greater weight to the figures experienced in recent months, and to reduce the weight given to older figures. Our first step is to settle on a number between 0 and 1 – say 0.2. We then perform the following calculation, using the figures from the example above.

$$
\begin{aligned}
\text{July cost} &= 0.2 \times £380 + (0.2 \times 0.8) \times £420 + (0.2 \times 0.8^2) \times £600 + \dots + (0.2 \times 0.8^5) \times £450 \\
&= 0.2 \times £380 + 0.16 \times £420 + 0.128 \times £600 + \dots + 0.066 \times £450 \\
&= £76 + £67.2 + £76.8 + £61.4 + £15.6 + £29.5 \\
&= £326.5
\end{aligned}
$$

1.18 The factor 0.8 is simply 1 minus our chosen factor of 0.2. How we chose the value of 0.2 – rather than 0.1, say, or 0.95 – is a matter of experience. We look back on known values from the past and we work out what factor would have given the best estimates if we had used it in the basic formula. We deduce that this is the value which best encapsulates the nature of the historical trend, and so we apply it for the future in the hope that it will continue to give good results.

1.19 Notice that this has given a lower estimate for the cost in July than the simple moving average. This is because the high values of March and April, being some months ago, have little weight in the calculations above, but were given full weight in the simple average calculation.

1.20 Of course, this formula uses the value 0.2 that we decided on in the case of this particular cost. In the case of another cost, we might have settled on a different value and the formula above would have to be amended accordingly.

Who should be involved?

1.21 One final consideration in this process of estimating costs is to determine who should be involved.

1.22 Certainly purchasing staff will be involved in relation to many categories of costs, in fact for all costs involving bought-in materials and services. This is because purchasing staff are most aware of the prices that they have been obtaining from the suppliers of such goods, and of any likely changes (arising, perhaps, from newly negotiated agreements with the suppliers).

1.23 Finance/accounting staff will also be involved. Estimates of costs are very much their province, and they have ready access to historical trends of costs. As we have seen above, historical trends are often an important starting point in estimating future cost levels.

1.24 Marketing staff will also be involved. They are in the best position to forecast the likely level of sales, which (as we have seen) is usually the principal budget factor. The level of sales has a knock-on effect on many cost areas – most notably on production costs, because the level of production will depend mainly on the level of expected sales.

2 Controlling costs

Standard costing and variance analysis

2.1 Managers use costing information to help them run operations more efficiently. An important technique in this regard is that of variance analysis. As the name implies, this is based on a comparison of what something **should have cost** with what it **actually did cost**, the difference being known as a variance.

2.2 In its usual form, variance analysis is based on the use of **standard costs**. Managers determine in advance what a unit of output should cost by drawing up standards for each of the cost elements comprised in it. For example, a company might determine that the standard cost of producing one widget is £4.40, made up as follows.

	£
Raw material X, 1.2 kilos @ £2.00 per kilo	2.40
Grade A labour, 20 minutes @ £6.00 per hour	2.00
Total	4.40

2.3 Suppose now that on a particular day 120 widgets were produced, with costs incurred as follows.

	£
Raw material X, 150 kilos	285.00
Grade A labour, 35 hours	217.00
Total	502.00

2.4 Based on standard costs, we would expect 120 widgets to cost £528.00 (ie 120 @ £4.40). In fact it has cost us less than that (good news). Variance analysis enables managers to pinpoint why.

2.5 The basic idea is to examine each input resource (in this case, raw material X and Grade A labour) and to compare actual results with standard, both in terms of the amount of resource used and in terms of the cost per unit of resource.

2.6 In relation to raw material X, the analysis is as follows.

120 widgets should use	144 kilos
but actually used	150 kilos
Usage variance (bad news)	6 kilos

At a standard cost of £2 per kilo, the excess usage means bad news of £12.

	£
150 kilos should cost	300.00
but actually cost	285.00
Price variance (good news)	15.00

We have paid less than expected for each kilo of material.

2.7 Overall, the good news on material X (the purchase price) outweighs the bad news (the excess usage) by £3. Sure enough, in producing 120 widgets we would expect to spend £288 on material X (ie 120 @ £2.40), whereas in fact we spent £3 less than that (£285). We say that there is an **adverse usage variance** of £12 and a **favourable price variance** of £15.

2.8 A similar analysis applies to Grade A labour

120 widgets should take	40 hours
but actually took	35 hours
Efficiency variance (good news)	5 hours

At a standard cost of £6 per hour, the improved efficiency means good news of £30.

	£
35 hours should cost	210.00
but actually cost	217.00
Labour rate variance (bad news)	7.00

We have paid our labour force £7 more than expected for the number of hours they have worked.

2.9 Overall, the good news on Grade A labour outweighs the bad news by £23. Sure enough, in producing 120 widgets we would expect to spend £240 on labour (ie 120 @ £2.00), whereas in fact we spent £23 less than that (£217). The favourable efficiency variance has outweighed the adverse rate variance.

2.10 The advantages of standard costing are chiefly to do with the improved management control it offers. Each product's costs are carefully analysed and listed out, and an expected amount allocated. In addition, budgeted figures for expected production are calculated, so altogether the standard costing system has encouraged the organisation to plan very carefully.

2.11 Once activities commence, standard costing requires regular and systematic comparison of actual with estimate so that variances are calculated. This should provide early warning signals regarding specific issues such as prices, efficiency and utilisation, which might go unregarded for a longer period were it not for standard costing.

2.12 The problems presented by standard costing are generally to do with the fact that the system is expensive to install and run effectively. In addition, a product's or service's standard costs can quickly become out of date, which renders the variances meaningless. Finally, while the system should mean that managers take more responsibility for the variances under their control, often the interrelatedness of variances means that direct responsibility cannot be taken on board by individual managers in quite such a straightforward way.

2.13 As an example of this, consider again the raw material X in the above example. Purchasing staff may well claim credit for the favourable price variance, and may blame production staff for the adverse usage variance. But it is rarely as simple as this. Production staff might retort that the buyer saved on price by skimping on quality. If an inferior grade of material X was purchased, the result might be higher wastage, which would account for the adverse usage variance.

Target costing

2.14 Another technique for controlling costs is target costing, which we discussed briefly in Chapter 4. To understand how this works, we need to consider how a firm fixes the selling prices for its products.

2.15 A traditional approach to this issue is known as cost-plus pricing. The firm attempts to work out all the costs incurred in producing and selling a product. These are totalled to arrive at an overall product cost. An amount is then added to this to reflect the firm's expected profit. The total is the selling price of that product.

2.16 Referring again to our previous example, suppose that the only costs involved in a widget are those we have already examined (raw material X and Grade A labour). For simplicity, we ignore any selling costs associated with the product. Since the total estimated cost of a widget is £4.40, the firm might set its selling price at, say, £6 per unit. At this price, the firm expects to make a profit of £1.60 per unit produced and sold.

2.17 A drawback of this method is that it takes costs as a given, which gives little incentive for buyers and production staff to seek reductions. Moreover, the selling price is arbitrarily set by adding on a hoped-for profit margin. This takes no account of what value the market places on the product, which may be higher or lower than £6.

2.18 To overcome this problem, some Japanese firms pioneered a different approach to setting prices: target costing. This differs considerably from the cost-plus approach.

- The traditional model builds up the cost of a product by analysing its components step by step. A profit margin is then added on and the result is the selling price of the product. With luck, this will be a price that the market can stand; if it is not, the product will be unsuccessful.

- Target costing starts at the other end. The manufacturer first estimates the selling price that the market will be willing to pay for a product with specific features. He then works backward to calculate the production cost that must be achieved in order to provide a reasonable profit.

2.19 The difference between these approaches is crucial.

- The traditional approach accepts costs as given, and calculates a selling price that must be achieved. We must then hope that the market will be willing to pay.

- Target costing starts with what the customer will pay, and then attacks costs so that they are reduced to the required level. This gives a strong incentive to buyers and production managers to achieve the lowest possible costs.

2.20 There are three important factors that may help in setting cost targets.

- Customer requirements. Producers should focus on the aspects important to their customers. Cost should not be incurred on features that customers consider unimportant.

- Competitors. Understanding the cost structure of competitor companies can help to identify areas for savings.

- Internal cost structure. We need a thorough understanding of our own cost structure so as to identify where costs are arising. We consider this issue further under the headings of absorption costing and activity based costing below.

Other techniques for the reduction and control of costs

2.21 Reduction and control of costs should be a concern for all departments in the organisation. In Table 8.1 we suggest various techniques that different departments can employ to achieve these objectives.

3 Review procedures and contingencies

Allowing for contingencies

3.1 Needless to say, any attempt to predict future costs or other outcomes is subject to uncertainty. This raises the issue of dealing with risks. In relation to costs, one familiar technique is simply to include a contingency allowance. For example, if we are considering investment in a new tailor-made computer system we might estimate the cost at £500,000, but our budget might include a 10% contingency, giving a total of £550,000.

Table 8.1 *Cost reduction and control*

Function	Techniques for cost reduction and control
Design/engineering	Value engineering Simultaneous engineering Continuous improvement (**kaizen**)
Purchasing	Pareto/ABC analysis of stocks Just in time purchasing Vendor managed inventory Make or buy decisions
Marketing	Market research Avoidance of over-specifying Market testing Effective market targeting
Distribution	Outsourcing transport Inventory management Appropriate use of distribution channels

3.2 Including an allowance of this sort means that we do not have to completely derail the project if costs are slightly above target. Nor do we have to begin again on our capital expenditure authorisation procedure, which may be time-consuming. Assuming the overspend does not exceed the amount of our contingency we are able to proceed to a successful completion.

3.3 Similar considerations may apply to non-cost items, such as deadlines. For example, if we are managing a project to move offices we might lay down a timeline, highlighting the main things to be done and the dates by which they are to be achieved. While we will try to be as accurate as possible in our estimates, it may make sense to allow a contingency.

3.4 As an example of this, suppose that major electrical rewiring is needed in the new building, and the estimated completion date for the work is 31 January. Once it is done, we will be ready to move in. It might appear tempting to book the removals firm for 1 February, but a more sensible approach might be to choose a slightly later date. This gives us a contingency allowance in case the rewiring work overruns.

Periodic checks

3.5 With cost budgets in place it is natural to carry out progress checks on a regular basis. This ensures that any departures from budget are quickly identified and allows remedial action sooner rather than later.

3.6 One method of achieving this has been described earlier: variance analysis. It should be a defined responsibility for someone – usually a member of the finance staff – to perform variance analysis at defined intervals, perhaps at the end of each month. Once variances have been identified, it is equally important to ensure that they are reported as swiftly as possible to the manager(s) responsible for them.

3.7 Similarly in project work, we can keep track of the resources consumed by periodic checks. For example, to track how much labour input has been used we can summarise timesheets prepared by the people involved in the project. This can be compared with some kind of benchmark – eg the total amount of labour input expected over the whole project life – to estimate whether we are within budget or not.

3.8 Another important consideration is the procedure for authorising procurement. (This is presumably what your syllabus is referring to in mentioning **procurement spend authorities**.) Every organisation of any size will have rules in place to regulate the amount that an individual can spend. There may well be different levels for different individuals. For example, a purchasing officer may be able to authorise expenditure of £5,000 by his own signature alone; whereas for expenditure between £5,000 and £50,000 he might have to obtain a counter-signature from the purchasing manager; and for even larger amounts the purchasing director might have to be involved.

3.9 With such a system in place it is still important to have periodic checks to ensure that staff have adhered to the rules. Instances where the rules have been breached should be investigated.

4 *Managing costs of the purchasing function*

Principles of cost management

4.1 Buyers are naturally keen to control costs, both in terms of their spend with external suppliers, and in relation to the costs of the purchasing function itself. However, in doing so they should not lose sight of some basic principles.

4.2 It is important that the accounting systems are giving the correct signals. Buyers can work with finance staff to ensure that costs are being allocated to account codes in such a way as to provide useful information for the buyer's purposes.

4.3 In some cases, it is not obvious how to account for a particular cost. Indeed, the cost may comprise several different elements that need to be allocated separately. Beware of treating an activity as unprofitable just because heavy costs have been allocated to it. It may be that the allocation system is at fault.

4.4 When using published accounts as a source of costing information, bear in mind that the costs displayed in such documents are calculated on a basis laid down in law as 'true and fair'. They are not necessarily calculated in a way that maximises their usefulness for decision purposes, so it may be important to analyse the costs in more detail than the published accounts provide.

4.5 Bear in mind also the problem of fixed costs and their absorption into product costs. In Chapter 5 we examined the misleading costs that might emerge from a traditional absorption cost accounting system. A more modern system, such as activity based costing, may provide more accurate results, but there is always an element of arbitrariness in the way that fixed costs are attributed to activities and products.

4.6 Finally, even when we are confident of having accurate and relevant cost information there are sometimes reasons for avoiding cost cuts. In some cases this may lead to side effects more expensive than the problem we were trying to cure.

Coordinating activities

4.7 One factor in boosting the effectiveness of the purchasing function is effective coordination of activities with other departments. Dobler and Burt point out that this can be achieved by evaluating the effectiveness of certain joint activities (eg the joint establishment of order quantities with production staff). But this kind of evaluation tends to cover only limited areas of cooperation.

4.8 A more systematic approach is for purchasing to conduct periodic reviews of the departments they serve. Often, the means of doing this is a questionnaire. Dobler and Burt suggest a number of questions that purchasing could address to other departments in such a questionnaire: see Table 8.2.

Table 8.2 *Questionnaire on coordination with other functions*

1	Does the purchasing department regularly provide you with a list of estimated lead times for the items you use?
2	Do you believe that the buyers who handle your requirements know enough about the key items to make intelligent purchasing decisions?
3	Is the quality of material the purchasing department obtains for you always suitable for your needs?
4	Does the buyer who handles your requirements periodically visit personally with your departmental staff?
5	Is he or she familiar with the operations and problems of your department?
6	Does he or she assist you in planning your materials requirements?
7	Does he or she keep you informed regarding delays, estimated delivery dates, and so on for materials that you have requisitioned?
8	Does he or she periodically bring a supplier's representative to your department to discuss cost-saving proposals?
9	Are you always treated in a friendly, courteous, businesslike manner by purchasing and supply personnel?
10	Do you believe that buyers are taking advantage of cost-saving ideas and recommendations of suppliers?
11	Do you think that buying personnel continually urge suppliers to develop new methods and ideas that will help you cut your costs and improve your operations?
12	Do the materials you requisition usually arrive on time?
13	How often do buyers arbitrarily change the quality specifications on your purchases without consulting you?
14	How long does it take, on the average, for the stores department to fill your requisition for items that are carried in inventory?
15	Additional comments and suggestions.

4.9 Equally, purchasing staff may review how well other departments have contributed to coordination. For example, they may check on such matters as unauthorised negotiations with suppliers, correctness and completeness of requisitions etc.

Planning, control and reporting

4.10   To improve effectiveness, the purchasing department typically devises a variety of control measures. Such a control system might involve the following stages.

- Planning: determining the appropriate factors to measure and setting a target for each measure

- Control: comparing the actual outcomes against the targets and identifying areas for improvement

- Reporting: reporting the results to appropriate managers for remedial action if required.

4.11   What factors might the purchasing department seek to measure? Some of the possibilities are listed below.

- Timeliness: percentage of on-time deliveries from major suppliers, average lead time per material and per supplier, number of production stoppages caused by late deliveries etc

- Quality: number of production stoppages caused by faulty materials, number of stockouts caused by poor JIT performance, service levels achieved in supply production departments etc

- Materials costs: actual costs paid against target prices, percentage value of items under long-term contracts etc

- Efficiency: average processing time to deal with a requisition, number of purchase orders not covered by long-term contracts, number of rush orders, average value of purchase orders (too many low-value orders may indicate inefficiency) etc

Budgeting

4.12   Clearly a key technique in controlling the costs of the purchasing function is effective budgeting. Often an incremental budgeting approach will be used. This means that we look at what happened last year and assume that the figures for the coming year will be similar. We make appropriate adjustments for known changes that have taken place or are expected.

4.13   This is a natural and straightforward approach, which has the merit of being understood by everyone. However, it has the disadvantage that last year's figures are simply accepted as reasonable. This is not always a sensible assumption: we may have been misallocating resources for years, and nobody has thought to challenge it. There is an argument for taking a zero-based approach to budgeting instead.

4.14   Assuming, even so, that the incremental method is used, how might we arrive at adjustments to last year's figures?

- Senior managers may impose targets that we simply have to accept. For example, they may insist on a 10% cut in all budgets.

- We may be aware of important changes, such as an expected 5% increase in the price of a major material that we purchase.

- We may have to allow for expected changes, such as new activities that are to be undertaken, or activities that are going to be abandoned.

4.15 More formally, it is possible to think of a defined series of steps in setting a budget for the purchasing function. See Figure 8.1.

Figure 8.1 *Stages in the budgeting process*

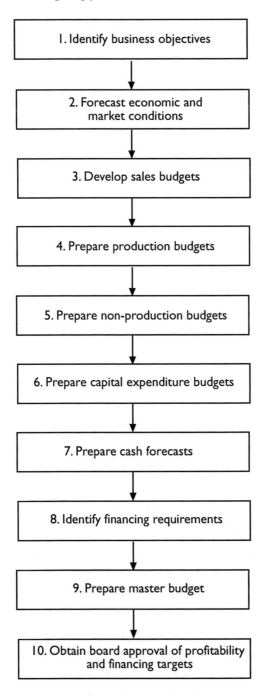

1. Identify business objectives

2. Forecast economic and market conditions

3. Develop sales budgets

4. Prepare production budgets

5. Prepare non-production budgets

6. Prepare capital expenditure budgets

7. Prepare cash forecasts

8. Identify financing requirements

9. Prepare master budget

10. Obtain board approval of profitability and financing targets

4.16 At all times during this process, we should be questioning the 'cost drivers', ie the activities that give rise to costs. Do we need the number of suppliers that we currently use? Do we really need to generate the number of purchase orders that we currently produce? Is a particular activity really necessary, or could we remove it or simplify it?

4.17 Usually, cost reduction will involve either producing the same output for less input, or producing increased output without increased input.

5   *Effective programme and project management*

Cost estimating techniques

5.1   This area of the syllabus appears to refer specifically to project work, rather than to the routine task of managing costs from day to day (which has been the subject of the rest of this chapter). To a large extent, the principles and techniques involved are similar.

5.2   Harvey Maylor (*Project Management*) describes two main approaches to the preparation of costing information in project work.

- Bottom-up costing, in which estimated costs for each task are prepared and totalled

- Top-down costing, in which a certain amount of money is allocated to the project and this must be divided among the various activities.

5.3   Maylor illustrates the two possibilities as shown in Figure 8.2.

Figure 8.2 *Preparation of costing information*

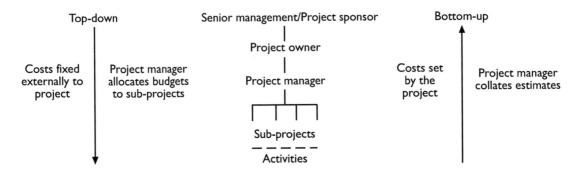

5.4   With bottom-up costing, the people who prepare the cost estimates are the people who will be expected to achieve the targets, which encourages them to feel ownership and commitment. Of course, this feeling may be diluted if the project owner adjusts their figures materially. To counter this, the estimators may build in an element of padding, expecting their first estimates to be trimmed.

5.5   With top-down costing, supervisors lower down in the chain will be competing for the finite resources allocated to the project as a whole. In some respects this may appear unhealthy, but many commentators regard it as beneficial in that it forces the supervisors to compile and present a persuasive case for the activities they have in mind.

5.6   The kind of costs that arise in project work include materials, labour, capital equipment, incidental expenses, and fixed overheads such as the provision of office space. For most of these costs, we have seen how estimates may be made either in this chapter or (in the case of capital equipment) we will be examining it in Chapter 10. But one additional point about labour costs in project work is worth mentioning: the **learning curve** effect.

The learning curve effect

5.7 The learning curve phenomenon has been observed in a number of industries, particularly in those where a high proportion of skilled labour is used to manufacture products of very great complexity and scale. The example cited most commonly is the construction of aircraft.

5.8 Often in such industries the products are manufactured expressly to the buyer's specification. It makes a great difference to the price quoted whether the buyer is ordering a small number or a large number of the products. The reason for this is that manufacture of the first unit tends to take up more labour hours than the second; the second unit is manufactured more quickly than the first, the third unit more quickly still and so on. As experience grows, the workforce become more adept and complete their tasks more quickly.

5.9 Where this occurs, it is clear that later units will cost less to manufacture than earlier ones. A buyer ordering a large number of units will benefit from this effect, and will find that the supplier can quote an average cost per unit that is much less than the cost of supplying just a single unit, where no learning effect would apply.

5.10 Of course, there are limits to this process. For one thing, it applies only to the labour element of total cost. There is no reason to suppose that material costs will fall as more units are produced, except for the minor point that the producer may benefit from bulk discounts from his own suppliers. And even the average labour cost will not continue to fall forever (we never reach a labour cost of zero, no matter how many we order).

5.11 Despite these limits, the effect on cost can be quite dramatic, as Figure 8.3 illustrates. The diagrams relate to an 80 per cent learning effect; the meaning of this will be explained later.

5.12 The first diagram shows how average labour hours decrease as the number of units produced increases. The fact that the slope of the curve is tailing off means that the decline cannot continue beyond a certain point. (It is of course the curved nature of this relationship that gives rise to the phrase 'learning curve'.) The same point is often illustrated on log-log graph paper, as in the second diagram. On this scale the rate of decrease is seen to be constant because the downward slope is a straight line.

5.13 The extent of the savings created by the learning effect can be computed mathematically. As you might expect, the key factor is just how quickly the average labour hours decline, and this will vary from one industry to another, and from one manufacturer to another in the same industry. It is often the difference in the learning curves between manufacturers that gives one of them a competitive advantage over the others.

Figure 8.3 *Learning curve*

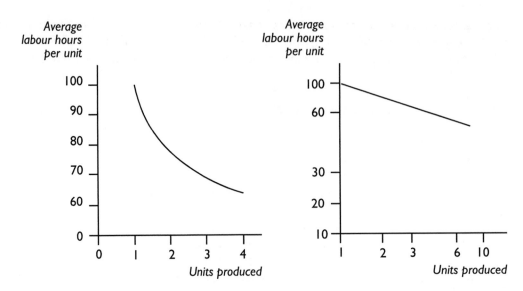

5.14 It is usual to talk of 'a 75 per cent learning curve', 'an 80 per cent learning curve' and so on. The graphs above illustrate an 80 per cent curve. This means that each time the number of units produced is doubled, the overall average time per unit is reduced by a factor of 80 per cent (or 75 per cent or whatever).

5.15 The implication of all this for buyers should be sufficiently clear. In the kind of industry discussed here, the price quoted for a single large item is not at all a good guide to what might be quoted for a batch of items or a recurring order. Buyers need to be aware of this effect when negotiating.

5.16 Another application for buyers is in estimating delivery times. If a first unit is scheduled to take six months to complete, it would be very misleading to assume that subsequent units would also take six months. The buyer should be alerted to discuss delivery schedules with the producer in the light of learning curve effects.

Cost management

5.17 In developing bottom-up costs, managers will focus separately on the areas already mentioned: materials, labour, incidental expenses, capital expenditure, overheads. In some cases (especially in public sector environments) this may be done on a zero base approach. This means that every proposed activity must be justified in detail. Until this is done, the budget for that activity is zero, even if it has always been done in the past.

5.18 In most cases, expenditure is tracked by means of a job costing system. Each job is allocated a code number. When expenditure is incurred on that job, it is coded appropriately on being input to the accounting system. If a budgeted cost for the job has been computed (as it should have been) the system will flag up any overspend immediately.

5.19 As in day-to-day cost control activities, project costs should also be reviewed periodically with a view to identifying any problem areas.

Project management and control

5.20 So far we have focused mainly on financial aspects of projects. However, CIPS guidance suggests that we should also look at general principles of project management and control. This is discussed in the paragraphs that follow.

5.21 Project management is a carefully planned and organised effort to accomplish a specific and (usually) one-time effort (for example, to construct a building, refurbish a hotel or implement a new computer system).

5.22 Here are two definitions of project management.

- 'An activity, or usually a number of related activities, carried out according to a plan in order to achieve a definite objective within a certain period of time and which will cease when the objective is achieved.' (Lysons)
- 'A unique set of co-ordinated activities, with definite starting and finishing points, undertaken by an individual or team to meet specific objectives within defined time, cost and performance parameters.' (Office of Government Commerce)

5.23 These definitions highlight areas such as co-ordination, related activities, definite start and finish, plan, specific objectives and achievement which are all key considerations with projects and project management.

5.24 Project management includes developing a project plan, which includes defining project goals and objectives, specifying tasks or how goals will be achieved, what resources are needed, and associated budgets and timelines for completion. It also includes implementing the project plan, along with careful controls to stay on the 'critical path', that is, to ensure the project is being managed according to plan and that project milestones are being met.

Characteristics of projects

5.25 A project is a unique set of co-ordinated activities that has the following characteristics.

- A finite and defined lifespan
- Defined and measurable deliverables or outcomes to meet the specified objectives
- A set of activities to achieve the specified objectives
- A defined amount of resources
- An organisation structure, with defined responsibilities, to manage the project

5.26 There are three main points that are most important to a successful project.

- A project must meet customer requirements.
- A project must be within budget.
- A project must be completed on time.

5.27 Lysons distinguishes four different types of project.

- **Manufacturing projects**: such as prototyping a new product, development work or any discrete application of machinery or equipment to attain a defined end goal.

- **Construction projects**: that are characterised by being based off-site from a headquarters or central location.

- **Management projects**: activities, often utilising cross-functional teams, that have a defined purpose, eg office relocation, simultaneous engineering teams etc.

- **Research projects**: aimed at the expansion of knowledge or the acquisition of new data or information.

5.28 How does project work differ from other tasks in the workplace?

- **A project is an instrument of change**. By their very nature projects will produce a different end result (eg a refurbished hotel). This will induce a change situation for the management and staff involved when they return to work.

- **A project is non-routine**. Projects have a high degree of uncertainty as a result. In most cases, a project will not have been done before and will therefore require careful and ongoing planning.

- **A project is complex**. Many different tasks are involved in order to complete the objective. The inter-relationships between these tasks can be difficult to organise and manage. Controlling these inter-relationships involves planning and adaptability by the project manager.

- **A project is unique**. Even in the case of a 'repeat' project (such as building the same model of a house) there will still be differences in the time taken, resources used, personnel involved, etc.

- **A project is composed of inter-dependent activities**. Each of these must be scheduled so that later activities can begin on time.

- **A project is carried out by people who don't normally work together**. Projects throw people together usually based on their expertise in a specific area (eg plumbers, bricklayers and carpenters on a construction project, or designers, purchasing, marketing and engineers when developing a new product). This can cause problems as it takes time to form personal relationships. However, if the function to be carried out is specific and defined then the joint achievement of common goals can provide a bond.

- **A project is temporary with defined start and end dates**. Projects have a defined beginning and end. This will mean that resources are concentrated for the life of the project and may then be redeployed on the next project.

- **A project is intended to achieve a specific outcome**. Projects have a specification or defined end goal from the outset. Problems can often occur when changes are made to the specification during the project that can cause delays and subsequent additional costs. A recent UK example is the Scottish Parliament in Edinburgh where changes in the design led to spiralling costs.

Critical success factors

5.29   Slack *et al* give a detailed list of requirements for successful project management.

- **Clearly defined goals**: which can include the overall philosophy or mission of the project, and the commitment to those goals from the project team members.

- **Competent project manager**: a project leader who has the necessary blend of interpersonal, technical and administrative skills.

- **Top-management support**: commitment that must be communicated to the project team.

- **Competent project-team members**: the selection and training of project teams who have the right blend of skills to successfully complete the project.

- **Sufficient resource allocation**: in the form of finance, personnel, logistics etc, which are available when required.

- **Good communication channels**: between those involved on objectives, status, changes, organisational conditions and client needs.

- **Control mechanisms**: put in place to monitor actual events and recognise deviations from plan.

- **Feedback capabilities**: all parties concerned are able to review the project status and make suggestions and corrections.

- **Troubleshooting mechanisms**: a system or set of procedures which can tackle problems as they arise, trace them back to their root cause and resolve them.

- **Project staff continuity**: the continued involvement of key project personnel through the project lifecycle. Frequent staff turnover can dissipate acquired learning and damage team morale.

5.30   Successful projects have the following features.

- A well-defined scope and agreed understanding of intended outcome.

- Active management of risks and issues, and timely decision-making supported by clear and short lines of reporting.

- Ongoing commitment and support from senior management.

- A senior individual with personal accountability and overall responsibility for the successful outcome of the project.

- An appropriately trained and experienced project team and in particular a project manager whose capabilities match the complexity of the project.

- Defined and visibly managed processes that are appropriate for the scale and complexity of the project.

5.31   For cross-company projects, there may be nominated senior owners from each organisation involved in the project and its delivery. Where this is the case, there must be a single owner who is responsible for the whole project.

Why projects fail

5.32 Experience has shown that projects are inherently at risk through overrunning on time and cost and/or failing to deliver a successful outcome. Such failures are almost invariably caused by some or all of the following shortcomings.

- Poor project definition by the project's owner, perhaps because of insufficient consultation with stakeholders or their failure to be specific about requirements and desired outcomes.
- Lack of ownership and personal accountability by senior management.
- Inadequately skilled and experienced project personnel.
- Inadequate reporting arrangements and decision-making.
- Inconsistent understanding of required project activities, roles and responsibilities.

5.33 Project management techniques help to reduce and manage risk. It puts in place an organisation where lines of accountability are short and the responsibilities of individuals are clearly defined. Its processes are clearly documented and repeatable, so that those involved in the project can learn from the experiences of others.

5.34 Project management uses various measurement tools to accomplish and track project tasks. These include Gantt charts, critical path analysis and program evaluation and review technique (PERT).

The project management process

5.35 Development of a project from conception through to fulfilment requires a considerable effort in terms of communication, organisation and control. The uniqueness of the project brings with it a degree of uncertainty to those involved and in consequence requires experienced management control.

5.36 Lysons identifies six stages in the project management process but we should be careful when applying this as all projects are different. Some stages will have more emphasis than others and some may not be prioritised in this order.

- **Definition**: the investigation into the feasibility of the project or identification of a problem that requires a solution. Define the goals and objectives of the proposal and submit the proposal for approval.
- **Planning**: prepare plans to see how the project will fulfil its business needs. Propose budgets and cashflow projections for the duration of the project. Develop planning tools such as CPA, PERT and work breakdown structures.
- **Initiation**: recruiting the correct staff and preparing for the project launch. Placing the infrastructure for the project in place is an important aspect of project management as it eases the potential problems when work commences and has a positive effect on morale.
- **Control**: project management tries to gain control over five variables (time, cost, quality, scope and risk). The control process involves monitoring all these variables against project progress and making changes as necessary.
- **Organisational processes**: with a focus on co-ordinating the resources to ensure delivery of the project's goals on time and within budget.
- **Closure/completion**: bringing the project to a successful close and ensuring that clients are happy with the outcome or ensuring that a change in processes is successfully integrated into the organisation.

5.37 The project objectives triangle is used as a tool to ensure that the requirements of the project are fulfilled. The three objectives of project management are cost, quality and time. The relative importance of each will vary with each project. In essence the triangle is used as a grid where the factors are 'traded-off' against each other.

Figure 8.4 *The project objectives triangle*

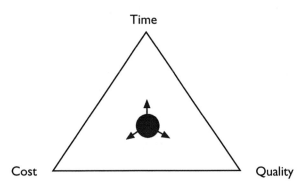

5.38 In order to achieve these objectives managers will use a variety of tools and techniques.

- **In relation to cost**: setting of budgets and budgetary control, variance reporting, activity based costing and auditing.
- **Quality**: quality assurance, quality control, specifications, quality manuals and quality audits.
- **Time**: Gantt charts, and network techniques such as CPA and PERT.

Project definition

5.39 A project requires a clear and unambiguous statement that encompasses three aspects.

- **Its objectives**: the end result that the project is trying to achieve. The objectives provide a focus to the project team. Good objectives will be clear, measurable and quantifiable. This may be made easier if they are broken into smaller staged sets of objectives that will come together to meet the overall objective at the end. Common objectives would be cost, time and quality.
- **Its scope**: the exact range and responsibilities covered by project management. The scope of the project serves to identify the work content and outcomes. This helps to set boundaries and will be set out in a specification. The scope of the project helps to define contractors or part of the organisation involved, time periods including start and end dates, commercial and legal responsibilities of those involved and the resources to be employed.
- **Its strategy**: how the project management role will ensure that the objectives will be met. The strategy enables an overview of the project and allows for phases of the project to be identified which then allows for milestones to be set. These can then be conveyed to those involved so as to provide a common understanding.

5.40 A **specification** is the definition of the project. The specification will initially contain errors, ambiguities and misunderstandings. In consequence, the specification will usually need clarification with everyone concerned with the project (from originator, through the workers, to the end-customer) to ensure everyone is working with the same understanding. The outcome of this deliberation should be a written definition of what is required, by when; and this must be agreed by all involved.

5.41 The agreement upon a written specification has several benefits.

- The clarity will reveal misunderstandings.
- The completeness will remove contradictory assumptions.
- The rigour of the analysis will expose technical and practical details which may otherwise be overlooked.
- The agreement forces all concerned to read and think about the details.

5.42 The work on the specification can be seen as the first stage of quality assurance since you are looking for and countering problems in the very foundation of the project. From this perspective the creation of the specification clearly merits a large investment of time. The specification will change as the project progresses but deviations will be agreed rather than imposed.

The project management plan

5.43 The project management plan is a document that embodies the project. It is the most important document in the overall planning, monitoring, and implementation of the project and should be 'owned' by the project manager and his team.

5.44 The plan should include the following elements.

- A definition of the objectives
- Statements as to how these will be achieved and verified
- Estimates of the time required
- Financial budget
- Safety, health and environmental policies
- Quality policy
- Risk management strategy
- Related items concerning technical, commercial or organisational aspects

5.45 The project management plan is a key document in establishing why, what, how, who, how much and when.

5.46 Project planning has four main purposes.

- It identifies and determines the duration and cost of the project. This enables decisions to be made regarding whether the project will commence and provides the basis for further development of specific activities.
- It determines the resources that will be required. This enables planning ahead to ensure the resources are available when required and gives time for an examination of costs quoted.
- Linking with the project strategy, it helps in allocating work, in setting phases and milestones, and in defining responsibilities.
- It forces those involved to consider potential risk areas and the possible impact on the project. The example of the Scottish Parliament showed the risk when the specification was changed on more than one occasion. The result was a project both over time and over budget. The risk was always present but to estimate the impact was difficult.

5.47 Most projects are too involved and complex to be planned effectively unless they are broken down to a manageable size. By instigating smaller projects as a series of work packages then each work package can be given its own objectives that can then be monitored appropriately.

5.48 This process is referred to as the work breakdown structure and is a key component of project management. The discrete work packages can then be monitored and managed more effectively by the project manager whose role will be to ensure that these work packages meet the key objectives in terms of quality, cost and time. The work breakdown structure also assists in scheduling the project, as smaller work packages can be more easily brought forward or put back allowing a greater degree of flexibility.

Project control

5.49 Project control is the administrative interface that ensures that the project is progressing as intended. Project control is there to make sure that the criteria detailed in the project plan are being met and (if not) to instigate remedial action.

5.50 Project monitoring means that the progress of the project must be continually measured against the established schedule. Monitoring does not mean holding to the schedule rigidly. Circumstances change and as the project develops new information becomes available that may require a change in plans. The schedules serve as a yardstick against which to measure progress, to show where and how plans must change. The schedule is a tool to keep attention on the final objective and goal.

5.51 Although monitoring against the schedule is of paramount importance it is not the only measure that can be applied. Monitoring against the main performance objectives of quality, time and cost is equally appropriate. Inspection rejection rates, costs against budget and activities not started on time are examples. The project manager must ensure that the monitoring infrastructure is in place and that prompt and accurate feedback is given. Monitoring is the only way to ensure that resources can be reallocated effectively and judiciously when required.

5.52 Control comprises those administrative measures that must be undertaken to get and keep a project on schedule. Controlling is the adjustment of the work when needed so the overall commitments are maintained or at least optimised. Controlling means taking the appropriate action in the light of the information gained from monitoring. The whole purpose of scheduling and monitoring is to permit intelligent control.

5.53 There are two key elements to the control of a project.

- Milestones (clear, unambiguous targets of what needs to have been achieved and by when)
- An established means of communication

Chapter summary

- To estimate costs we need to distinguish between fixed and variable costs. In a mixed cost, we can analyse the fixed and variable elements by means of the high-low method.

- Other methods for estimating future cost levels on the basis of historical trends include simple moving averages and exponential smoothing.

- The process of estimating costs should include personnel from various departments, especially purchasing, finance and marketing.

- A standard cost is the amount we expect a product to cost, based on an analysis of the resources it should use and their costs. Standard costs are used as the basis of variance analysis.

- A traditional approach to price setting is cost-plus pricing: establish the total cost of a product, add on a profit margin, and the result is the selling price. A more modern approach is target costing: establish the price that the market will pay, take off the amount required for profit, and the remainder is our cost target.

- Absorption costing is a process of allocating fixed costs to units of output on some 'fair' basis. This helps to establish the total cost of a product. (Marginal costing, by contrast, values products at the total of their variable costs only, and makes no attempt to include a share of fixed costs.)

- Traditional absorption costing has been criticised for giving misleading costs. Activity based costing is a more modern system for dealing with fixed costs and attempts to overcome the criticisms levelled at traditional absorption costing.

- It is common when estimating costs and deadlines to allow for contingencies.

- The costs reported by an accounting system may not always be a good guide to purchasing action. Even when accurate cost information is available, care must be taken when seeking to cut costs.

- One measure of purchasing effectiveness is the department's success in coordinating its activities with other departments.

- In project management, it is useful to distinguish between bottom-up and top-down approaches to cost estimating.

- The learning curve effect can have a material impact on costs and deadlines in project work.

- Three key requirements for a successful project: it must meet customer requirements; it must be completed within budget; it must finish on time. This is the project objectives triangle: quality, cost, time.

- Lysons identifies six stages in the project management process: definition; planning; initiation; control; organisational processes; closure/completion.

Self-test questions

Numbers in brackets refer to the paragraphs where you can check your answers.

1   Give an example of a mixed (or semi-variable) cost. (1.5)

2   What is meant by a moving average? (1.14)

3   Describe the process of exponential smoothing. (1.17)

4   Why should marketing staff be involved in the estimation of costs? (1.24)

5   What is meant by a standard cost? (2.2)

6   What are the drawbacks of a standard costing system? (2.12)

7   Distinguish between cost-plus pricing and target costing. (2.18)

8   Why is it sensible to allow an amount for contingencies when estimating future costs? (3.2)

9   List questions that purchasing may address to other departments in order to assess effective coordination of activities. (Table 8.2)

10   What efficiency factors may the purchasing department seek to measure? (4.11)

11   Distinguish between bottom-up costing and top-down costing. (5.2)

12   What is meant by an 80% learning curve? (5.14)

13   List characteristics of a project. (5.25)

14   How does a project differ from other tasks in the workplace? (5.28)

15   List reasons why projects fail. (5.32)

16   What are the four purposes of project planning? (5.46)

CHAPTER 9

Purchasing Capital Items

Learning objectives and indicative content

5.3   Evaluate the most appropriate decision making tools for projects across a variety of sectors

- Whole life costing
- Target costing
- Value engineering
- Value for money (VFM)

5.4   Evaluate the roles of the functions of an organisation in the reduction and control of costs

- Design and engineering
- Purchasing
- Marketing
- Distribution
- Finance

Chapter headings

1   Capital buys analysis

2   Whole life costing

3   Value analysis and value engineering

4   Reduction and control of costs

5   Authorisation of capital expenditure

Introduction

Much of the work of a buyer is in purchasing routine, recurring items such as production supplies. However, a buyer must also be involved in the acquisition of major assets. Buying such an asset, or undertaking a large-scale project, is described as a capital investment. Special techniques of evaluation are needed before such commitments are entered into.

In this chapter we look at the general principles involved in this kind of investment decision. In the next chapter we examine the computational techniques that may be used to assess the likely financial outcome of the decision.

1   *Capital buys analysis*

Purchase price as one element of total cost

1.1   Changing perceptions of the role of purchasing have led to broader perspectives on the elements of cost that arise from purchasing activities. There has been a move away from the perception that purchasing is a function divided from other departments by boundary walls. That earlier perception dictated that purchasing must be evaluated on its success in the activities that belonged specifically within its own remit. In other words, the success of purchasing was evaluated solely on the amount paid for incoming materials.

1.2   A newer emphasis on overall corporate performance has reduced the importance of functional boundaries. Senior managers have focused on eliminating what are called **suboptimal decisions**: that is, decisions which make sense in the light of functional targets but have a damaging effect on overall performance.

1.3   This can be illustrated by very simple examples drawn from purchasing.

   •   It would be easy for purchasing to reduce the price of incoming materials by ordering an inferior quality. However, while this might look like a success for purchasing, the increased costs elsewhere (rejects, rework, disruption to production, customer dissatisfaction etc) would outweigh any savings achieved.

   •   Similarly, purchasing staff might be tempted to take advantage of discounts for bulk purchases, without taking account of the stockholding costs this incurs.

1.4   What these simple examples show is that basic purchase price is just one element in the total costs that are attributable to bought out materials. Managers must take a broader view which does not focus on one particular function, but crosses functional boundaries to look at the organisation as a whole. Indeed, some would go further and argue that even boundaries between organisations in the supply chain should be disregarded in order to reduce costs for everyone.

1.5   The implications of this way of thinking are far-reaching. Instead of concentrating on minimising purchase price, buyers must focus on total acquisition cost, which includes such additional costs as those already illustrated above. Instead of operating as a closed function, separate from the rest of the organisation, buyers become part of a multi-functional team.

The purchase of capital assets

1.6   One type of purchase illustrates the difference between purchase price and total costs particularly clearly. This is the purchase of a capital asset such as a large machine. In the nature of things, such an asset is expected to be used in the purchaser's business for a number of years. Over that time, it will give rise to many costs of maintenance and repair in addition to the original cost of purchase. There will also be costs associated with any inefficiency or actual failure in the machine. In choosing between one asset and another buyers must take into account the costs arising over the whole life of each.

1.7   These costs include any or all of the following elements in addition to the basic purchase price.

- Costs of delivery, installation and commissioning
- Costs of routine maintenance and periodic overhauls
- Costs of energy and labour involved in running the machine
- Costs of time lost during breakdowns

1.8   Another element in the total cost – in effect, a negative cost – is the disposal value of the asset, if any, when the time comes to replace it. An asset with a high disposal value has a lower total cost, other things being equal, than an asset with little resale value at the end of its life.

1.9   The relatively long time period involved, combined with the subjectivity of estimates for most of these elements of cost, make it difficult to assess the lifetime costs of a capital asset. One technical difficulty is that the relevant cashflows occur not immediately but in years to come; we will see later that such cashflows are not easy to evaluate in today's terms even if they are known with certainty (which they never will be).

1.10   Another difficulty is that the purchase of most capital assets is of a non-recurring nature. That is to say, a similar asset is not likely to have been purchased in the very recent past and there is therefore no relevant experience to draw upon. Then too there is the fact that purchase of such an asset generally means purchase of a service too – installation, training of operators, after-sales maintenance and so on. This introduces a whole series of new problems.

1.11   As well as estimating the costs of ownership, it is also important to estimate the benefits. Otherwise, the comparison between different assets will be incomplete. However, this is even trickier than estimating the costs of ownership, partly because of the conceptual difficulties involved in valuing intangible benefits such as improvements in quality.

2   *Whole life costing*

Costs over the life of a capital asset

2.1   The monetary value of capital asset purchases is often very significant. This means that, despite all the difficulties just mentioned, buyers must make a systematic attempt to assess costs and benefits. The technique of whole life costing (otherwise referred to as **lifecycle costing**) has been developed to cope with this problem. It is relatively simple in principle, though the calculations can appear complicated. In practice, these would always be carried out on a computer.

2.2   The buyer makes assumptions (inevitably subjective) about the level of costs that will arise in each year of the asset's useful life. Obviously a large element, namely the basic purchase price, will be paid at once (in Year 0 as it is usually described). Other elements will arise as maintenance, repair and overhaul are required. These are all estimated in advance.

2.3   At the same time, the buyer attempts to quantify the benefits that will arise from ownership of the asset. This will be done in conjunction with personnel from other departments. The total benefits must be allocated to each year of the asset's useful life, exactly as was done in the case of costs.

2.4   At this point the calculations begin, usually on computer. We discuss the principles of these calculations (called discounted cashflow) in the next chapter. Briefly, the idea is that costs and benefits arising in some future period are equivalent to a smaller amount in today's money. All costs and benefits are converted to today's values. Then an annual equivalent is computed. This is a single figure which measures the cost of ownership of the asset over a period of one year.

2.5   The point of computing the annual equivalent is that it enables buyers to compare assets with different useful lives. In principle, if the annual equivalent cost of owning Asset X is £10,000, while the figure for Asset Y is £11,000, then Asset X is chosen.

2.6   The procedure is described in more detail by Dobler and Burt (*Purchasing and Supply Management*). They identify the following stages.

-    Determine the operating cycle for the equipment, including factors such as the interval at which servicing will be required.
-    Identify and quantify the factors that affect costs, such as power consumption, average time between failures etc.
-    Calculate all costs at current rates and prices.
-    Project all costs and disposal value if any to the future dates at which they will be incurred.
-    Discount all amounts to today's values.
-    Calculate the total cost in today's values.

2.7   You may well be thinking that things cannot possibly be so difficult in practice. Do buyers really invest the large amounts of time that such calculations seem to imply? The answer is that in some cases there is no alternative, because the amount of money at stake is so great. However, there is one way in which things can be simplified, and that is the use of **guaranteed maintenance contracts**.

2.8   Some suppliers, appreciating the difficulties that buyers experience in comparing different capital assets, attempt to remove some of the trouble and some of the uncertainty by offering to sell on terms of guaranteed maintenance. With such a contract the buyer can ignore at least some of the costs discussed above, namely the costs of service and maintenance, because they are borne by the supplier. Obviously the supplier compensates by increasing the selling price, and indeed the total price would usually be expressed as a combination of basic price plus service elements.

Benefits of whole life costing

2.9   The point of calculating whole life costs is to identify the option that costs us least over the long term. This is often not at all apparent from the original purchase price. Of course, cost is not the only consideration relevant to a capital purchase and other factors must also be taken into account. But cost is invariably one of the important issues and whole life costing gives us a broad perspective on this one factor at least.

2.10 Several benefits of whole life costing may be identified.

- As described already, it clarifies the total costs of ownership.

- It enables realistic budgeting, not just for the original purchase but over the life of the asset.

- It highlights, at an early stage, any risks associated with the purchase.

- It promotes communication and cooperation between user departments, purchasing, finance and other interested parties.

- It enables us to achieve the best possible value for money.

Target costing

2.11 In earlier chapters we have looked briefly at the technique of target costing. Briefly, the approach is to begin by determining a selling price for a product that will be acceptable to the market. We then aim to drive down the costs of producing the product to a level that affords us an acceptable profit.

2.12 This technique is particularly relevant at the time when a new product is launched. **New product development** (NPD) is a strategic issue and most organisations follow a structured approach, similar to that shown in Figure 9.1.

Figure 9.1 *The NPD process*

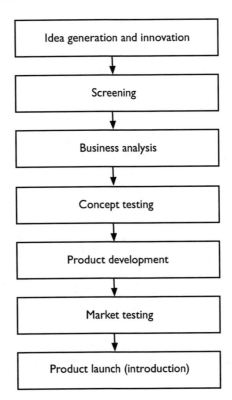

2.13 Within such a framework, target costing is likely to be applied from an early stage, certainly no later than the 'Business analysis' phase. But fine tuning will continue to take place during later stages as well. The aim is to 'close the cost gap', ie to reduce costs down to a level where the profit margin is acceptable. This will be an iterative process.

2.14   What techniques might we use to close the cost gap? Any or all of the following are possibilities.

- The use of new materials, possibly sourced from new suppliers
- Improving designs
- The use of new equipment and/or tooling in production
- Greater automation of production
- Standardisation of parts
- Reduction in stockholdings

3   *Value analysis and value engineering*

The meaning of value analysis and value engineering

3.1   Value analysis has been defined as 'the organised, systematic study of the function of a material, part, component or system to identify areas of unnecessary cost. It begins with the question "What is this item worth?" and proceeds to an analysis of value in terms of the function the item performs'. (Gary J Zenz, *Purchasing and the Management of Materials*)

3.2   The origin of the technique lies in the Second World War when it was developed by Larry Miles of General Electric in the USA as a response to wartime shortages of materials. His idea was that careful attention to the make-up of products could lead to changes which would save money. At the same time, he believed that quality would not suffer; indeed, a more critical investigation of what was included in a product, and why, would lead to actual improvements in quality.

3.3   Nowadays, the concept has been adopted in a large number of manufacturing firms. Alongside it there is a technique referred to as value engineering. There is some confusion between the terms and usage is not consistent. For many people the difference lies in the status of the product being analysed. When the process is applied to a product that is being designed for the first time, the term value engineering is preferred. When the task is to look afresh at a product already in existence the term chosen is value analysis.

3.4   This is the distinction adopted in this text, but you should be aware that other authors distinguish the terms differently. For example, in some accounts you will find that the distinction lies in who initiates and manages the process. If it is the engineering department, then the term used is value engineering; on the other hand, it tends to be purchasing personnel in charge of value analysis exercises. Clearly, this method of distinguishing the terms overlaps with the previous one. Unless it is important to distinguish the two in a particular context, we will usually refer simply to value analysis and leave the reader to infer that the same applies to value engineering.

3.5   A possible problem with value analysis in the sense used above is that changes in the configuration of a part or subassembly may make it difficult to use in other products of which it forms one element. Another shortcoming is that each value analysis exercise, to the extent that it leads to change, is in effect shortening the lifecycle of the product that is being changed. The effect may be to cancel out the economic benefit that was supposed to arise.

3.6 For these reasons, among others, there is merit in the value engineering approach because, in effect, it gets things right from the beginning and minimises the need for later change. Many firms take great pains to value engineer all new products to the extent that it is feasible. However, where the process was not used at the design and engineering stage, there is greater scope for fruitful value analysis later.

3.7 Whichever term is used, the process is the same. The idea is first to establish what function a particular part is fulfilling; then to consider the various design options for achieving this function to the desired standard; and finally, to analyse the cost of alternatives.

3.8 This approach is summarised in the five 'tests for value' that were developed in General Electric's pioneering use of the technique.

- Does use of the material, part or process contribute value?
- Is the cost of the material, part or process proportionate to its usefulness?
- Are all the product features actually needed?
- Can a lower-cost method be used while still retaining the features and functions that add value?
- Is anyone paying less for this part?

3.9 A more detailed checklist is quoted by Dobler and Burt (*Purchasing and Supply Management*).

- Can the item be eliminated?
- If the item is not standard, can a standard item be used?
- If it is a standard item, does it completely fit the application or is it a misfit?
- Does the item have greater capacity than required?
- Can the weight be reduced?
- Is there a similar item in inventory that could be substituted?
- Are closer tolerances specified than are necessary?
- Is unnecessary machining performed on the item?
- Are unnecessarily fine finishes specified?
- Is 'commercial quality' (ie the most economical quality) specified?
- Can the item be made more cheaply? Can it be bought out more cheaply?
- Is the item properly classified for shipping purposes to obtain lowest transportation costs?
- Can the cost of packaging be reduced?
- Are suppliers being asked for suggestions to reduce cost?

3.10 The specific outcomes of a value analysis exercise may be reduced costs and/or improved quality, but this is not the only benefit to the organisation. Individuals involved in this kind of exercise find that they look at their work in a different way, no longer regarding previous decisions on design and engineering as binding, but taking a fresh approach. The whole process of value analysis therefore fosters a positive approach towards innovation and overcomes the entrenched resistance to change that may otherwise be encountered.

Organising for value analysis

3.11 Value analysis is based on teamwork. It depends on inputs from purchasing, design and engineering, production and other personnel from within the organisation, as well as drawing on assistance from suppliers. It works by encouraging free exchange of opinions on the various alternatives. Staying in touch with developments in production techniques and materials is essential, and clearly purchasing staff, using their contacts with other organisations, are well placed to assist in this.

3.12 The teamwork aspect means that management must institute a framework within which the team can function at its optimum. There are various ways in which this can be organised. At its least formal, this could simply mean training and encouraging operating personnel to be alert for value analysis opportunities. This could become slightly more formalised if the chance of feedback were offered, perhaps through regular value analysis meetings.

3.13 Other firms prefer to organise on a committee basis. Representatives of the various functions likely to have an input are co-opted under the guidance of an appointed committee head. The team could well include members from purchasing, design and engineering, production, quality control, finance and marketing.

The role of suppliers

3.14 Involving suppliers in a value analysis exercise is a regular procedure for many firms. Often the firm simply displays value analysis projects on boards, and invites current and potential suppliers to study the exhibits. Suppliers may then come up with suggestions for how quality and/or cost could be improved. Their reward is the likelihood of further business as a result.

3.15 Zenz quotes a checklist for buyers to observe when they seek to involve suppliers in value analysis.

- Make sure that suppliers understand the principles.
- Provide suppliers with the means to update their knowledge of value analysis techniques and how to apply them to the firm's products.
- Authenticate the buyer's interest in value analysis and make it apparent to suppliers.
- Make it easy for suppliers to submit value analysis ideas. Use of a simple standard form such as that shown in Figure 9.2 below is an important step.
- Prompt suppliers with ways they can help.
- Include suppliers in make-or-buy discussions.
- Assign value analysis projects to promising suppliers.
- Recognise the limits of supplier expertise.
- Rate suppliers on value analysis contributions.
- Give adequate rewards for value analysis help.

Figure 9.2 *Supplier checklist for value analysis study*

Fictional plc: supplier checklist for value analysis study			
Part name and number _____			
Estimated annual usage _____ Buyer _____			
QUESTIONS	Yes	No	Recommendations
Do you understand the part function? Could costs be reduced by relaxing requirements: • Tolerances? • Finishes? • Testing? • By how much?			
Could costs be reduced through changes in: • Material? • Ordering quantities? • The use of castings, stampings, etc? • By how much?			
Can you suggest other changes that would: • Reduce weight? • Simplify the part? • Reduce overall costs?			
Do you feel that any of the specifications are too stringent?			
How can we help to alleviate your greatest element of cost in supplying this part?			
Do you have a standard item that could be substituted for this part? • What is it? • What does it cost?			
Other suggestions _____			
Supplier _____ Date _____ Address _____ Signature _____ Title _____			
Additional comments may be made on the back of this sheet			

The contribution of purchasing to value analysis

3.16   As we have progressed through the discussion of value analysis the involvement of purchasing staff has been mentioned several times. In this final section we recapitulate and develop the ideas on purchasing's contribution.

3.17   Two general principles stand out to begin with. Firstly, value analysis is only a particular (highly formalised) example of what purchasing staff are doing in their everyday work. Every time a purchasing manager decides to order component X rather than component Y he is in effect conducting a miniature value analysis exercise. Secondly, it is purchasing staff who in general will bring to the process the most consistent drive towards lower costs, because reducing costs is such an important part of the entire purchasing discipline.

3.18 Specific contributions that can be made by purchasing staff include the following.

- From their contacts with outside organisations, purchasing staff are aware of and can advise on developments in materials and processes. They can advise on the costs of alternative materials and methods.

- When the value analysis team considers how to make improvements, one question to ask is 'how do others do it'? It is purchasing staff who are best placed to answer this question.

- As we have seen, suppliers can make a large contribution to value analysis and it is clearly purchasing staff who should marshal their efforts. In other cases, purchasing staff may be able to suggest new suppliers who can provide more suitable and/or less expensive materials.

- Finally, purchasing will usually take the overall responsibility for project leadership. The form this will take may vary depending on the organisational structure adopted for the value analysis activity, and this has been discussed earlier.

Value for money (VFM)

3.19 Value for money is a term used particularly in the public sector (though it is equally relevant to private sector firms). Organisations must ensure that they get the best possible value for the money they spend. Often this has been measured in terms of the 'three Es'.

- Effectiveness – achieving appropriate objectives by the best possible deployment of resources used

- Efficiency – using the least possible amount of resources while achieving objectives

- Economy – spending the least amount possible in acquiring the resources to achieve objectives

3.20 A commitment to VFM should go beyond the obvious functions of finance and purchasing. It should be integrated into all organisational functions until it is a part of 'business as usual' for all members of staff. Often, different departments will be required to report on the application of VFM principles within their own activities. This is to ensure that all departments are aware of their responsibility in this area.

3.21 The risk in leaving VFM considerations entirely in the hands of finance and/or purchasing is that these functions are not necessarily best placed to see the full scope for savings. Individual departments will be aware of which measures are likely to be effective in their own sphere of activities. Their contribution to achieving VFM must not be allowed to be passed over.

4 Reduction and control of costs

The role of design and engineering

4.1 As we have already emphasised, the costs of acquiring and owning a capital asset extend far beyond the original purchase price. It is a priority for purchasers to ensure that the costs of the asset over its whole life are reduced to the minimum compatible with effective operation. Various departments within the organisation are able to contribute to this: your syllabus specifies design and engineering, purchasing, marketing, and distribution.

4.2 As far as design and engineering are concerned, you should refer back to the earlier section of this chapter on value analysis and value engineering.

The role of purchasing

4.3 That same section has a good deal to say about the role of purchasing in minimising the costs of capital assets. This topic is also covered in Sections 1 and 2 of this chapter.

The role of marketing

4.4 There is a traditional conflict between the roles of marketing staff and operations and purchasing staff. Typically, it is said that marketing staff wish to maximise the variety of their firm's product offerings so as to meet the demands of as many potential customers as possible. Meanwhile, operations and purchasing staff are said to favour minimal product variety, because this streamlines their activities and keeps down costs.

4.5 Of course, this is a conflict that needs sensitive handling, based on a careful appraisal of both views in the particular circumstances of the organisation concerned. But it is clear that the 'marketing' approach can lead to high costs in the purchase of a capital asset (because the conventional requirement of marketing would imply purchase of a machine with the facility for highly varied production, ie for a machine with a high specification).

The role of distribution

4.6 The distribution function has a role to play in cost reduction and control (see Table 8.1 in the previous chapter), but this is not closely linked to the specific case of capital assets.

The role of finance

4.7 Not surprisingly, the finance function is closely involved in the reduction and control of costs for capital assets. This begins in the earliest stages: finance staff are ideally placed to evaluate the financial costs and benefits of potential asset acquisitions. This may take the form of the investment appraisal techniques to be discussed in the next chapter.

4.8 Finance staff are also, of course, deeply involved in the process of drawing up and monitoring budgets, including budgets for capital expenditure. They are well placed to take a view on the type of financing required (whether purchase from funds on hand, raising of share or loan capital, finance leasing or whatever). If necessary, it is the finance function who will have contacts with the organisation's bank. This is important because the bank may need to be kept aware of the reasons why the organisation is incurring heavy outgoings.

4.9 In the case where loan capital is to be used, finance staff will be responsible for agreeing the schedule of interest payments and repayment of capital. Their general budgeting duties will include accounting for these payments and ensuring that there is sufficient income for the purpose.

5 *Authorisation of capital expenditure*

5.1 Before a major investment is undertaken it will be necessary to go through certain authorisation procedures. The extent and formality of such procedures will reflect the large amount of organisational resources that are to be committed.

5.2 Often the first stage is undertaken as part of the budgeting process. We have seen earlier that budgets are used as a mechanism for control, and this extends to capital expenditure as much as to operating expenditure. Most firms of reasonable size will have a capital expenditure budget within which major projects will be considered.

5.3 Given that a capital budget exists, there is still a need for defined procedures to be completed before any particular project is entered into. One control often encountered in practice is the use of a standard requisition form showing the nature and amount of the expenditure and the rationale for it. This would be signed by a manager of appropriate seniority before it could be progressed.

5.4 In general, defined levels of authority should be laid down. For example, a manager at a particular grade in the hierarchy should be authorised to initiate expenditure up to a certain level, whereas for a manager at the next higher grade a slightly higher authorisation level would be set.

5.5 Other procedures may include a requirement to obtain more than one quotation for an item of capital expenditure. In addition, it helps control to insist that the person authorising the expenditure should not be the same person who is using the asset.

5.6 It should be clear that a capital purchase involves the expertise of a number of different departments. This is appropriate in view of the importance of such purchasing decisions.

5.7 The steps involved, and the departments responsible, are tabulated in Table 9.1.

Table 9.1 *The steps in a capital purchase decision*

Step		Departments/personnel involved
1	Initial request for capital item	User department
2	Sourcing	Purchasing function, often with input from the user department
3	Authorisation	Finance department, working to guidelines laid down by senior management
4	Investigation	Purchasing function, possibly represented by a buying team set up for the purpose
5	Appraisal and evaluation	Finance department and purchasing
6	Buying decision	Purchasing function (buying team)
7	Purchase contract	Purchasing function

Chapter summary

- The large sums of money involved in capital projects, and the fact that cashflows will take place over an extended period, make it essential to adopt formal techniques of investment appraisal.

- This is seen especially clearly in the case of capital assets. The total costs of acquiring, owning and running a capital asset may be vastly more than the basic purchase price.

- To deal with the problems of costing capital assets, the technique of whole life costing has been developed. This takes into account all the categories of cost that may be incurred at different stages of the asset's total useful life and uses discounted cashflow principles to evaluate them in today's terms.

- Target costing is particularly relevant in the context of new product development. NPD is a strategic issue and is normally approached in a highly structured manner.

- Value analysis is an organised and systematic study of the function of a part, process, material etc. The idea is to assess the value of the part in terms of the functions it performs. When applied at the design stage value analysis is often referred to as value engineering.

- The outcome of a value analysis exercise should be improved quality, but may also be reduced costs. The process also helps to focus the minds of staff on value issues.

- Value analysis is usually conducted by means of multi-functional teams. Often the involvement of suppliers is appropriate.

- The task of minimising whole life costs of a capital asset involves many different departments, including: design and engineering, purchasing, marketing, distribution.

- The financial impact of acquiring a capital asset makes it essential to follow strict authorisation procedures.

Self-test questions

Numbers in brackets refer to the paragraphs where you can check your answers.

1   What is meant by a suboptimal decision? (1.2)

2   What types of cost are involved in the purchase of a capital asset? (1.7)

3   What is meant by a guaranteed maintenance contract? (2.7, 2.8)

4   List benefits of whole life costing. (2.10)

5   What techniques might we use to reduce costs as part of a target costing exercise? (2.14)

6   Distinguish between the terms value analysis and value engineering. (3.3, 3.4)

7   List as many as you can of the five tests for value developed in General Electric. (3.8)

8   What organisational structures might be chosen to implement a value analysis exercise? (3.11–3.13)

9   What principles should buyers observe when they involve suppliers in value analysis? (3.15)

10 What are the specific contributions that purchasing staff can make to a value analysis exercise? (3.18)

12 List the main steps in a capital purchasing decision, together with the main organisational functions involved at each step. (5.7)

CHAPTER 10

Appraisal of Capital Investments

Learning objectives and indicative content

5.1 Evaluate the nature and importance of investment decision making for home and international markets.

- Accounting rate of return (ARR)
- Payback period (PP)
- Discounted cashflow (DCF)
- Net present value (NPV)
- Internal rate of return (IRR)
- Opportunity costs of capital
- The impact of depreciation on running costs

5.2 Assess the impact of external factors upon the decision making process and how these might be factored into the modelling and ultimate business case.

- Inflation
- Customs and Excise
- Taxation
- Exchange rates and currency management
- Social and political factors
- CSR and sustainability
- PESTLE and regulatory factors

Chapter headings

1 Cashflows associated with capital investments

2 The payback method

3 The accounting rate of return (ARR) method

4 Principles of discounted cashflow

5 Computer modelling and simulation

6 The impact of external factors

Introduction

In the previous chapter we looked at general principles relating to the acquisition of capital assets. In this chapter we move on to the tools of financial analysis that are used to evaluate the capital acquisition decision. You should always bear in mind that financial factors are not the only ones with relevance to the decision, but naturally they carry great weight.

These techniques necessarily have a mathematical flavour, and in some cases are quite difficult to understand conceptually. We begin with the simple methods of payback period and accounting rate of return, but more sophisticated analysis requires the use of discounted cashflow techniques (Section 4 of this chapter). Needless to say, such analysis is nowadays invariably carried out by means of a computer and in Section 5 of the chapter we look at the use of computer modelling and simulation in the appraisal of capital investments. Finally, in Section 6, we look at a number of external factors that may affect the capital investment decision.

1   Cashflows associated with capital investments

The nature of capital investments

1.1   When a business spends money to acquire assets it does so in order to generate revenue which will more than cover the money expended. In other words, businesses invest cash in productive assets in order to make profits. This applies to virtually any cash expended by the business: spending on wages and raw materials (to manufacture products which will sell at a profit), spending on office buildings, factory premises and plant (to make such manufacture possible) and so on.

1.2   On this analysis, every penny spent by a business is an investment. In principle, each item of expenditure should be subject to detailed appraisal: is this 'investment' the best possible use of the cash? In practice, of course, this would bring most businesses to a standstill. Detailed techniques of investment appraisal are reserved for occasions when large sums of money are at stake. The term 'investment' in this chapter is reserved for this type of expenditure.

1.3   As an example, a company might be considering the acquisition of more modern plant which would improve productivity and quality. Or it might be quoting for a large project to be carried out for a customer, possibly involving the acquisition of major assets, hiring of employees and other significant expenditure.

1.4   The size of the sums involved makes it vitally important for the business to evaluate such investment projects rigorously, and a number of techniques have evolved to help with this.

1.5   The nub of the question in investment decisions is the (usually) extended time period involved. In the case where a large capital asset is acquired heavy expenditure takes place up front, but benefits of quality and productivity are expected over years to come. Our concern is with ways of evaluating such costs and benefits in financial terms.

1.6 The starting point is to estimate the types and magnitude of the cash inflows and outflows that will arise if the investment goes ahead. Clearly, this is a very subjective process, especially if the cashflows relate to periods in the distant future. Nevertheless, detailed appraisal cannot even begin without this first step.

Types of cashflow

1.7 What kinds of cashflows might be involved?

- Cash outflows might include the cost of capital equipment, any loan interest payable, wages and salaries of new employees taken on as part of the project, and tax payable on the profits arising.

- Cash inflows might include increased cash receipts from customers, savings in operating costs arising from increased efficiency, and possibly any reductions in tax bills. Such reductions are possible because of tax incentives offered by governments in order to stimulate investment by businesses.

- Net cashflows in any period are the cash inflows less cash outflows for that period. Typically the net cashflow is negative in early years (because of upfront payments for capital assets), while in later years net cashflow should become positive (as operating benefits take effect).

- Your syllabus also mentions the **opportunity costs of capital**. This means the benefit forgone by investing in the chosen project rather than the next best alternative. In other words, one of the costs involved in adopting Investment A is the benefit forgone by **not** investing in Investment B. In practice, rather than considering this as a separate cost, it makes better sense to evaluate the two investments separately and to choose the one that is more profitable.

- Finally, your syllabus mentions the impact of **depreciation**. Depreciation is not a cashflow – it is merely a 'book entry', reclassifying capital expenditure as operating expenditure. The cashflows relevant to the cost of equipment are its initial cost, usually paid up front in full, and (sometimes) the proceeds from scrapping or re-selling the asset at the end of its useful life.

1.8 It might appear that an investment should always be approved if expected net cashflows are positive. However, things are not as simple as that. There is invariably a limit on the amount of funds available for investment; even a project with a positive cashflow profile may be rejected if other projects look more attractive. The timing of cashflows is also important; in general, the negative cashflows in early years are reasonably certain, while positive cashflows expected later are inevitably more speculative. The longer the period before cashflows become positive, the less attractive the project will seem.

1.9 To evaluate these various factors businesses use a variety of investment appraisal techniques. Below, we look at three: the payback method; the accounting rate of return (ARR) method; and the use of discounted cashflow techniques to determine the net present value of a project.

2 *The payback method*

2.1   We now begin our discussion of the particular numerical approaches that are used to evaluate investment proposals. We begin with the payback method.

2.2   The great virtue of this method is its simplicity. The idea is to assess how long a project will take to 'pay back' the initial investment. An example will make this clear. Suppose that a company proposes to purchase a replacement machine for £200,000, payment to be made immediately. The new machine is much more productive than existing plant, and this will lead to financial benefits of £50,000 per annum for each of the five years that the machine is expected to be in use.

2.3   The net cashflows associated with this project are shown below. (Note that negative cashflows are shown in brackets. The initial outlay of funds takes place 'now', ie year 0. The operating savings in subsequent years are assumed to arise at the end of the year in question. All of this is conventional in investment appraisal.)

	Net cashflow each year £	Cumulative cashflow £
Year 0	(200,000)	(200,000)
Year 1	50,000	(150,000)
Year 2	50,000	(100,000)
Year 3	50,000	(50,000)
Year 4	50,000	0
Year 5	50,000	50,000

2.4   The pattern here is clear. In Year 1, the initial negative cashflow of £200,000 is only partly compensated by financial benefits of £50,000. This negative is gradually wiped out by benefits in later years. By the end of Year 4 the net cumulative cashflow is zero. We say that the project has paid back by the end of Year 4. By the time the machine's useful life is finished the cumulative net cashflow has reached a positive figure of £50,000.

2.5   Managers favour the use of this method partly because of its simplicity, but partly also because of its relative safety compared with other methods. In the above example, we expect to recoup our investment after four years, which is not a long time in investment terms. Projects which appear very profitable, but which will not pay back until well into the future, are regarded with suspicion: after all, there must be considerable uncertainty whether the distant benefits will ever be realised.

2.6   The payback method has a valid place in preliminary screening of potential projects. For example, managers might adopt a rule of thumb that any project not expected to pay back within ten years should be rejected without further investigation. But it is an unsophisticated guide to investment decisions. The reason for this becomes clear if we suppose that our fictional company above has an alternative use for its £200,000.

2.7   Suppose that an alternative project offers financial benefits of £20,000 per annum in years one to three and £80,000 per annum in years four to six. The cashflow profile looks like this.

	Net cashflow each year £	Cumulative cashflow £
Year 0	(200,000)	(200,000)
Year 1	20,000	(180,000)
Year 2	20,000	(160,000)
Year 3	20,000	(140,000)
Year 4	80,000	(60,000)
Year 5	80,000	20,000
Year 6	80,000	100,000

2.8 Using the payback criterion, this project looks less attractive: it does not pay back until some point during Year 5. But overall, this project generates a positive cashflow of £100,000, compared with £50,000 for the previous investment. The effect of using the payback criterion is clear: it gives preference to projects which pay back quickly, even if other projects offer better returns in the long term. For this reason it should be used only as a supplement to more sophisticated methods.

3   The accounting rate of return (ARR) method

3.1 This is another relatively simple method, easily understood by managers faced with investment decisions. The idea is simply to calculate the average rate of return earned by the money invested. This procedure is familiar to anyone who has ever compared rates of interest offered by building societies and banks on their savings accounts.

3.2 As the name suggests, the relevant rate of return is based on the accounting profits generated by the investment. Accounting profits are not identical with cashflows, but for simplicity we will ignore this distinction and illustrate the procedure using the cashflow figures already given above.

3.3 For the first project, the overall return over five years is £50,000, being savings of £250,000 compared with expenditure of £200,000. This means that average annual returns of £10,000 are expected on an investment of £200,000, a 5 per cent rate of return.

3.4 For the second project, the overall return over six years is £100,000. This means that average annual returns of £16,667 are expected on an investment of £200,000, a rate of return of 8.3 per cent per annum. On this criterion, the second project is preferable.

3.5 Notice that this conflicts with the choice suggested by the payback method, under which the first project was preferable. This again illustrates the main shortcoming of the payback method, which is that only the rapidity of repayment is considered, and not the overall level of return.

3.6 Strictly speaking, it is incorrect to use £200,000 as the investment figure in the ARR calculation. This is because the business is not investing this entire sum for the duration of the project. Indeed, in both cases the whole of the initial investment is recouped before the project ends. This means that the average amount invested over the lifetime of the project is far less than £200,000. These complications do not affect the general principles involved. However, it is just worth mentioning that if we did do more accurate calculations the payback method and the ARR method would not be so far apart as appears in the analysis above.

3.7   A number of criticisms can be made of the ARR approach.

- It takes no account of the project's life. A 20 per cent return may seem more attractive than a 15 per cent return, but a project offering 15 per cent for five years may be more attractive than one that offers 20 per cent for only two years.

- It takes no account of the timing of cashflows. Later cashflows are more speculative than earlier ones, but all are given equal weight in the ARR calculation.

- The measurement of accounting profits is subjective. (We avoided this problem above by using cashflows instead of accounting profits.)

4   Principles of discounted cashflow

The time value of money

4.1   The methods of investment appraisal described so far are relatively crude. Although they are in widespread use (particularly the payback method) they should really be regarded as providing only preliminary criteria for evaluation. If a large-scale capital project warrants detailed appraisal, the use of discounted cashflow (DCF) techniques is essential.

4.2   The reason for this is the crucial importance of timing in the generation of cashflows. To understand this you need to be familiar with the concept of the **time value of money**. This can be illustrated by considering the difference between a sum of £1,000 receivable today and the same sum receivable in one year's time. Which would you prefer?

4.3   Clearly there are several reasons why £1,000 right now is preferable. One reason is the element of risk. Perhaps circumstances will change over the next year, and the promised £1,000 will not materialise at the end of that period. Another reason is inflation. In most developed economies inflation erodes the value of money over time. The amount you can purchase with £1,000 today is greater than you will be able to purchase in one year's time. Finally, if the money is received today it can be put to work immediately. If it is invested it will amount to more than £1,000 by the end of the year.

4.4   This final point is easy to illustrate. Suppose your local bank is offering interest of 5 per cent per annum on savings accounts. If you receive £1,000 today and invest it, your account will be worth £1,050 after a year. In this sense it is fair to say that £1,000 today is worth £1,050 in one year's time. If you leave the cash on deposit for a further twelve months you will receive a further interest payment of £52.50 (£1,050 × 5% = £52.50). This boosts the value of the account to £1,102.50, so we can say that £1,102.50 receivable in two years is equivalent to £1,000 receivable today.

4.5   To put this the other way around, what is the value in today's terms of £1,000 receivable twelve months hence? This can be calculated by working out the amount you would need to deposit in the savings account in order for your balance to reach £1,000 in one year's time. The answer is £952.38, because this sum plus 5 per cent interest will amount to £1,000 in twelve months. We say that the **present value** of £1,000 receivable after a year at a discount rate of 5 per cent is £952.38.

4.6   These calculations illustrate the main principle of discounted cashflow. Cashflows arising in the future must be **discounted** to arrive at their present value, ie their value in today's terms. The exact rate of discount reflects the time value of money. This value may be different at different times, or even for different firms at the same time. It reflects the fact that a particular firm at a particular time may have a stronger or weaker preference for receiving money now rather than in the future. But whatever the circumstances, there is always some preference for receiving cash now.

4.7 This is an important point which often causes difficulties for students coming to the subject for the first time. Such students sometimes come away with the confused notion that DCF techniques are a way of dealing with inflation. They believe that the current rate of inflation is the appropriate discount rate to use. The logical conclusion is that in an economy with no inflation, no discounting would be necessary, because firms would be indifferent between cash now and cash in the future.

4.8 The above discussion should have made it clear that this is quite false. Inflation is only one of many reasons why money today is better than money tomorrow. Other reasons for discounting will always be present even if inflation is not.

4.9 So far we have illustrated the time value of money by reference to cash receivable. However, similar principles apply in reverse to cash payable. In this case firms prefer to pay money in one year's time rather than now. For example, a firm which is due to pay a bill of £1,000 in one year's time can pay £952.38 today into a building society account at 5 per cent interest. After a year there will be £1,000 in the account to pay the bill. From the firm's point of view the liability of £1,000 is equivalent to a liability of only £952.38 in today's terms. Notice again that this has nothing to do with inflation.

Using DCF tables

4.10 These calculations are greatly simplified in practice by the use of published tables. The present value of a future sum of money depends on two things: the discount rate, and how far in the future the money will be paid or received. Published tables are arranged in the form of a grid in which any combination of these two factors can be identified and a 'discount factor' read off. This is illustrated by an extract from published tables; see Table 10.1.

4.11 The discount factor in each case shows the present value of £1 receivable or payable after the stated number of years at the stated rate of discount. For example, with a discount rate of 5 per cent, a sum of £1 receivable in two years time has a present value of £0.907 or 90.7p. Using this information it is easy to calculate that £1,000 receivable in two years has a present value of £907. Allowing for a small rounding difference, this is the amount that you calculated in the exercise above.

Table 10.1 *Discount factors for DCF calculations*

	5%	6%	7%	8%	9%	10%
Year						
0	1.000	1.000	1.000	1.000	1.000	1.000
1	0.952	0.943	0.935	0.926	0.917	0.909
2	0.907	0.890	0.873	0.857	0.842	0.826
3	0.864	0.840	0.816	0.794	0.772	0.751
4	0.823	0.792	0.763	0.735	0.708	0.683
5	0.784	0.747	0.713	0.681	0.650	0.621
6	0.746	0.705	0.666	0.630	0.596	0.564

Rate of discount

4.12 Notice that 'Year 0' refers to cashflows arising immediately; 'Year 1' means cashflows arising one year from now, and so on.

Net present value

4.13 We illustrate the use of DCF in investment appraisal by reference to the two projects already mentioned; we will distinguish them as Project A and Project B. In each case the idea is to take the estimated net cashflows for each year and apply the appropriate discount factors to evaluate the present values of all cashflows over the life of the projects. By totalling these we arrive at the net present value (NPV) of the project.

4.14 A positive NPV is good news, suggesting that the project is worth undertaking; a negative NPV suggests that the project costs more than it is worth. We assume that the discount rate for each project is 8 per cent. In practice, it is a difficult exercise to decide on an appropriate discount rate. (Later in this chapter we will look briefly at how to calculate an appropriate discount rate.)

Year	Discount factors	— Project A — Cashflows £	Present values £	— Project B — Cashflows £	Present values £
0	1.000	(200,000)	(200,000)	(200,000)	(200,000)
1	0.926	50,000	46,300	20,000	18,520
2	0.857	50,000	42,850	20,000	17,140
3	0.794	50,000	39,700	20,000	15,880
4	0.735	50,000	36,750	80,000	58,800
5	0.681	50,000	34,050	80,000	54,480
6	0.630			80,000	50,400
Net present value			(350)		15,220

4.15 At the discount rate of 8 per cent Project A should not be undertaken: its NPV is negative. The NPV of Project B is positive, and in the absence of factors indicating otherwise it is worthwhile undertaking.

4.16 Notice that the NPV is far less in each case than the 'profit' shown by the figures before discounting (respectively £50,000 and £100,000). This is because the discounted figures correctly indicate that the benefits from the projects, arising as they do in the distant future, are not as valuable as they appear at first sight.

Internal rate of return

4.17 The NPV for Project A is such a small negative as to be virtually equal to zero. The discount rate at which a zero NPV occurs is called the **internal rate of return** (IRR) of a project. Effectively, this rate can be used as a way of deciding for or against an investment project. If the firm considering Project A can borrow funds for the project at less than 7 per cent, then the project is viable; its internal rate of return at 7 per cent would be greater than zero and so the return is greater than the cost of financing the project at 7 per cent – the firm's **hurdle rate**. On the other hand if the firm would suffer interest charges of, say, 9 per cent on its borrowings, the project is not viable. It is certain that the NPV at 9 per cent would be a much greater negative than the return at 8 per cent.

Advantages of DCF

4.18   The elaborate nature of DCF calculations may have already led you to wonder about how common they are in practice. The answer is that they are very common in most large organisations. Of course, to use this kind of technique every time a salesman needs a new company car would make no sense: the amount involved could not possibly justify the trouble. But for larger investment decisions the sums involved suggest that careful appraisal is essential.

4.19   Given that careful appraisal is needed, DCF offers significant advantages over other methods.

- Unlike the payback method, DCF takes account of all cashflows over the life of the project, not just those in the early years.

- Unlike the ARR method, DCF concentrates on the most relevant factor: actual cashflows rather than accounting profit or loss.

- DCF is the only method to take account of the crucial factor of the time value of money.

4.20   Despite this it is sensible to recognise the limitations of DCF techniques. The apparent precision of the calculations should not mask the subjective assumptions on which they are based. The cashflows estimated to arise in the future are necessarily uncertain in amount, and this uncertainty increases as the time horizon becomes more distant. Moreover, we have entirely ignored the very great practical difficulties of determining an appropriate discount rate in respect of a particular firm or a particular investment. We look briefly at this issue below.

What discount rate should be used in a DCF calculation?

4.21   To determine an appropriate discount rate we really need to know the cost to the firm of the capital that will be invested in the project. In some cases this might be fairly simple. For example, a small business may fund a new project simply by going along to the bank manager and asking for the required amount of capital in the form of a loan. The 'cost of capital' in this case is simply the interest rate attaching to the loan.

4.22   In other cases it is more complicated than this. For example, a large company may fund its operations by means of several different sources of finance: share capital, reserves, loans and debentures etc. For a particular investment it is not easy to say which of these sources is providing the capital required.

4.23   In a case like this it makes more sense to talk about the **weighted average cost of capital** (WACC). Any form of funding has a cost, which will be related to the level of return expected by the investor or lender who provides the funds. This in turn will be influenced by the level of risk perceived by that provider.

4.24   If we can establish the cost of each source of funds, and we know the proportion of each type of funding in the total funds owned by the organisation, we can calculate the WACC. For example, if an organisation is funded by £100,000 of loan capital, with an interest rate of 9%, and £200,000 of equity capital, with shareholders expecting a return of 12%, we can calculate a WACC of 11% (being one third of 9% plus two thirds of 12%).

5 *Computer modelling and simulation*

5.1 The number-crunching aspect of DCF is beyond the scope of this syllabus, but you should be aware that readily available computer programs make all the calculations for you. For instance, in some versions of the Microsoft Excel spreadsheet package you can access the *Business Planner Template* menu from the **File>New** menu. Included in the templates is the *Capital Budgeting for a New Project* worksheet, in which you simply have to put in the figures available to you. The programme then calculates the undiscounted net cash flow of the project, plus the net present value at its end, using two different discount rates. It then also presents the internal rate of return of the project, which can be compared with the firm's target or hurdle rate of return for new projects.

Example

5.2 A new asset can be purchased and installed by Waddy plc for £100,000. It is expected to have a life in use of five years, at the end of which time it will be sold for £5,000. Waddy plc has a hurdle rate for new capital projects of 4 per cent, which is the interest rate at which it can borrow the money for the new asset. During its life the asset will generate the following income and incur the following costs:

Year	Sales income £	Maintenance costs £
1	25,000	5,000
2	30,000	6,000
3	50,000	8,000
4	30,000	12,000
5	20,000	15,000

5.3 By convention the initial expenditure is treated as occurring 'now', which is called Time 0. All other cash flows are treated as occurring at the end of each subsequent year. As Waddy plc can borrow at 4 per cent, this is a sensible figure to use as the lower discount rate, which is asked for by the calculation table part of the spreadsheet. We have used 6 per cent for the higher one, but you can use whatever rates you wish to achieve a result.

5.4 By putting the figures into the appropriate areas of the Business Planner spreadsheet, the following calculations are made.

New asset cashflow

Year	0	1	2	3	4	5
	£	£	£	£	£	£
Receipts						
Sales income	0	25,000	30,000	50,000	30,000	20,000
Disposal proceeds	0	0	0	0	0	5,000
Total receipts	0	25,000	30,000	50,000	30,000	25,000
Maintenance costs	0	5,000	6,000	8,000	12,000	15,000
Total payments	100,000	5,000	6,000	8,000	12,000	15,000
Net cashflow	-100,000	20,000	24,000	42,000	18,000	10,000

Calculation table

Discount rates

Lower discount rate: 4%
Higher discount rate: 6%

Net present value at lower discount rate, 4%   £2,364
Net present value at higher discount rate, 6%   –£2,778

Internal rate of return: 5%

5.5   We know that the hurdle rate is 4 per cent, and this calculation shows a positive NPV at the hurdle rate, so the project should be accepted. The spreadsheet also tells us that the IRR is 5 per cent; we know that this exceeds the hurdle rate, so on this criterion as well the project should be accepted.

5.6   Obviously this form of computer modelling can be used for all types of capital project, and is particularly useful for comparing alternative projects and working out how much can be paid for an asset initially for the project as a whole to be viable. However, one must always bear in mind that all the costs and revenues (except for the initial outlay) are estimates only. Matters can turn out very differently in reality, and it is good practice to do **sensitivity analysis** on the results of DCF calculations. This calculates how sensitive the decision is to changes in estimates – for instance, what the effect will be if revenue is £1,000 lower each year, and maintenance costs are £1,000 higher.

6   *The impact of external factors*

Introduction

6.1   Your syllabus refers to a number of so-called 'external factors' that might affect the decision making process in relation to capital assets. Although it is not always clear what effects the author of the syllabus had in mind, we provide brief notes on each of these factors below.

Inflation

6.2 In a time of price inflation the minimum return required by an investor will increase. For example, a return of 5% might be satisfactory in an inflation-free economy, but if inflation is running at 10% per annum a much higher return would be sought. In other words, what we have previously described as the hurdle rate for capital investments will alter as a result of inflation.

6.3 In this situation, we have to be careful about what kind of cashflows we are considering.

- If we have settled on a 'real' rate of return required, we need to ensure that we are dealing with 'real' cashflows in our investment appraisal. This means that actual amounts of cash expected to be received or paid in the future must be adjusted for inflation so as to express them in today's values. In other words, if we are using a **real** rate of return, we must use **real** cashflows.

- If we have settled on a 'money' rate of return required, we can use actual money amounts received and paid.

6.4 Needless to say, the use of discounted cashflow techniques – which you may feel is complicated enough already – becomes even more difficult when inflation must be taken into account.

Customs and Excise

6.5 H M Customs and Excise no longer exists as a separate government department in the UK, having merged with the former Inland Revenue to become H M Revenue and Customs. The syllabus caption is presumably a reference to one of the main functions carried out by the Customs authorities, namely the administration of value added tax (VAT).

6.6 In most cases (such as the purchase of an item of machinery) VAT will not be a factor, because the organisation will normally be able to reclaim the VAT paid on acquiring the asset. However, VAT is not always recoverable in this way. For example, an organisation whose services are VAT-exempt (most banks and financial institutions fall into this category) is not able to recover VAT paid to its suppliers.

6.7 VAT is a cashflow like any other and in cases where it is not recoverable the organisation should include it as a cost of the acquisition. Moreover, if the organisation's future cashflows from operating activities are affected by VAT this must be factored into the discounted cashflow calculations.

Taxation

6.8 In many cases, the purchase of a capital asset will have an effect on the organisation's liability to pay tax. For example, in the UK there is a system of **capital allowances**, whereby the price paid for such an asset is deducted from taxable profits over a period of years. This reduces the amount of tax payable by the organisation.

6.9 This tax saving should be shown as a favourable cashflow in the DCF calculations.

Exchange rates and currency management

6.10 The main effect under this heading concerns the case where we are buying the asset from an overseas supplier. The supplier will normally quote a price in his own currency, and we will need to purchase such currency in order to pay for the asset.

6.11 This creates a problem because the exchange rate prevailing between the home currency and the overseas currency at the time of the payment will be impossible to predict with certainty. The situation is even more complicated if stage payments are to be made.

6.12 One possibility would simply be to estimate the rate that will apply and perform the calculations accordingly. Another approach would be to use one of the available tools of currency management, such as a **forward exchange contract**. Under this arrangement the organisation contracts now to purchase the overseas currency at the required future date, at a rate of exchange agreed now. This takes the uncertainty out of the situation.

PESTLE and regulatory factors

6.13 Changes in social, political and environmental factors can disturb the assumptions on which the investment appraisal is made. For example, a change in the regulations on harmful emissions might require changes in a company's manufacturing processes. This might mean that a machine we are planning to invest in becomes obsolete more quickly than expected.

Corporate social responsibility (CSR) and sustainability

6.14 The effect here is similar to the above. In recent years, there has been increasing emphasis on the need for organisations to be good corporate citizens. This has far-reaching effects on the ways in which it conducts its business. In the nature of things, a capital investment has an expected life of several years. It may be difficult to predict what changes will arise over such a period as a result of CSR influences.

6.15 This is particularly evidenced by the recent focus on sustainability. Organisations are now expected to plan their purchases with due regard to the effects on limited natural resources. This has a double effect on the planning of capital purchases. On the one hand, buyers may be restricted in the suppliers they feel able to select – only those with a good record on sustainability will be considered. And secondly, the type or model of asset they decide to purchase must be one designed to limit the organisation's impact on the natural environment.

Chapter summary

- Capital investments invariably give rise to a number of cashflow effects extending over a period of years. Various techniques have been developed to evaluate such cashflows.

- The payback method discloses how quickly the initial expenditure on a project will be recouped, but does not reflect cashflows arising after that point.

- Like the payback method, the ARR method takes no account of the time value of money, and is also dependent on subjective estimates of accounting profits.

- The most sophisticated methods of investment appraisal are based on discounted cashflow (DCF). This procedure recognises that cashflows arising in the future must be discounted back to today's terms in order to enable decision-making.

- The basic procedure in DCF is to estimate all the relevant cashflows over the life of the project, to discount them to today's terms, and to calculate the net present value (NPV) of the project. A positive NPV suggests that the project is worthwhile; a negative NPV suggests that it should not be undertaken. An IRR that is higher than the organisation's target or hurdle rate suggests that the project should be undertaken.

- DCF calculations are invariably carried out by means of computer software. Apart from doing the basic calculations efficiently, such software also permits sensitivity analysis.

- External factors such as inflation and taxation can have important effects on the assumptions underlying a discounted cashflow analysis.

Self-test questions

Numbers in brackets refer to the paragraphs where you can check your answers.

1   What kinds of cashflow might be involved in a capital investment? (1.7)

2   Describe the payback method. (2.2)

3   What are the limitations of the payback method? (2.6–2.8)

4   What are the criticisms of the ARR method? (3.7)

5   Why is £1,000 now preferable to £1,000 in a year's time? (4.3)

6   What is meant by the discounting of cashflows? (4.6)

7   What is meant by the net present value of an investment? (4.13)

8   What is meant by the internal rate of return? (4.17)

9   What are the advantages of DCF as compared with other appraisal techniques? (4.19)

10   What is sensitivity analysis? (5.6)

11   How does inflation affect the appraisal of a capital investment? (6.2–6.4)

12   What is a forward exchange contract? (6.12)

CHAPTER 11

Managing Risk

Learning objectives and indicative content

6.1   Assess the different types of risk and their impact on each of the following:

- Suppliers
- Own organisation
- Customers

6.3   Evaluate and select financial risk management options

- Debt
- Futures and derivatives
- Insurance

Chapter headings

1   Supply risk

2   Supplier appraisal

3   Financial risk

4   Specialised risk management options

Introduction

The management of risk has increasingly become a focus of management attention. There are many different ways of classifying risk, but in this chapter we distinguish simply between the risks relating to supply and the risks arising from financial factors. In all cases we consider how the organisation itself is affected, but we also keep an eye out for possible impacts on customers and suppliers. In the final section of the chapter we look at some specialised tools of risk management specified in the syllabus.

1   Supply risk

Single sourcing

1.1   Kit Sadgrove (in *The Complete Guide to Business Risk Management*) states that supply risk can be divided into two categories.

- Risk from suppliers (eg the supplier is unreliable, or runs into financial difficulties)
- Risk from the organisation's procurement policies (eg the buyer sources from far away, possibly overseas)

1.2 We begin our discussion by looking at the issue of single sourcing, which arguably incorporates both of these categories: if the supplier is unreliable, we have compounded the risk ourselves by relying on a single source.

1.3 The traditional adversarial model of supplier relations encouraged use of many different suppliers for each material, particularly in the case of critical materials. The idea was to avoid over-dependence on a single supplier. This reasoning has not lost its validity as a result of changes in strategic outlook. It remains true that a buyer who depends on a single supplier for a material is at risk if that supplier experiences fire, flood, strikes or other disruption to production. For this reason most buyers continue to avoid single sourcing in the case of many or even all materials.

1.4 What has changed is buyers' readiness to accept single sourcing when circumstances suggest it.

- This may happen for example when the total amount needed is too small to justify splitting orders among several suppliers, because unit costs of handling and processing would rise as a result.

- Similarly it may happen that one supplier is so far ahead of others in terms of reputation, quality, price etc that it would make no sense to use anyone else.

- Another possible case is where expensive tooling is required: it may not make sense to pay for such tooling several times over by using several different suppliers.

- A final, and very important, consideration is that in times when a material is in short supply the buyer is likely to be treated more favourably by a single supplier than by any one of several suppliers.

1.5 The other major change in this area is that when buyers decide against single sourcing, they do not now generally opt for multiple sourcing either. Instead, they pursue the objective of a slimmer supplier base by choosing just two or three (not 10 or 20) different suppliers.

1.6 A related problem is where the market for a particular material is dominated by a single supplier (monopoly) or by just a small number of suppliers (oligopoly). Clearly the risk to supplies can have an impact not just on the organisation itself, but also on its customers if production is disrupted.

Partnership sourcing

1.7 Partnership sourcing has become an important trend in modern purchasing, and offers advantages in terms of access to the supplier's specialist knowledge and skills, together with the opportunity of significant price reductions. However, it also carries risks.

1.8 Without proper screening, much time can be wasted in developing close relations with suppliers who turn out to be unsuitable. Moreover, suppliers may gain detailed knowledge, which can be used to win contracts with competitors. This risk must be addressed by careful contractual arrangements, preventing disclosure or restricting the supplier's ability to trade with competitors.

Reputation issues

1.9 Suppliers can damage an organisation's reputation if it turns out that they are guilty of unethical practices. For example, suppliers located in the developing world may not observe employment practices that are mandatory in Western economies; they may employ child labour or offer inadequate conditions of work.

1.10 Many organisations try to avoid this by implementing a system of auditing their suppliers, but the distances involved and (often) the lack of effective local controls make this an imperfect solution.

1.11 Another problem is the use of overseas call centres. It is difficult to ensure the adequacy of overseas call centre staff in dealing with customers, and many customers resent it when they find that the person handling their call is based overseas.

Supplier quality issues

1.12 Suppliers may fail in quality terms if their deliveries are late, or if the materials delivered are substandard. Clearly a supplier who fails to meet quality standards must be brought up to the mark. If quality failures persist, the ultimate sanction is removal from the approved supplier list.

1.13 Ideally, the buyer will spot quality problems before they become critical. This assumes that there is a system in place for flagging delivery failures (in terms of either deadline or materials quality). It is also helpful to have agreed on quality standards with the suppliers, so that failures can be easily identified. Some companies go further, and require suppliers to bear the costs of warranty work that can be traced to their materials.

1.14 These issues are particularly important in a JIT environment, and Kit Sadgrove (in *The Complete Guide to Business Risk Management*) states that many companies are now reducing the scale of their JIT activity as a result. However, there are also risks in moving too far along the scale away from JIT: overstocking also causes risks. This is mainly because of the amount of cash tied up in stock, which can cause cashflow problems.

1.15 No doubt the best solution lies in a stock policy somewhere between the two extremes, relying on a reasonably systematic approach to forecasting sales demand and the stock requirements needed to support it.

Outsourcing and offshoring

1.16 Some organisations attempt to manage the risks of poor quality by outsourcing operations, particularly those operations that are not core to the business. They hope (among other reasons for outsourcing) that they can draw on specialised skills of an external supplier to reduce the risks, or at any event to transfer the risk onto someone else's shoulders.

1.17 A development of this trend is **offshoring**: transferring jobs once done in the home country to areas of lower labour cost in the developing world. The easiest jobs to transfer in this way are those that are not 'customer-facing' (though overseas call centres have also increased in number), and which involve routine work such as data processing.

1.18 Clearly this kind of activity carries risks of its own. The organisation surrenders a measure of control over the operations that are outsourced or offshored and must work closely with the external partner to ensure that this leads to no loss of quality.

2 *Supplier appraisal*

Evaluating suppliers and potential suppliers

2.1 Buyers must carefully evaluate potential suppliers before entering into business relationships with them. Even when suppliers are on stream, buyers should continually monitor their performance.

2.2 CIPS examiners have identified eight main areas of evaluation (gathered together under the mnemonic FACE 2 FACE, indicating that there are two factors corresponding to each of the letters F, A, C, E).

- **F** relates to Fixed assets (or physical resources) and Financial stability
- **A** relates to Ability to deliver the goods or service required and Ability to work productively with the buyer
- **C** relates to Cost and Commitment to quality
- **E** relates to Efficiency and Environmental considerations

2.3 The importance of adequate **fixed assets** (physical resources) is that without these the supplier will be unable to meet the buyer's requirements. The buyer can find information on this topic in the supplier's balance sheet. A point to look out for is the age of the supplier's main fixed assets: are they due for replacement soon, and if so is there finance available to replace them?

2.4 **Financial stability** is also important, and again the accounts of the supplier are an obvious source of information. Apart from the profit and loss account and balance sheet, the accounts will also include a cashflow statement, which contains important information on how successful the supplier is at generating funds from operations. Another useful source of information on financial stability is a report from a credit reference agency such as Dun and Bradstreet.

2.5 **Ability to deliver** can be tested by seeking references from existing customers of the supplier. The buyer will also want to look at some of the output produced by the supplier to ensure that it meets quality standards.

2.6 **Ability to work with the buyer** will depend partly on compatible cultures in the buying and supplying organisation. The buyer will form an impression on this point during negotiations and on site visits.

2.7 **Cost** is obviously vital. The supplier's prices must be competitive, but this should be seen in the modern perspective of total acquisition cost, not just basic purchase price.

2.8 The supplier's **commitment to quality** will partly be evident from the control systems they have in place (eg statistical process control, total quality management systems). Do they have ISO 9000 certification?

2.9 The buyer will also be concerned about the supplier's **efficiency**. The supplier's published accounts will contain information permitting calculation of efficiency ratios, eg speed of stock turnover, speed of collecting debtor balances etc.

2.10 Finally, buyers will want to examine the supplier's **environmental policies**. Modern thinking emphasises the importance of environmentally friendly production processes, and to some extent this is embodied in legal requirements.

Financial information about suppliers

2.11 Financial information about a supplier or potential supplier is an important element in appraisal. Buyers need to be certain that they will not be let down by a supplier with financial difficulties.

2.12 Potential benefits of this procedure include the following.

- Financial information, at least for UK companies, is easy to come by. It is a simple matter to access published accounts by visiting the Companies House website. Similarly, credit information can be accessed (for a charge) via agencies such as Dun & Bradstreet. Although such information is even more important in relation to credit customers, its importance should not be overlooked even in the case of suppliers.

- Published accounts provide useful information about the supplier, particularly if ratio analysis is used. By examining the accounts carefully, the buyer can obtain an insight into the company's liquidity, gearing (and hence financial risk), profitability, financial stability, asset backing, sources of funding, etc. The fact that comparative figures are also published (ie figures relating to the previous year as well as the current year) enables the buyer to spot trends over time. We look at this in more detail in the next chapter.

2.13 However, financial information is not the be all and end all.

- The published accounts display the level of detail required by the Companies Acts and accounting standards. This may be far less than the buyer needs. For example, published accounts will rarely, if ever, give the buyer sufficient information about the supplier's cost structure. The buyer will undoubtedly want to supplement his enquiries by further questioning of the supplier.

- The published accounts display historical information, which may be out of date even when published, and in any event may not be a reliable indicator of future financial strength.

- By definition, the financial information is restricted in its scope. It says nothing about other points of vital importance to buyers: quality procedures, delivery times, reliability, etc.

3 *Financial risk*

Capital investment appraisal

3.1 In the previous chapter we examined techniques for evaluating capital investments. In view of the large sums involved, this is an area where risk assessment is particularly important.

3.2 In considering investment appraisal techniques we made the assumption that predictions can be made about future outcomes. For example, we considered the adoption of Projects A and B which we claimed would give rise to certain cashflows over a future period of six years.

3.3 In reality, of course, there is no way we can be certain that such cashflows will materialise. In other words, there is risk attached to our forecasts. A problem that managers must address is how to analyse the amount of risk involved. This obviously has an impact on the attractiveness or otherwise of any project we are considering.

3.4 One way of dealing with risk is simply to adopt very prudent criteria in deciding whether to make an investment. For example, if we think the likely positive cashflow in Year 3 is £120,000, we could scale this estimate down by, say, a factor of one third, to £80,000. If the project continues to look attractive on these pessimistic forecasts we can invest in it with some confidence: we have left ourselves a good margin for error.

3.5 A similar technique would be to impose an overriding criterion for acceptance of a project, eg a maximum payback period. For example, we might adopt a rule of never investing in a project that will take more than three years to pay back. Using this criterion we would reject even very attractive projects unless their positive cashflows were expected to arise in the first three years. Of course, this means we may lose out on high payouts further down the line, but we minimise the risk of expensive disasters.

3.6 Another possible technique would be to calculate not just one net present value, but a range of NPVs based on different discount rates and different estimates of future cashflows. For example, instead of forecasting that the positive cashflow in Year 3 will be £120,000 we might forecast that (with a high degree of likelihood) the amount would lie between £90,000 and £140,000. We could then compute the consequences at these extreme values and estimate how our decision would be affected in each case.

3.7 More sophisticated than all of these approaches would be the use of **sensitivity analysis**. This is defined as 'a modelling and risk assessment procedure in which changes are made to significant variables in order to determine the effect of these changes on the planned outcome'. This is essentially an extension of the technique described in the paragraph above.

3.8 As an example of sensitivity analysis, we could focus on one factor influencing our estimates of future cashflows. For example, we might consider the likely unit production cost of a new product that we intend to produce on a machine we contemplate purchasing. Our initial estimate of the unit production cost might suggest that the new machine is well worth buying, because it enables us to produce a product that can be sold profitably.

3.9 Use of sensitivity analysis would allow us to probe more deeply. By setting up the formulae on a spreadsheet we could estimate the degree of 'tolerance' in our forecasts. For example, in a particular case it might turn out that the production cost is absolutely critical, and even a small mistake in our estimate would make a big impact on the investment decision. In such a case, we would revisit our estimate and look at it very carefully indeed.

3.10 In another case, it might turn out that our decision is barely affected by the production cost. Even if our estimate understates the true production cost by 20 per cent the machine is still worth buying. In this case we would conclude that we are not much at risk from a mistake in forecasting this particular variable, and we should therefore concentrate our attention on other factors involved in the forecast (eg the volume of sales we might achieve).

3.11   In practice, all of these techniques have a strongly mathematical flavour and use of a computer would be routine nowadays. In the exam you are unlikely to be confronted with numerical work, but you should be aware of the principles involved.

Interest rate risk and currency risk

3.12   Interest rate risk arises when an organisation's borrowing is such that a change in interest rates might expose it to interest charges that are unacceptably high. For example, if a company has loan finance at a fixed interest rate, but which is due to be repaid and replaced in the near future, the company is exposed to a sudden change in interest rates.

3.13   Foreign exchange risk applies to organisations that trade with overseas countries. Unless all transactions are denominated in the home currency – unlikely – then the organisation could find itself paying more for its imports than it had budgeted if the overseas currency strengthens against the home currency.

3.14   In each of these cases it is open to the company to use one of a variety of financial instruments that have been devised to protect against adverse movements in the interest rate or exchange rate. We look at some of these in the next section of the chapter.

Risks associated with the method of finance

3.15   Many organisations finance their assets and their activities by means of loan finance. Loans may be either secured or unsecured.

    •   A secured loan means that the lender has protected his funds by taking a 'charge' (rather like a mortgage) over an asset or assets owned by the organisation. If the organisation defaults on its repayments, the lender can exercise his rights over the charged assets, and in the last resort is entitled to sell them in order to recover what he has lent.

    •   An unsecured loan is more risky for the lender, in that it is not protected by any charge over the borrower's assets. If the borrower defaults the lender may take action in the courts to recover what he has lent, but this is a more cumbrous procedure than recovery through disposal of a charged asset.

3.16   From the borrower's point of view it is important to plan carefully for payment of interest on loans, and (eventually) repayment of the capital sum. Failure to do so could expose the borrower to financial penalties at best. In worse cases the borrower might be forced to sell vital assets in order to pay off the debt, or could even be forced to cease trading.

3.17   Lenders will naturally be concerned about the company's ability to repay the amount owing. Often they will perform a credit check (with a company such as Dun & Bradstreet) before granting the loan.

Equity vs debt

3.18   Potential providers of finance may be deterred if they see that an organisation already relies heavily on loan finance (debt). This is because an organisation of this sort – 'highly geared' in the jargon – is at risk if trading takes a turn for the worse. The point is that much of the company's profits must be set aside for unavoidable interest payments, leaving not much margin for safety if profit levels fall.

3.19 This is particularly a worry in the case of borrowers who have high levels of fixed costs. We saw in an earlier chapter how companies like this are more exposed to risk when trading deteriorates. A company with a low base of fixed costs is a more attractive proposition for a potential lender.

3.20 Considerations of this sort indicate that a company must be very careful in balancing any debt finance with an appropriate level of equity finance. Providers of equity will naturally expect a return on their investment (in the form of dividends). However, a key distinction is that payment of dividends is not compulsory – if times are lean, a company may decide to forgo paying dividends. This is not an option with interest payments on debt.

3.21 There are other factors too in the choice of equity as compared with debt financing.

- Debt invariably has to be repaid by a defined date. Equity usually remains in the business indefinitely.

- Debt finance must often be supported by security. In other words, the business must accept a charge over its assets (in effect, a mortgage).

- In favour of debt finance, the interest paid on debt is tax-deductible. In other words, although we have to pay the interest, at least our tax bill reduces. This is not the case with dividends paid out on equity capital.

- Another advantage of debt is that lenders remain outside the business. If instead, we attract new equity finance, the providers become part-owners and have a say in the running of the business. The original owners find their ownership diluted.

- A final advantage of debt is that it is usually cheaper and simpler to arrange than equity finance.

Bad debts

3.22 We mention one more possible risk before moving on to consider methods of reducing and managing the dangers. This is the risk of bad debts.

3.23 Most organisations (other than retailers) make sales to their customers on credit terms. The danger is that the customers will be unable or unwilling to pay when the debt falls due.

3.24 This is rarely an area of concern to buyers. It is invariably someone within the finance department (perhaps a dedicated credit controller) who takes action to minimise the risk of bad debts. Even so, for the purpose of this syllabus you should be aware of some of the measures that can be taken to avoid bad debts.

3.25 To begin with, companies should screen potential customers before granting them credit. It should be standard practice to seek references from the potential customer's bank and from other trade creditors. In some cases it may be appropriate to get a full-scale credit reference from one of the specialist firms providing that service. An appropriate credit limit should then be set.

3.26 Once trading begins, the order processing system should automatically flag any occasion when an order would push the customer over his agreed limit. This can then be assessed by credit control staff and a decision taken as to whether the sale should proceed.

3.27 Where sales have been made, credit control staff should have procedures for chasing payment in timely fashion to avoid debts becoming old.

4 Specialised risk management options

Insurance

4.1 Most of the risks faced by an organisation can be insured against. Naturally, it is usually sensible to take out appropriate insurance, and in respect of some risks this is a legal requirement on organisations. For example, UK companies are required to take out a policy of employer's liability insurance for the benefit of their employees.

4.2 There are numerous other risks that can be, and usually are, covered by insurance. Here are just a few of them.

- Theft
- Fraud
- Damage to property
- Fire and flood
- Public liability (eg to cover the case where a member of the public suffers injury on the company's premises)
- Product liability

4.3 The range and extent of the risks faced by a modern organisation has led some of them to set up their own insurance companies. This means that they retain the risks within the organisation, but set aside sufficient funds to cover them (in the form of premiums paid to their own internal insurance subsidiary). They save money because they avoid the profit element contained in premiums paid to an outside party.

4.4 Of course, this option implies that the organisation is of sufficient scale to justify its own insurance company. There is also a need for specialist expertise, though this can be provided by third-party businesses if necessary.

Futures contracts

4.5 Some risks are not suitable for insurance cover. In areas such as the purchase of commodities, or in dealing with foreign exchange, more specialised risk management techniques have emerged to fill the gap. One such technique is futures contracts, which we will illustrate in connection with the purchase of commodities.

4.6 Futures contracts are a form of forward buying. Forward buying in itself is a fairly simple concept. Rather than wait until stocks are actually needed, a buyer will sometimes see advantage in buying ahead of demand. This may be because a large order will trigger a discount, or because the buyer wishes to use an economic order quantity. More speculatively, a buyer may buy today because he foresees that prices are likely to rise tomorrow. In all these cases the buyer has to reckon with the usual disadvantages of holding stock, but on balance it may still pay him to buy forward if the circumstances are right.

4.7 It is this last issue of price fluctuations which is central to the specialised form of forward buying known as futures contracts. Both producer and buyer can benefit if the effects of such fluctuations can be ironed out in advance. In particular, both can budget with confidence. The detailed workings of such contracts are the province of specialists and would take us outside the scope of the exam syllabus. However, a broad knowledge is useful as most buyers are likely to be faced with this kind of transaction on occasion.

4.8 To begin with it is worth asking why futures contracts are needed at all. Surely an ordinary commercial insurance contract could be taken out to cover the risk of price fluctuation? Unfortunately this is not so. The reason is that an insurer makes his money from the people who do **not** make claims; their premiums enable the insurer to pay out to the unfortunate minority who suffer loss. But in a commodity market **all** parties stand to lose if, for example, supply suffers through a crop failure. There are no winners in this situation and no fund from which to pay the losers.

4.9 Futures contracts provide an alternative to insurance. The subject of a futures contract is not a quantity of a physical commodity such as wheat or iron ore; it is the right to purchase or sell a quantity of such a commodity. It is used by a buyer or a seller to 'hedge' a contract in the physical commodity by making sure that any movement in price has self-cancelling effects on his financial position.

4.10 To see how it works, note that a **buyer** of a commodity today fears a price **fall** in the future. This is because when he later comes to sell the product in which the commodity is incorporated his customers will expect a low selling price. Conversely, a **seller** of coffee today fears a price **rise** in the future – 'If only I had delayed selling!'.

4.11 The fact that buyers and sellers have opposite fears is what makes futures contracts work. The idea is that a buyer of the physical commodity should make himself also a seller of that commodity by means of a futures contract. Then if the price falls, he loses as a buyer but gains as a seller. In a perfect hedge these effects would cancel out exactly and the buyer would make neither profit or loss as a result of the price change. His profitability would reflect his trading ability, and would not depend on price fluctuations beyond his control.

4.12 To illustrate this, suppose a buyer needs 5,000 bushels of wheat on 1 January, when the price stands at £3 per bushel. This will be incorporated in products for sale two months later on 1 March. Clearly the price the buyer will be able to charge his customers will depend crucially on the price of wheat on that date. Suppose that by then the price of wheat has fallen to £2 per bushel. In broad terms, the buyer will only be able to sell his products for £5,000 less than expected.

4.13 To protect against this disaster the buyer could enter a futures contract on 1 January under which he agrees to **sell** 5,000 bushels of wheat on 1 March. The 'forward price' of wheat for delivery in two months time will not in practice be exactly the same as the 'spot price', but to illustrate the perfect hedge we will assume it is.

4.14 Now what happens on 1 March? First, the buying company sells its finished products for £5,000 less than expected – bad news. However, the company can also purchase 5,000 bushels of wheat at the March price of £2, knowing that under his futures contract he has a guaranteed customer for this quantity at a price of £3 – good news. Result: he gains £5,000 on the futures contract, which exactly offsets his loss on the physical purchase of wheat.

4.15 The detail of these computations is not so important as the general principle. A buyer of a physical commodity can protect himself against price fluctuations in the commodity. He does so by entering a futures contract under which, in effect, he becomes a seller as well as a buyer. Any price fluctuation then has equal and opposite effects on his financial position.

4.16 This is an undeniably complex area of the purchasing profession and the discussion has inevitably glossed over many practical points. However, this is likely to be sufficient for any question you are likely to meet in the exam.

4.17 Similar financial instruments are used by importers and exporters to protect against adverse movements in exchange rates. In this context, the most common type of arrangement is called a forward exchange contract.

Derivatives

4.18 Referring back to our example of the commodity dealer, notice that he protects his position by entering into two contracts. One is based on the purchase or sale of a physical commodity, and one on the purchase or sale of something less tangible: the right to buy or sell at a particular price. This second type of contract – where the subject matter is not the physical commodity but some entitlement related to it – is called a **derivative**.

4.19 In modern finance a huge variety of derivative products has emerged, catering for the many specialised transactions that arise in a developed economy. The futures contracts and forward exchange contracts already mentioned are examples of these.

4.20 Another area where derivatives are in common use is in guarding against adverse interest rate movements. This can be a particular concern, as mentioned earlier in the chapter, to an organisation relying heavily on debt finance.

4.21 Interest rate futures offer a means of hedging against the risk of interest rate movements. Such contracts are effectively a gamble on whether interest rates will rise or fall. Like other futures contracts, interest rate futures offer a way in which speculators can 'bet' on market movements just as they offer others who are more risk-averse a way of hedging risks. They are not essentially different from the futures contracts already discussed.

4.22 To illustrate the sophistication of developments in the derivatives markets we mention briefly another method of hedging interest rate movements: **interest rate swaps**.

4.23 This is a type of derivative that exploits different interest rates in different markets for borrowing, to reduce interest costs for either fixed or floating rate loans. A swap is an arrangement whereby two companies, or a company and a bank, swap interest rate commitments with each other. In a sense, each simulates the other's borrowings, with the following effects.

- A company with debt at a fixed rate of interest can make a swap so that it ends up paying interest at a variable rate.

- A company with debt at a variable rate of interest (floating rate debt) ends up paying a fixed rate of interest.

4.24 Finally on the subject of derivatives we mention the use of **options**. An option is an intangible asset consisting of the right to buy (or sell) an underlying asset at a particular price on a particular date (or within a defined period of time). An option conferring the right to buy is a **call option**; an option conferring the right to sell is a **put option**.

4.25   The underlying asset could take a wide range of forms. It might be a batch of shares in a listed company. Or it could be a quantity of a raw commodity or many other things. The owner of the option, as the name suggests, has the right (but not an obligation) to buy or sell a quantity of the underlying asset. This contrasts with a futures contract, where both parties to the deal are obliged to carry out the transaction agreed in advance. With an option, the owner will exercise his right if the price is such that he can make a profit, and will decline to exercise if it would cause a loss.

4.26   As with futures contracts, there are two main reasons why people trade in options. Some traders are speculative – their business is to guess what market movements will be like in the future and they use options to make profits if their guesses are correct. Others – and this is where the topic is relevant to your work as a buyer – use options and futures to hedge risk. The aim is to minimise the effects of adverse market movements.

4.27   Both options and futures are particularly relevant to organisations engaged in overseas trade. The international dimension adds to the risks faced by, say, an importer in the UK. Such a buyer has to deal with the possibility of movements in currency exchange rates, movements in interest rates both at home and in the overseas market, and (if he is buying commodities) the uncertainties of the weather, natural disasters, political upheavals etc.

Chapter summary

- Single sourcing is consistent with modern trends in supplier relations, but carries the risk of being let down by the supplier.

- Other risks connected with supply issues include partnership sourcing, reputation issues, supplier quality issues, and the risks connected with outsourcing and offshoring.

- Buyers must carefully evaluate potential suppliers before entering into business relationships with them.

- Because of the large sums involved, the risks attached to capital investments deserve particular attention. Sensitivity analysis is an important technique in this connection.

- Importers (and perhaps exporters) suffer the risk of adverse exchange rate movements. Organisations that depend to some extent on debt financing suffer the risk of adverse interest rate movements. These risks can be alleviated by specialist risk management techniques.

- Organisations with high levels of debt finance and/or high levels of fixed costs are vulnerable to downturns in trading.

- The risk of bad debts must be managed by careful credit control techniques.

- Specialised tools of risk management include insurance and derivatives.

- Derivatives include such tools as futures contracts, forward exchange contracts and interest rate swaps.

Self-test questions

Numbers in brackets refer to the paragraphs where you can check your answers.

1   Into what two categories does Kit Sadgrove analyse supply risk? (1.1)

2   How can suppliers damage a company's reputation? (1.9)

3   What is meant by offshoring? (1.17)

4   Explain what is meant by FACE 2 FACE. (2.2)

5   Explain the limitations of financial information in supplier appraisal. (2.13)

6   What is meant by sensitivity analysis? (3.7)

7   In what circumstances is an organisation subject to interest rate risk? (3.12)

8   What is meant by a highly geared company? (3.18)

9   What measures of credit control should an organisation implement? (3.25–3.27)

10   List some of the risks that can be covered by insurance. (4.2)

11   Why is it not possible to insure against fluctuations in commodity prices? (4.8)

12   What is a derivative? (4.18)

CHAPTER 12

Financial Appraisal

Learning objectives and indicative content

6.2   Carry out a financial appraisal and risk analysis of suppliers, own organisation, and customers, using a range of financial performance ratios:

- Profitability ratios
- Efficiency ratios
- Liquidity ratios
- Investment ratios

Chapter headings

1   The purpose of ratio analysis

2   Profitability ratios

3   Liquidity ratios

4   Efficiency ratios

5   Investment ratios

Introduction

Financial statements are prepared not as an end in themselves but in order that users can make better decisions. To do this, users must interpret the financial statements. By calculating ratios (the main subject of this chapter) we can more clearly see the relationships between different parts of the financial statements.

One small point of terminology is worth making. Strictly a ratio is a relationship between two numbers, often expressed in the form 2:1, 0.7:1 etc. However, some of the indicators we calculate in this chapter are expressed in the form of percentages, and some in other forms. For simplicity, we refer to them all as 'ratios' even though the term is not always applicable in its strict mathematical sense. This usage is very common in accounting.

1   The purpose of ratio analysis

A basis for decision making

1.1   In Chapter 2 we looked at the make-up of the main financial statements published by companies. Our interest is not specifically in how these statements are compiled, or in the regulations governing their form or content. Like most users of accounts, buyers are interested in this kind of information because they need to draw conclusions which will form the basis for decisions in the future.

1.2   Much of this information will be gathered by calculating ratios and making comparisons with:

- the performance of the business in previous years
- the budgeted or planned performance in the current year
- the performance of similar businesses.

The ratios themselves do not tell users what to do, but they do help to point in the right direction. Ratios should, therefore, make it easier to make better decisions.

1.3   The various users of financial statements require information for quite different purposes. There are a large number of ratios, not all of which will be relevant to a particular situation. It is therefore important to determine the precise information needs of the user, and the decisions he has to take after analysing the relevant information.

Sources of information

1.4   So far we have assumed that all the information we need is ready to hand, and that all we have to do is to carry out the analysis. In practice, a buyer must first of all obtain the raw material for this kind of analysis. What sources of information are available?

1.5   In an ideal world, buyer and supplier are operating on an open book basis. In such a case the supplier himself will make detailed accounting information available to the buyer. This is likely to include more detail than would appear in the financial statements published by the supplier and lodged with the Registrar of Companies.

1.6   In other situations the buyer will have to access the Registrar's files himself. It is easiest to do so by means of the internet (www.companieshouse.gov.uk). The internet is also a useful source for other types of information For example, a buyer may be interested in the credit rating of a potential supplier. Such information is available – for a fee, of course – via a number of websites, eg www.experian.com, or www.dnb.com (the website of Dun & Bradstreet).

Possible drawbacks of ratio analysis

1.7   Ratios may highlight significant trends, but they do not in themselves provide reasons for the trends. To do this effectively, the interested party may need more information and a deeper insight into the affairs of the business. Often this may be difficult to obtain, because the amount of information available is limited unless the user is a manager within the organisation.

1.8   Another problem is the date at which the accounts are drawn up. Accurate information can only be obtained with any degree of certainty from up-to-date figures. Furthermore, seasonal variations in the particular trade should be taken into account.

1.9   Accounting is not an exact science. Despite efforts by the accountancy profession to standardise accounting practice there is still room for a variety of methods in particular cases. This may affect the comparability of different accounts.

1.10 In his comments on the May 2009 exam, the Senior Assessor suggested a number of other difficulties attaching to ratio analysis. The large number of possible ratios may become confusing. Specialist financial training may be needed to understand the results. Ratios demonstrate trends, but do not indicate the causes of them. Seasonal trends may be masked by the ratios. Any of these may be cited in your answers to questions in this area.

Guidance for tackling exam questions

1.11 In the past, examiners have placed emphasis on the ability of students to make use of accounting information. Unfortunately it is a difficult area for which to prepare, as a wide variety of situations can be encountered. Here are some tips to remember in the exam room.

- If a ratio is computed, consider defining what items have been included in the numerator and denominator, because for some ratios definitions vary.

- Compute only the ratios required by the examiner. If no particular ratios are specified, do not compute a huge number of ratios. Remember that ratios are only a means to an end: they are computed in order that a comment can be made. The marks are gained by making the comments.

- Do not be frightened of making what may be regarded as an obvious comment. Thus, a statement that 'the gross profit to sales ratio has increased from last year' is stating something important – that the business is more profitable. It is only an obvious comment because the computation of a ratio made it so obvious. That is the main point of ratios – to highlight trends.

- If you are asked to suggest reasons why a ratio has changed, use your common sense. If, for instance, the gross profit percentage has increased from 32 per cent to 35 per cent, state that it has improved (not worsened) and suggest that, say, prices have been raised or stock has been purchased more efficiently.

Types of ratio

1.12 Ratios fall into several groups, the relevance of particular ratios depending on the purpose for which they are required. The groups we consider below are as follows.

- Profitability ratios – measuring the extent to which the business has traded profitably

- Liquidity ratios – measuring the extent to which the business has liquid assets sufficient to meet its short-term and long-term liabilities

- Efficiency ratios – measuring the efficiency with which the business is managing its assets

- Investment ratios – measuring the attractiveness of the business to potential investors

1.13 The number of ratios that can be calculated may easily lead to confusion. Try to organise your thoughts in this area by mentally dividing them into the categories above. This will help you to give structure to the solutions you write in the examination.

1.14 Remember above all that the ratios are not an end in themselves. The examiner is interested in your ability to draw conclusions from accounts. Calculating a ratio is not the same as drawing a conclusion, but it can point you towards a conclusion.

1.15 The above ratios will be illustrated by reference to the following set of accounts. In practice, the small amount of detail disclosed in a set of published accounts places limits on the analysis that you can perform. However, in the present case we will assume that fairly full information is available.

X PLC – SUMMARISED BALANCE SHEETS AT 30 JUNE

	20X7		20X6	
	£000	£000	£000	£000
Fixed assets		130		151
Current assets				
Stock	42		37	
Debtors	29		23	
Bank	3		5	
	74		65	
Creditors: amounts falling due within one year				
Trade creditors	36		55	
Taxation	10		10	
	46		65	
Net current assets		28		-
Total assets less current liabilities		158		151
Creditors: amounts falling due after more than one year				
5% secured loan stock		40		40
		118		111
Capital and reserves				
Ordinary share capital (50p shares)		35		35
8% Preference shares (£1 shares)		25		25
Share premium account		17		17
Retained profits		41		34
		118		111

X PLC – SUMMARISED PROFIT AND LOSS ACCOUNT FOR THE YEAR ENDED 30 JUNE

	20X7	20X7	20X6	20X6
	£000	£000	£000	£000
Turnover		209		196
Opening stock	37		29	
Purchases	162		159	
	199		188	
Closing stock	42		37	
Cost of sales		157		151
Gross profit		52		45
Depreciation	11		11	
Sundry expenses	14		11	
		25		22
Operating profit (profit before interest and taxation)		27		23
Interest on 5% loan stock		2		2
Profit before taxation		25		21
Taxation		10		10
Profit for the year		15		11
Note				
Dividends on ordinary shares		6		5
Dividends on preference shares		2		2
		8		7

2 Profitability ratios

Gross profit percentage

2.1 Many ratios are expressed as a relation between a particular item and the level of sales turnover. Placing items in the context of turnover is a useful technique, because turnover tends to be a good guide to the overall size of a business.

2.2 The first ratio we look at is the gross profit percentage. This expresses the gross profit as a percentage of turnover. The ratio is in very common use, and is calculated as follows.

$$\frac{\text{Gross profit}}{\text{Sales}} \times 100$$

2.3   Using our example of X plc, the ratios for the two years are as follows.

20X7: $\dfrac{52}{209} \times 100 = 24.9\%$

20X6: $\dfrac{45}{196} \times 100 = 23.0\%$

2.4   What can be learned from these figures? Clearly, the gross profit percentage has improved but it is not known why. Nor is it obvious whether these figures are better or worse than those which would be expected in a similar type of business. Before coming to definite conclusions one would need further information.

2.5   For example, most businesses sell a wide range of products, usually with different gross profit percentages (or profit margins). It may be that in 20X7 the sales mix changed and that a larger proportion of items with a high profit percentage were sold, thus increasing the overall gross profit percentage of the business.

Net profit percentage

2.6   As the name suggests, this ratio relates the amount of net profit to the amount of sales turnover. It is calculated as

$$\dfrac{\text{Profit before taxation}}{\text{Sales}} \times 100$$

2.7   In the example of X plc, the ratios for the two years are as follows.

20X7: $\dfrac{25}{209} \times 100 = 12.0\%$

20X7: $\dfrac{21}{196} \times 100 = 10.7\%$

2.8   Note that when analysing the accounts of a limited company it is usual to use the profit before taxation in calculating this ratio, as we have done here. However, where a company has significant loans ('gearing'), it is often also useful to calculate this ratio based on operating profit, also known as 'profit before interest and tax'. For 20X6 this would be 23/196 = 11.7%; for 20X7 it would be 27/209 = 12.9%. The difference between these ratios calculated on these alternative bases reflects the effect of gearing on the company's profits.

2.9   What conclusions can be drawn from this apparent improvement between 20X6 and 20X7? Very few! Since operating profit equals gross profit less expenses, it would be useful to tabulate the various expenses for each of the two years, and to express them as a percentage of sales. These are known as **costs to sales ratios**. A suitable tabulation might be as follows.

	20X7		20X6	
	£000	%	£000	%
Sales	209	100.0	196	100.0
Cost of sales	157	75.1	151	77.0
Gross profit	52	24.9	45	23.0
Depreciation	(11)	(5.3)	(11)	(5.6)
Sundry expenses	(14)	(6.7)	(11)	(5.6)
Operating profit	27	12.9	23	11.7

2.10   Given a detailed profit and loss account, the above type of summary could be very useful. Care must be taken in interpreting the results, particularly since sales (£) are used as the denominator. An increase in sales (£) could be due to a combination of price and quantity effects.

Return on capital employed (ROCE)

2.11   This is an important ratio as it relates profit to the capital invested in a business. Finance for a business is only available at a cost. For example, loan finance requires interest payments, and further finance from shareholders requires either the immediate payment of dividends or the expectation of higher dividends in the future. Therefore a business needs to maximise the profits per £ of capital employed.

2.12   Owing to its importance the ROCE is sometimes referred to as the **primary ratio**.

2.13   There are several ways of measuring ROCE, but the essential point is to relate the profit figure used to its capital base. A sensible formula is as follows.

$$\frac{\text{Profit before interest and tax (operating profit)}}{\text{Average capital employed}} \times 100$$

In the case of X plc for 20X7 we have:

$$\text{ROCE} = \frac{27}{(158+151)/2} \times 100 = 17.5\%$$

2.14   Average capital employed in this case includes long-term finance but does not include short-term finance such as bank overdrafts.

2.15   Note the following points about this ratio.

- The interest referred to is the interest payable on the long-term liabilities. Any interest on short-term liabilities, such as a bank overdraft, is deducted from the profit. This ensures that the numerator and the denominator are computed on a consistent basis.

- The denominator could alternatively be calculated as total assets less current liabilities (to give the same figure as above).

- The calculation is based on the average capital employed during the accounting period. This is computed by averaging the capital employed in the opening and closing balance sheets.

- Profit before interest and tax (or operating profit) may also be called **earnings before interest and tax** (abbreviated to EBIT).

Return on assets

2.16 While ROCE focuses on the return the company makes on the amounts invested in it, by shareholders and the suppliers of debt capital, return on assets looks at how well the total assets of the company are being used.

2.17 The calculation is:

$$\frac{\text{Profit before interest and tax (operating profit)}}{\text{Total assets (fixed assets + current assets)}} \times 100$$

In the case of X plc:

20X7: $\dfrac{27}{130+74} \times 100 = 13.2\%$

20X6: $\dfrac{23}{151+65} \times 100 = 10.6\%$

2.18 This ratio highlights the fact that X plc is successfully making an increased profit out of the same level of assets from 20X6 to 20X7.

3 Liquidity ratios

Short-term liquidity (or stability) ratios

3.1 We have referred already in this text (see Chapter 2) to the difference between profits and cash. To prosper, a business must ensure that it has plenty of cash and other liquid assets, as well as being profitable. This will enable the business to pay short-term liabilities which would otherwise endanger its survival.

3.2 The two main ratios relating to short-term liquidity are the **current ratio** (also called the **working capital ratio**) and the **quick ratio** (also called the **acid test ratio** or **liquidity ratio**). Both ratios measure the relationship between the organisation's liquid assets and its current liabilities. Liquid assets means cash plus other assets that can quickly be converted into cash, for example amounts owing from debtors or stocks of finished goods which can be sold.

3.3 The current ratio is calculated as follows.

$$\frac{\text{Current assets}}{\text{Current liabilities}}$$

3.4 In the case of X plc the ratio for 20X7 is calculated as:

$$\frac{74}{46} = 1.61$$

3.5 The quick ratio (or acid test ratio, or liquidity ratio) is calculated as follows.

$$\frac{\text{Current assets - stock}}{\text{Current liabilities}}$$

3.6 The point of this is to emphasise that stock, though a current asset, is the least liquid of such assets. Before stock can be converted to cash it must be sold. Even when it is sold the customer may enjoy credit terms, which means that cash may not be received for some time. The quick ratio therefore focuses only on current assets (mainly cash and debtors) that can be used quickly to pay off liabilities.

3.7 In the case of X plc the ratio for 20X7 is calculated as:

$$\frac{32}{46} = 0.7$$

3.8 The current ratio and quick ratio in 20X6 were 1.0 and 0.43. Both of these ratios show a strengthening from 20X6 to 20X7. The extent of the change between the two years seems surprising and would require further investigation. It would also be useful to know how these ratios compare with those of a similar business, since typical ratios for supermarkets, say, are quite different from those for heavy engineering firms.

3.9 What can be said is that in 20X7 the current liabilities were well covered by current assets. Liabilities payable in the near future (creditors), however, are only half covered by cash and debtors.

3.10 Conventional wisdom suggests that an ideal current ratio is 2 and an ideal quick ratio is 1. It is very tempting to draw definite conclusions from limited information or to say that the current ratio should be 2, or that the liquidity ratio should be 1. However, this is not very meaningful without taking into account the type of ratio expected in a similar business.

Medium- and long-term solvency ratios

3.11 Being able to pay immediate liabilities is important, but a business must also be concerned about liquidity into the long term. Our next group of ratios help to assess this.

3.12 **Gearing** is a widely-used term in accounting. Unfortunately it can be defined and calculated in several different ways. It is essential to state the definition used.

3.13 Gearing is relevant to the long-term financial stability of a business. There are different ways of calculating a gearing ratio, but always the idea is to consider the relationship between:

- ordinary shareholders' funds (or equity interest);
- fixed-return capital – comprising loans and preference share capital.

3.14 The term 'fixed-return capital' may require some explanation. The best starting point is to contrast loans and preference shares with equity (ordinary) shares.

3.15 A holder of ordinary shares has no clear idea of how much money he may receive in dividends from one year to the next. If a company is very profitable in a particular year, or has a surplus of liquid assets, there may be a big dividend for ordinary shareholders. In another year profits or liquidity may be poor, and the ordinary shareholders may get very little or no dividends. Over the years the return they earn from their investment may be very variable.

3.16 For preference shareholders the picture is clearer. Although they may receive no dividends in very bad years, in most years they can count on receiving a dividend of known amount. Certainly they are entitled to their full rate of dividend if any dividend at all is paid to ordinary shareholders – preference dividends have priority over ordinary dividends. Indeed, if the preference shares are of the special type known as 'cumulative preference shares' then any preference dividend not paid in previous years must also be made good before an ordinary dividend can be declared.

3.17 For these reasons a preference shareholder enjoys a reasonably fixed return on his investment. This is even more so with providers of loan finance. They must be paid their agreed rate of interest whether the company is enjoying profitable times or not. Otherwise, they can take drastic action against the company.

3.18 Having to meet the demands of fixed-return investors may place strain on a company if times are lean. For this reason it is advisable to restrict the proportion of such finance in the total financial structure of the company. In other words, fixed-return capital must be balanced with a good measure of equity capital.

3.19 The gearing ratio measures the proportions in which these two different types of capital are present. A high gearing ratio means that there is a lot of fixed-return capital in the overall mix, and may be a danger signal in the long term. A low ratio means that the company is relying mainly on equity capital and should have less difficulty in weathering difficult years.

3.20 In this text we calculate the gearing ratio as follows.

$$\frac{\text{Preference share capital} + \text{loan capital}}{\text{Ordinary share capital and reserves}}$$

3.21 In this formulation, the top line is the fixed-return capital and the bottom line is the equity capital. (Remember that reserves belong to the ordinary shareholders.) The total of ordinary share capital and reserves is sometimes referred to as the **net worth** of a company. For X plc in 20X7 the gearing calculation is as follows.

$$\frac{25 + 40}{118 - 25} \times 100 = 69.9\%$$

In 20X6, the figure was 75.6%.

3.22 Gearing may have an important effect on the distribution of profits. For example, consider two companies with the same profit record but different capital structures. A plc is highly geared, while B plc is financed entirely by equity capital. The return earned by the ordinary shareholders can vary considerably, as shown in the following example. We will ignore taxation since it will not affect the comparison that we are making.

	A plc £	B plc £
Capital structure:		
10% Loan stock	20,000	-
Ordinary share capital and reserves	10,000	30,000
	30,000	30,000
Year 1 – Profits £4,000 before interest		
∴ Returns to investors:		
10% Interest	2,000	-
Ordinary shares – balance	2,000	4,000
	4,000	4,000
Year 2 – Profits double to £8,000 before interest		
∴ Returns to investors:		
10% Interest	2,000	-
Ordinary shares – balance	6,000	8,000
	8,000	8,000

3.23 The doubling of profits in year 2 has the effect of tripling the return to the equity shareholders in the highly-geared company. The effect would be even more dramatic if the profits fell below £2,000 because then there would be no return at all to the ordinary shareholders in A plc. Thus an investment in ordinary shares in a highly-geared company is a far more speculative investment than a purchase of ordinary shares in a low-geared company.

Interest cover

3.24 Interest on loans (debentures) must be paid whether or not the company makes a profit. The interest cover ratio emphasises the cover (or security) for the interest by relating profit before interest and tax (operating profit) to interest paid. It indicates the extent to which profits are sufficient to meet interest payments. A high ratio means that profits are more than sufficient to cover the interest that must be paid. A low ratio is a danger signal: it suggests that the company is only just able to meet its interest payments.

3.25 The ratio is calculated simply by dividing the relevant profit figure by the amount of interest. The relevant profit figure is the profit before deduction of interest itself and before deducting tax and dividends. For X plc in 20X7 the interest cover is as follows.

$$\frac{27}{2} = 13.5 \text{ times}$$

3.26 This indicates that the company is earning enough profit to meet its interest payments more than 13 times over, a comfortable position. From the point of view of medium- and long-term solvency, the company is in a strong position as regards the payment of interest. Profit would have to drop considerably before any problem of paying interest arose.

4   *Efficiency ratios*

Asset turnover

4.1   Asset turnover is a measure of how well the assets of a business are being used to generate sales. A business that 'turns over' its assets frequently is getting good value from them, so high turnover ratios suggest efficient management, though there are dangers in taking this idea too far.

4.2   The meaning of asset turnover will be clearer after we have shown how to calculate the ratio. Looking at all of the operating assets within a business, asset turnover is calculated as follows.

$$\frac{\text{Sales}}{\text{Operating assets}} = \text{times per year}$$

4.3   Operating assets can be defined in various ways but the most sensible approach is to use the same amount as computed for capital employed. In the case of X plc this was £154,500, the average of the 20X6 and 20X7 figures. Asset turnover for 20X7 is then computed as follows.

$$\frac{209}{154.5} = 1.35$$

4.4   The meaning of the ratio may now be clearer: for every £1 of assets employed in the business X plc is generating £1.35 in sales revenue. Clearly it is desirable to generate as much sales revenue as possible for as little investment as possible, so a higher ratio is preferable to a lower one. A ratio of 1.35 does not seem particularly impressive.

Elements of working capital

4.5   We do not need to include all of the operating assets of a business in calculating turnover ratios. Similar calculations are often applied to individual asset categories to focus attention on particular areas where asset management could be improved.

4.6   We will look at three areas in particular: stock, debtors and creditors. Note that stock plus debtors plus cash less creditors is often referred to as the working capital of a business, so that the ratios we are about to explain may be referred to as working capital ratios. Creditors of course are a liability, not an asset, so we will find that ratios relating to creditors are interpreted in a way that is a mirror image of the interpretation relating to stocks and debtors.

4.7   We begin with stock. Companies have to strike a balance between being able to satisfy customers' requirements out of stock (which suggests a need for high stock levels) and the cost of having too much capital tied up in stock (which suggests that stock levels should be kept low).

4.8 By calculating a stock turnover ratio, and monitoring it from one period to the next, managers can assess how successfully they are balancing these conflicting needs. The calculation is as follows.

$$\frac{\text{Cost of sales}}{\text{Average stock in period}} = \text{times per year}$$

4.9 Notice that in this case the relevant benchmark is cost of sales rather than sales. The bottom line of the fraction is average stock, but often it is convenient to use closing stock. In some cases (especially in exam questions) the closing figure may be the only one available. However, if you have access to the opening figure as well it is preferable to base the calculation on the average of opening and closing stock.

4.10 In the example of X plc the calculation for 20X7, based on average stock value, is as follows.

$$\frac{157}{\frac{1}{2}(37+42)} = 4.0 \text{ times per year}$$

4.11 An alternative calculation of the stock turnover ratio is to show the result in days. The calculation is as follows.

$$\frac{\text{Average stock during the accounting period}}{\text{Cost of sales}} \times 365 \text{ (ie length of accounting period)}$$

$$\frac{\frac{1}{2}(37+42)}{157} \times 365 = 92 \text{ days}$$

4.12 This means that the stock held by the company is on average sufficient to last for 92 days of business activity, which seems a high level of stock. However, much depends on the nature of the business. A jeweller would stock items that might well remain in stock for 92 days, or even much longer. At the other extreme, a fishmonger's stocks would obviously turn over much more quickly.

4.13 Next we look at debtors. Businesses which sell goods on credit terms specify a credit period. Failure to send out invoices on time or to follow up late payers will have an adverse effect on the cashflow of the business. In general, a business will try to ensure that customers take as few days credit as possible.

4.14 The debt collection period relates closing trade debts to the average daily credit sales. It indicates how many days' sales are represented by the debtors figure – in other words, how many days worth of sales we still have not been paid for.

4.15 For X plc in 20X7 we assume that all sales were credit sales and calculate as follows.

Credit sales per day $\quad \dfrac{£209,000}{365} = £573$

Closing trade debtors $\qquad\qquad = £29,000$

Debt collection period $\quad \dfrac{£29,000}{£573} = 50.6 \text{ days}$

4.16　This indicates that customers pay for goods about 51 days after purchasing them. This should be compared with:

- the credit period actually offered by X plc. If the company usually offers 60 days credit, then collecting debts within 50 days on average is very efficient; on the other hand if the usual credit period offered is 30 days, then most customers appear to be taking more credit than they are entitled to

- the similar ratio for the previous year, to indicate whether matters are improving or worsening.

4.17　A quicker way to compute the debt collection period is to use the following formula.

$$\frac{\text{Closing trade debtors}}{\text{Credit sales for the year}} \times 365$$

4.18　Finally we perform a similar calculation for creditors. In this case we relate closing creditors to average daily credit purchases. In the case of X plc in 20X7 the calculation is as follows.

Credit purchases per day $\dfrac{£162,000}{365} = £444$

Closing trade creditors　　　　= £36,000

Average period of credit
allowed by suppliers　　　　　= 81.16 days

4.19　The quicker method of calculation is as follows.

$$\frac{\text{Closing trade creditors}}{\text{Credit purchases for the year}} \times 365$$

$$\frac{36,000}{162,000} \times 365 = 81.1 \text{ days}$$

4.20　Often, suppliers request payment within thirty days. X plc is taking nearly three months to pay for its supplies. Trade creditors are thus financing much of the working capital requirements of the business which is beneficial to the company.

4.21　However, there are three potential disadvantages of extending the credit period.

- Future supplies may be endangered.
- The possibility of discounts for prompt payment is lost.
- Suppliers may quote a higher price for the goods knowing the extended credit taken by the company.

ROCE revisited

4.22 In the light of our calculations on working capital ratios it is useful to take another look at the primary accounting ratio: return on capital employed. There are two factors that affect ROCE.

- Profitability of sales.
- Rate of asset utilisation.

4.23 Note that multiplying the ratios for these two factors gives the return on capital employed.

$$\frac{\text{Operating profit}}{\text{Sales}} \times \frac{\text{Sales}}{\text{Operating assets}} = \frac{\text{Operating profit}}{\text{Operating assets}} = \text{ROCE}$$

4.24 In the example of X plc for 20X7:

$$\frac{\text{Operating profit}}{\text{Sales}} = \frac{£27,000}{£209,000} = 12.9\%$$

$$\frac{\text{Sales}}{\text{Operating assets}} = \frac{£209,000}{£154,500} = 1.35$$

12.9% × 1.35 = 17.5%

4.25 This is the ROCE we calculated earlier. It follows that to improve the primary measure of accounting success one must either increase the profit margin achieved on sales or increase the rate of asset turnover.

5 Investment ratios

The nature of investment ratios

5.1 So far our emphasis has been on the use of ratios as management tools. We have shown how calculation of ratios can help managers study profitability, liquidity and asset utilisation. Where the indicators are poor or deteriorating managers can take action to reverse the unwelcome trends.

5.2 In this final section of the chapter we look at another use of ratios. We consider the position of a potential investor wondering whether to purchase shares or lend money to a company. How can he assess the financial position of the company and the likely return he may expect from his investment?

5.3 Similar questions might be asked by an investment analyst whose job is to advise clients on suitable companies to put their money into.

5.4 The ratios we have dealt with so far are all relevant to this kind of analysis. However, you should bear in mind that the kind of accounts users we are now considering are 'outsiders' without access to financial information about the company except for that contained in their published accounts. Not all of the ratios that we have discussed could be calculated with this limited information.

5.5 In addition to this point, there are also certain other ratios which we have not covered yet and which have a particular bearing on the decisions of potential investors. We will look at six of these.

- Dividend per share
- Dividend yield
- Earnings per share
- Dividend cover
- Price earnings ratio
- Return on shareholders' funds

Dividend per share

5.6 Obviously a key consideration in the mind of a potential shareholder is the amount of dividend he can expect from the company. It is common to quote an amount of dividend per share. An investor holding 1,000 shares can then simply multiply by 1,000 to calculate how much he will receive.

5.7 In the published accounts of large companies this amount is invariably quoted, so no calculation is necessary. However, in an exam question you might be expected to do the calculation yourself, so you need to understand how it is done.

5.8 First of all, determine which shares are relevant. If the examiner is asking about the dividend per ordinary share then you should ignore any information about preference shares. We will assume that it is the dividend per ordinary share that is required. The profit and loss account will show the amount of the ordinary dividend for the year. It does not matter whether it is being paid in two or more instalments (interim dividends); all we are interested in is the total figure for the year. In the case of X plc in 20X7 the amount is £6,000.

5.9 The next thing we need is the number of ordinary shares in issue. We can derive this from the balance sheet. Notice that the figure for ordinary share capital in X plc's balance sheet in 20X7 is £35,000. However, we cannot conclude that there are 35,000 ordinary shares in issue. This is because we are told that the ordinary shares have a nominal value of 50p each. That means there must be 70,000 ordinary shares in issue.

5.10 We can now calculate the amount of ordinary dividend per share: it is simply

$$\frac{£6,000}{70,000} = 8.6\text{p per share (approximately)}$$

A holder of, say, 2,000 shares could expect to receive about £172 (more exactly £171.43). Of course, this information relates to the year just ended, so it is only a starting point for making predictions for the future.

Dividend yield

5.11 By itself the figure of dividend per share does not help the potential investor very much. Knowing that he may earn about £172 per year on a holding of 2,000 shares is only part of the story. The next thing he needs to know is how much that investment will cost him. Clearly that depends on the price of a share in X plc.

5.12 Remember that the price of a share depends on market conditions, in particular on the market's assessment of the value of X plc and its future prospects. It has no connection at all with the nominal value of the share, which is just an arbitrary amount selected probably at the time the company was first formed.

5.13 The reason why this is important is that our investor wishes to compare his likely return from different potential investments. If banks are paying 4 per cent interest per annum on deposit accounts the investor knows that placing £4,300 on deposit will earn him £172 per year (4% x £4,300 = £172), and this is a risk-free investment. Buying shares in X plc is a much riskier investment, and will not be attractive to the investor unless he can buy 2,000 shares for much less than £4,300.

5.14 The point here is that the **yield** from the bank deposit account is known – it is 4 per cent per annum, ie £4 for every £100 invested. The potential investor needs to do a similar calculation for shares in X plc, comparing the price to be paid with the dividends to be expected. This is called the **dividend yield**.

5.15 In simple terms, the dividend yield is calculated as follows:

$$\frac{\text{Amount of dividend per share}}{\text{Price of one share}}$$

5.16 In the case of X plc we have already calculated the dividend per share in 20X7: 8.6p per share. Suppose that a share in X plc is currently priced at £1.90. We calculate the dividend yield as:

$$\frac{8.6p}{190p} = 4.5\%$$

This is slightly better than our (fictional) yield of 4 per cent from bank deposits, but perhaps not enough to compensate for the additional risk from this kind of investment.

Earnings per share

5.17 Earnings per share (EPS) is a key ratio in investment analysis. It is calculated just like dividend per share, except that earnings are usually not exactly equal in amount to dividends.

5.18 Earnings means the profits left to the company after tax has been paid and after the preference dividend has been paid. In other words, it is the profit remaining to benefit ordinary shareholders. The reason why this amount is not equal in amount to ordinary dividends is simply that companies rarely pay out all of their earnings in the form of dividends. Some earnings will be retained in the business. For example, a company with earnings of £50,000 may decide to pay dividends of only £20,000, retaining £30,000 for use in the business.

5.19 In the case of X plc the profit after tax for 20X7 was £15,000. Of this, £2,000 goes in dividends to the preference shareholders. This leaves £13,000 earnings belonging to the ordinary shareholders. We know that there are 70,000 ordinary shares in issue, so the earnings per share is:

$$\frac{£13,000}{70,000} = 18.6p$$

Dividend cover

5.20   The ordinary shareholders may need to know how 'safe' the dividend payment was, ie how many times the current year's earnings could have covered the dividend payment. If the dividend cover falls to very low levels, ordinary shareholders may not be able to rely on the current level of dividends being maintained in the future.

$$\text{Ordinary dividend cover} = \frac{\text{Earnings (profits after interest, tax and preference dividends)}}{\text{Ordinary dividend for the year}}$$

Notice that the numerator in the calculation, the earnings, is the amount of the current year's profit that the directors could have paid out as ordinary dividend if they had wished.

For 20X7 the dividend cover is:

$$\frac{£13,000}{£6,000} = 2.2 \text{ times}$$

Price earnings ratio (P/E ratio)

5.21   Again, this is a vital ratio in investment analysis. It is calculated exactly as its name suggests: divide the price of a share by the earnings relating to the share.

5.22   For X plc in 20X7 we know that the price of an ordinary share is £1.90. We have just calculated the earnings per share as 18.6p. The P/E ratio is simply price divided by earnings:

$$\frac{190p}{18.6p} = 10.2$$

5.23   A high P/E ratio is an indication that the market is impressed with the potential of a company. In effect, an investor buying a share in X plc is expecting to wait 10.2 years before he gets his money back. If a similar company has a price ratio of, say, 6.5, then this indicates that investors are only prepared to pay an amount which will return to them within 6.5 years: in other words, they are less impressed with this company than with X plc.

5.24   P/E ratios vary enormously between different industry sectors. You would not expect a publishing company to have a similar ratio to a heavy manufacturer. But by looking at the P/E ratios of companies of similar size and operating in a similar industry sector useful comparisons can be made.

Return on shareholders' funds

5.25   It could be argued that this ratio belongs with the profitability ratios in Section 2 of this chapter. However we have included it here as an investment ratio since, like the other ratios in this section, it focuses on the returns generated for ordinary shareholders. Return on shareholders' funds (ROSF) is calculated as follows.

$$ROSF = \frac{\text{Earnings (profits after interest, tax and preference shares)}}{\text{Ordinary share capital} + \text{reserves}} \times 100\%$$

For 20X7, ROSF is:

$$\frac{£13,000}{£(35,000 + 17,000 + 41,000)} \times 100\% = 14\%$$

In 20X7 the company generated a return of 14 per cent on shareholders' funds invested.

5.26 The formula we have used above calculates net ROSF, ie after taxation. Some analysts calculate gross ROSF, ie based on profit before taxation. If you are required to calculate ROSF in an examination you should use the formula shown above, but state that you are aware that the calculation may also be based on profit before taxation.

Chapter summary

- Ratios are a useful method of assessing the performance of a business, especially when used in comparison with similar ratios from other businesses or from earlier years.

- Profitability ratios measure the extent to which the business has traded profitably. They include gross profit percentage, net profit percentage and return on capital employed (ROCE), the primary accounting ratio.

- Liquidity ratios measure the extent to which the business has liquid assets sufficient to meet its short-term and long-term liabilities. They include current ratio, quick ratio, gearing ratio and interest cover.

- Efficiency ratios measure the efficiency with which the business is managing its assets. They include operating assets turnover, stock turnover, debtors collection period and creditors payment period.

- Investment ratios measure the attractiveness of a business to potential investors. They include dividend per share, dividend yield, earnings per share, dividend cover and price earnings ratio.

Self-test questions

Numbers in brackets refer to the paragraphs where your answers can be checked.

1   List possible drawbacks of ratio analysis as a means of assessing business performance. (1.7 – 1.10)

2   How is gross profit percentage calculated? (2.2)

3   What is meant by the term 'costs to sales ratios'? (2.9)

4   How is ROCE calculated? (2.13 – 2.15)

5   What is the difference between the working capital ratio and the acid test ratio? (3.3, 3.5)

6   What items are included in the term 'fixed-return capital'? (3.14)

7   What items are included in the term 'working capital'? (4.6)

8   What is the quick formula for calculating the debtors collection period? (4.17)

9   What are the potential disadvantages of taking extended credit from suppliers? (4.21)

10   How is dividend per share calculated? (5.10)

11   What is meant by the dividend yield? (5.14)

12   What is meant by 'earnings' in the context of company accounts? (5.18)

CHAPTER 13

Mock Exam

THE EXEMPLAR PAPER

The exam paper below was published by CIPS in 2006 as an illustration of what might be expected under the new syllabus. If you are able to make a good attempt at the paper you should be very well prepared for the live examination.

The examination is in two sections.

Section A has two compulsory questions, worth 25 marks each.

Section B has four questions; answer two. Each question is worth 25 marks.

SECTION A

You are strongly advised to carefully read and analyse the information in the case study before attempting to answer questions 1 and 2.

Minter plc

Introduction

Minter plc is a UK-based retail grocery business, comprising supermarkets and convenience stores. It was established in 1910 by Ebenezer Minter to offer quality and value for money, as well as high standards of customer service in food retailing. The business has subsequently grown into 120 stores in the UK, employing nearly 8,000 people.

Products

Every Minter store contains some of the best known brand names in food and drink, as well as its own branded products. It gives priority display space to popular, high-margin products, and encourages competition for the best display spaces among suppliers. Quality is seen to be of the utmost importance. Minter therefore has established quality control procedures at key points in the retailing process, particularly in new product development and product appraisal.

Minter buys, packs and distributes all fruit and vegetables sold in its stores. Fresh produce is delivered into temperature-controlled warehouses and packing plants, before despatch to stores nationwide. It also has a meat processing facility, where produce can be prepared and supplied direct to the butcher section in the stores.

Structure

Minter classifies its stores according to three different formats.

- Main outlets – these are stores of approximately 10,000 to 20,000 square feet, offering a broad range of grocery items, and catering for the weekly family shop.

- Traditional shop – these are stores of approximately 5,000 to 10,000 square feet and are mostly located in town and city centre locations.

- Rapid shop – these are stores of up to 5,000 square feet and which are locally based, offering a limited range of items, mostly sandwiches, ready-made meals, wines and spirits.

It has no superstores, occupying in excess of 20,000 square feet. However, in line with growth aspirations, as part of the corporate strategy these are currently being considered by the Board. Nonetheless, the growth of large, out-of-town developments in the UK is becoming more difficult for supermarkets, owing to stricter planning laws and the lack of suitable sites.

By tradition, it has not entered into non-food retailing such as clothing, books, CDs or household items. Similarly, unlike other major food retailers, Minter has not established a home service, where customers place orders either online or by telephone, and then select when and where to have their shopping delivered.

Loyalty card

Shoppers can accumulate 'Minter points' on a registered loyalty card, which can then be redeemed on purchases in-store. It also provides Minter with a means of gathering customer intelligence on buying habits. This supports customer/market segmentation by tailoring what Minter offers in terms of goods and services to the appropriate market segment. Customers are also offered incentives, usually to purchase new products, related to their segment/buying habits.

Vision and strategy

The current focus is to improve the performance of the core UK supermarket chain, whilst at the same time to develop growth opportunities through increasing the number of stores, enhancing the range of products, and by extending existing premises, where possible. Management see sales as being a key indicator of customer satisfaction and are therefore committed to increasing sales. It is expected that, by increasing supply chain efficiencies, cost savings can be passed on to customers to offer greater value for money.

Corporate social responsibility (CSR)

CSR is seen to be integral to business and embodied in Minter's corporate governance framework. Minter aims to maintain the highest standards of corporate behaviour by taking account of social, environmental and ethical matters that are central to its commercial activities.

CSR priorities incorporate three key themes: society and community investment; environmental responsibilities; and employment (including health and safety). The Board of Directors also considers strategic risks at every meeting, including financial and business risks and control procedures. The Business Ethics Group, which comprises directors and senior managers, has a remit to oversee, review and advise on CSR matters, reporting directly to the Board.

The UK retail grocery market

The UK grocery market is worth nearly £120 billion, with groceries accounting for 13.1% of all household spending. There are over 10,200 (*sic*: could mean either 10,200 or 102,000) grocery stores operating in a fiercely competitive environment. Consequently, retailers try to position themselves in the market by differentiation, particularly through product development and branding. Moreover, changes in demographics (for instance, ageing population) have resulted in retailers focusing on added value products such as ready meals, ranges of premium quality products and extending the range of own-brand products.

It is felt that the UK grocery sector will continue to grow at an average rate of 2.7% over the next five years. However, retail sales can be affected by an economic downturn, changes in interest rates and reductions in disposable income. There has been a fall in retail sales in the UK recently, and as a result many retailers have cut prices to maintain levels of sales, while at the same time they have sought cost reductions through operational improvements in the supply chain.

Financial performance

PROFIT AND LOSS ACCOUNTS FOR THE YEAR ENDED	2005 (£M)	2004 (£M)
Turnover	4,290	4,770
Cost of sales	3,946	4,293
Gross profit	344	477
Operating expenses	206	262
Operating profit	138	215
Other costs	2	4
Profit before interest and tax	136	211
Net interest payable	12	19
Profit on ordinary activities	124	192
Tax on profit on ordinary activities	43	67
Profit after tax	81	125
Dividends	59	116
Retained profit	22	9

BALANCE SHEETS	2005 (£M)	2004(£M)
Fixed assets		
Intangible assets	65	70
Tangible assets	1,727	1,554
Total fixed assets	1,792	1,624
Current assets		
Stock	190	188
Debtors	100	136
Short-term investments	551	481
Cash at bank and in hand	92	118
Total current assets	933	923
Creditors: amounts falling due within one year	1,177	1,081
Net current liabilities	244	158
Total assets less current liabilities	1,548	1,466
Creditors: amounts falling due after more than one year	(487)	(432)
Provisions for liabilities	(58)	(59)
Net assets	1,003	975
Capital and reserves		
Called up share capital	121	120
Share premium	355	350
Other reserves	39	39
Profit and loss account	488	466
Total capital employed	1,003	975

The information in this case study is purely fictitious and has been prepared for assessment purposes only.

Any resemblance to any organisation or person is purely coincidental.

QUESTIONS

Questions 1 and 2 relate to the case study and should be answered in the context of the information provided.

Question 1

Critically evaluate Minter's aspirations for growth. Use the financial and non-financial data to support your answer. **(25 marks)**

Question 2

Examine the importance of corporate social responsibility (CSR) to Minter, in relation to economic performance, and discuss possible future developments in CSR activities that Minter could consider. **(10 marks)**

SECTION B

Answer **TWO** questions from section B.

You are strongly advised to carefully read all the questions in section B before selecting **TWO** questions to answer.

Question 3

Analyse the factors that should be taken into account when choosing between equity finance and long-term debt as a means of financing investment in new equipment. **(25 marks)**

Question 4

'The purpose of budgeting is to ensure the accountability of managers for their actions.' Critically discuss this statement. **(25 marks)**

Question 5

Evaluate the use of market prices as a means to price manufactured goods transferred between separate divisions of a company. **(25 marks)**

Question 6

Discuss how you might analyse the risks involved in a capital investment decision.

(25 marks)

CHAPTER 14

Mock Exam: Suggested Solutions

SOLUTION 1

Tutorial note: In the marking scheme for this question, 13 marks were allocated to the analysis of Minter's financial position, especially by means of ratio analysis. Your objective in analysing the ratios is to determine whether Minter is financially sound enough to contemplate expansion. The remaining 12 marks were allocated to non-financial factors: whether growth is a sensible objective, whether market factors suggest potential for growth, possible means of achieving growth. The question specifically asks you to use both financial and non-financial data, and the mark scheme reinforces how important it is to deal with both aspects.

The starting point for a solution here is to examine the accounts of Minter so as to establish the financial strength of the company.

Looking first at the profit and loss account, the first thing to catch the eye is the significant fall in turnover this year (down £480m, or 10.1%). This is especially worrying when we read that 'management see sales as being a key indicator of customer satisfaction and are therefore committed to increasing sales'. There is no specific information in the scenario to account for the very significant sales decrease, though the general remarks about the overall fall in UK retail sales and recent price cuts may apply to Minter.

Such price cuts may explain the very worrying fall in gross profit percentage: down from 10.0% of sales in 2004 to 8.0% in 2005. Operating profit has also fallen (down from 4.5% to 3.2%), as has profit on ordinary activities (down from 4.0% to 3.1%). Return on capital employed (taken here as profit on ordinary activities divided by net assets or capital and reserves) is 12.4% in 2005 compared with 19.7% in 2004, a very significant fall. Companies are normally reluctant to reduce the level of dividends, but in this case dividends in 2005 (£59m) are barely half of what was paid to shareholders in 2004 (£116m). This is a strong indication that management have recognised a degree of financial frailty.

So far, the picture suggests that Minter has had difficulties in recent years, and this is supported by analysis of the balance sheet. The company's current ratio (current assets divided by creditors due within one year) is 0.79 at the end of 2005, down from an already worrying 0.85 in 2004. The company's short-term liabilities exceed the short-term assets, giving serious concerns about liquidity. Taking stock out of the current assets figure we can calculate the acid test ratio in 2005 as a mere 0.63 (2004: 0.68). We should not place too much emphasis on the difference between current ratio and acid test ratio, because in Minter's sector stocks are converted into cash quite quickly. Even so, the liquidity position is worrying.

On the positive side, the company is managing to work its assets very hard. Total capital employed of £1,003m has led to sales of £4,290m in 2005, an asset turnover rate of 4.3 times per year (though even here, the picture was better in 2004: 4.9 times per year). The company appears to be managing its current assets quite effectively: stock at the end of 2005 amounted to just 17.6 days cost of sales (2004: 16.0), while debtors are also low, as we would expect in a retailer (8.5 days sales in 2005, 10.4 days in 2004).

A strength of the balance sheet is the very high figure for tangible fixed assets, no doubt mostly made up of the company's freehold retail outlets. These appear in the balance sheet at £1,792m at the end of 2005. There is no sign of any significant revaluation reserve in the balance sheet, so it is safe to assume that this figure is the historical cost of the properties. Their true value may be very much higher.

The company is financed by a mix of shareholders' funds (£1,003m in 2005, assumed to represent equity capital since there is no mention of preference shares in the scenario) and long-term liabilities (£487m in 2005). We are not told the nature of the long-term liabilities. We would normally assume them to be loans, but the interest paid in 2005 was only £12m: if the whole amount of £487m is loans the company must be enjoying very favourable interest terms! More likely, a part of this sum represents provisions for deferred liabilities, but we can't really tell in the absence of more detailed information.

The company's gearing ratio may be calculated by comparing the long-term liabilities with the shareholders' funds: the ratio is 48.5% (2004: 44.3%). This appears quite high, but might fall materially if the true value of tangible fixed assets is greater than they appear at in the balance sheet.

Overall, the financial analysis suggests that there is some cause for concern. The difficult question to answer is whether the proposed expansion will be a solution to current problems or an addition to them.

So much for the financial analysis. There are also important non-financial factors affecting Minter's plans.

Firstly there is the issue of whether growth is a sensible objective in itself. Shareholders who have seen their dividends hit this year may be inclined to think that a strategy of consolidation could be more important. Minter's management might respond that further damage to margins may occur unless the group can achieve greater economies of scale. This is indicated by the statement in the scenario that 'by increasing supply chain efficiencies cost savings can be passed on to customers to offer greater value for money'.

Even if shareholders accept that growth is the right way forward, there are limits on what Minter can do. The scenario points out that stricter planning laws and the lack of suitable retail sites may be a block on growth plans. Another possible limiting factor may be the need for new funds: as we have seen, it may be difficult to attract further loan finance when the gearing ratio is already quite high and the company's financial performance has been stuttering.

What the scenario says about the general economic climate suggests that growth may be possible. Although the retail sector as a whole has been in decline recently, the grocery sector is forecast to enjoy growth 'at an average rate of 2.7% over the next five years'. (Presumably this is intended to mean growth of 2.7% per year for five years running.) Minter's expansion plans may be an important element in taking a share of this growth.

Supposing that Minter does adopt a strategy of growth, where exactly will the growth come from? Management apparently intend to develop 'through increasing the number of stores, enhancing the range of products, and by expanding existing premises, where possible'. In terms of Ansoff's matrix (tutorial note: you may have studied this in Strategic Supply Chain Management) this is primarily a strategy of market penetration (increasing sales of existing products in existing markets), with elements of a product development strategy tacked on. Some of the possibilities are mentioned in the scenario: Minter has not in the past entered non-food retailing, nor has it offered a home service. Both of these areas have been exploited by its competitors and could represent avenues for growth.

In summary, there are many opportunities for Minter to grow, but the company's financial situation is not so strong that these should be pursued without careful thought about the financial consequences.

SOLUTION 2

Tutorial note: Note that the question is effectively in two parts.

First we must discuss the impact of CSR in terms of the company's economic performance. A prime consideration here is the extent to which Minter (or any company) should voluntarily do more than they are compelled to do by regulations if to do so would damage profitability. To some extent this can be answered in general terms, and we draw on material from the Course Book (Chapter 1) in order to do so. However, note that in this kind of question you must always relate the general considerations to the specifics of the case.

In the second part we must identify new elements of a CSR policy that Minter might wish to adopt.

The term 'social responsibility' is used to describe a wide range of obligations that an organisation may feel it has towards the society in which it operates: its 'secondary' stakeholders (ie those not directly connected with the organisation, but affected by its operations). This is sometimes expressed in terms of 'externalities': the costs of business activities which are not absorbed in a product/service or paid for by consumers, but which are borne by the wider community – such as the costs of pollution, including associated costs of illness, environmental degradation and so on.

Milton Friedman and Elaine Sternberg took the view that 'the social responsibility of business is profit maximisation': to give a return on shareholders' investment. Spending funds on objectives not related to shareholder expectations is irresponsible: regard for shareholder wealth is a healthy discipline for management, providing accountability for decisions. The public interest is served by profit maximisation, because the State levies taxes. 'Consequently,' argued Friedman, 'the only justification for social responsibility is enlightened self interest' on the part of a business organisation. This argument suggests that Minter should do no more in the area of CSR than they are obliged to do by law and regulations. By doing so, they will avoid financial and operational penalties.

However, there may be economic reasons for going beyond the bare minimum.

- Voluntary measures (which may in any case only pre-empt legal and regulatory requirements) may enhance corporate image and build a positive brand.

- Above-statutory provisions for employees and suppliers may be necessary to attract, retain and motivate them to provide quality service and commitment – particularly in competition with other employers/purchasers.

- Increasing consumer awareness of social responsibility issues creates a market demand for CSR (and the threat of boycott for irresponsible firms).

All of these considerations are highly relevant to a company such as Minter, operating in a highly competitive market and needing to find ways of distinguishing itself favourably from its rivals. And the scenario appears to indicate that management have already decided to do more than bare compliance: 'Minter aims to maintain the highest standards of corporate behaviour'. The company pays particular attention to three themes: society and community investment; environmental responsibilities; and employment (including health and safety).

Given this approach to CSR, what future developments might Minter consider? As many firms have already done, the company could set social responsibility objectives, in relation to matters such as:

- Sustainability issues: the conservation and perpetuation of the world's limited natural resources

- Environmental issues: the reduction of environment pollution, waste management, the avoidance of environmental disfigurement, land reclamation, promoting recycling, energy conservation and so on

- Ethical trading, business relationships and development: consumer protection, improvement of working (and social) conditions for employees and subcontractors (particularly in developing nations), avoidance of exploitation, debt minimisation, contribution to local communities and so on.

SOLUTION 3

Tutorial note: According to the marking scheme, no fewer than 10 marks were available for introductory remarks followed by an explanation of what is meant by the two forms of finance. If you meet a question like this in the exam – with 25 marks on offer and apparently not very much to be said – bear in mind that the examiner may be expecting some kind of introduction and explanation before you proceed to answer the question actually set.

Organisations must ensure that they have an appropriate mix of equity and debt finance to suit their circumstances. In some cases an organisation may be so rich in cash resources that it apparently has no requirement for debt, but this is uncommon. Even in such a case there may be an argument for taking on a limited amount of debt finance if it enables equity funds to be deployed in more profitable avenues. In general, an organisation needs to think carefully about the structure of its funding.

In the present case, the choice is between equity finance and long-term debt. Both of these are long-term in nature, and this is appropriate in view of the fact that the funds are to be invested in new capital equipment. The reason for this is that the new equipment is presumably expected to generate enough cash to cover its own cost, but it may not do so until towards the end of its (presumably long) life. In the meantime, it might cause problems if we had to repay short-term finance before this happened.

Equity finance is that provided by ordinary shareholders in a limited company (or the ordinary capital provided by partners in a partnership). The ordinary shareholders own the company, and it is this element of ownership that is denoted by the term equity. By contrast, holders of debt have a claim against the company in that they are entitled to expect payment of interest and eventually repayment of the debt, but they do not in any way own the company or its assets.

Long-term debt finance is provided by persons other than the business owners and advanced for a substantial period before repayment is expected, certainly for more than 12 months. The lenders will in the meantime expect to be rewarded in the form of interest payments from the borrower.

A number of factors may be relevant in choosing between the two possibilities.

- The cost of finance. The cost of debt finance is essentially the rate of interest payable. This is in turn affected by the general economic climate and by the particular circumstances of the borrower. A borrower perceived as a low risk will be able to attract debt finance more cheaply than a high-risk borrower. The cost of debt is reduced by the effect of taxation, because interest on debt attracts tax relief. In relation to equity, the cost essentially comprises the dividends that shareholders will expect to receive as their reward for investing equity funds. (It is sometimes argued that equity finance is in effect free, but all investors will expect and demand a return on their money.) Dividends do not attract tax relief.

- The impact of gearing. A company that takes on long-term debt increases the level of its gearing. There are some disadvantages attached to this. The company may be perceived in future as more of a risk. Profits will be dented by amounts required to be paid in interest. The company will be more exposed to the risks of a downturn in trading, which affect high-geared companies more than low-geared companies. On the other hand, if the company chooses equity finance it will remain ungeared, or it will dilute any gearing that it already has.

- Cashflow implications. There are two aspects to this. In the immediate term, it may take longer to raise the equity finance than to take out debt. This is because there may well be extensive formalities associated with, for example, a rights issue. More crucially, there is a cashflow implication in the future: equity capital does not have to be repaid (or at least not until the company is eventually wound up). By contrast, the principal amount of the debt finance will have to be redeemed at a defined point in the future.

- Previous financing decisions. These have an impact in two ways. For one thing, if the company has already taken on substantial debt in the past, it may be reluctant to increase its gearing any further. This could tilt the balance in favour of equity finance. And for another thing, there may be implications concerning the company's track record. If the company has a good track record in paying interest and repaying loans it should be easy to raise debt finance again; if the company has a good track record in maintaining dividend levels it should be easy to attract further equity investment.

- Links to strategic objectives. All of a company's decisions, not just those in relation to financing, should reflect the overall strategic objectives laid down by top management. The company may see strategic advantage in using debt finance, perhaps because it is relatively cheap and enables them to gear their earnings capacity to the benefit of existing shareholders, without the need to allow new shareholders in. On the other hand, the company's strategic objectives may be based on avoidance of risk, in which case the risks attached to debt capital may be unacceptable.

SOLUTION 4

Tutorial note: In an exam question, a statement such as the one in this question is invariably meant to offer just part of the truth. In this case, the statement offers one good reason for why we prepare budgets, and it is appropriate in your answer to refer to this. However, you should also argue that budgets have other purposes too.

The question is essentially 'bookwork' and in the solution below we draw on material from Chapter 7 of the Course Book.

A budget is a plan expressed in financial and/or quantitative terms either for the whole of a business, or for the various parts of a business, for a specified period of time in the future. A budget is prepared within the framework of objectives and policies that have been determined by senior management as part of its own planning activities.

A budget centre is a section of an organisation for which control may be exercised and budgets prepared. A budget centre is a clearly defined part of an organisation for the purposes of operating a budgetary control system. Each function within an organisation will be sub-divided into appropriate budget centres.

In determining budget centres it is important to be able to define them in terms of management responsibility. The manager responsible for a budget centre (eg the machining department within the production function) will be involved in the planning stage of setting the budget for his area of responsibility and he will be the recipient of control information in due course. This is referred to as **responsibility accounting.** Thus to this extent the statement in the question is true: budgets are indeed a tool to ensure the accountability of managers.

However, it would be misleading to think of this as the only purpose of budgeting. Budgets are an essential element in the general regime of planning and control that all organisations ought to establish.

Essentially the budgetary control process consists of two distinct elements.

- **Planning.** This involves setting the various budgets for the appropriate future period. Managers at the various levels in an organisation should be involved in the budgetary planning stage for their own areas of responsibility. There is a need to coordinate the budgets of the various parts of a business to ensure that they are all complementary and in line with overall company objectives and policies.
- **Control.** Once the budgets have been set and agreed for the future period under review, the formal control element of budgetary control is ready to start.

This control involves comparison of the plan in the form of the budget with the actual results achieved for the appropriate period. Significant divergences between the budgeted and the actual results should be reported to the appropriate managers so that the necessary action can be taken.

The purposes of budgets and budgetary control are numerous.

- **Planning**. Budgetary control provides a formal framework for planning, which involves making sure that problems are anticipated and that steps are taken to avoid or reduce them. The organisation develops a plan of what it will aim to achieve in terms of costs and revenues, and management has a formal set of objectives to work towards, ie management by objectives.

- **Coordination**. The system integrates budgets for the various sections of a business into a master budget for the whole business. Individual managers will, therefore, recognise the overall objectives in forming their plans.

- **Authorising and delegating**. Approval of the master budget explicitly authorises the policy represented by the budget. The responsibility for carrying out the policy is delegated to individual managers.

- **Evaluating performance**. The budget represents a target against which the performance of managers can be assessed.

- **Communicating and motivating**. Preparing budgets involves communication between top management and lower levels on how to attain the objectives. Agreement motivates managers to achieve the targets set.

- **Control**. Continuous comparison of actual against plan indicates where control is needed. Budgetary control reports can be designed to focus management attention where it is most needed, for example where there are major differences between budgeted and actual performance. Following the principles of management by exception in this way means that control attention is directed where it will be most worthwhile and those areas of the business which are proceeding according to plan are not subjected to unnecessary scrutiny.

SOLUTION 5

Tutorial note: Once again, there is a large element of 'bookwork' in this question and in the solution we make use of relevant material from Chapter 4 of the Course Book. As with earlier questions, the examiner's comments suggest that significant marks are available for discussion not specifically required by the question (such as an introduction on what a transfer price actually is, and a comparison of market prices with other bases for transfer pricing).

A transfer price is an amount charged by one division to another within a single organisation. For example, in a very simple case a company might consist of just two divisions: a manufacturing division and a sales division. The manufacturing division produces output which it transfers to the sales division at an agreed transfer price. This price represents revenue to the manufacturing division and a cost to the sales division.

One reason for doing this is so that each division can be regarded as a profit centre. This may help to stimulate improved performance, particularly if divisional managers are appraised on the basis of the profits earned by their divisions. The level of transfer price may have a significant effect on the profitability of both the transferring division and the receiving division. If the transfer price is very high, the transferring division will appear very profitable, whereas the high cost of 'purchase' in the receiving division will depress its profits. A low transfer price of course has the opposite effect.

There are three main considerations for a firm when setting the transfer price for goods.

- **Goal congruence.** Within a divisionalised company, divisional managers will have responsibility for and will be judged on their division's performance. It is the task of the management accounting system in general and the transfer pricing policy in particular to ensure that what is good for an individual division is good for the company as a whole.
- **Performance measurement.** The transfer pricing system should result in a report of divisional profits that is a reasonable measure of the managerial performance.
- **Maintaining divisional autonomy.** One of the purposes of decentralisation is to allow managers to exercise greater autonomy. There is little point in granting additional autonomy and then imposing transfer prices that will affect the profitability of the division.

A perfect market means that there is only one price in the market, there are no buying or selling costs and the market is able to absorb the entire output of the primary division and meet all of the requirements of the secondary division. In this situation the optimum transfer price is the market price (less any savings achieved by transferring internally as compared with selling externally).

The aim is to set a transfer price that will give a fair measure of performance in each division. When transfers are recorded at market prices divisional performance is more likely to represent the real economic contribution of the division to total company profits. If the supplying division did not exist, the intermediate product would have to be purchased on the outside market at the current market price. Alternatively, if the receiving division did not exist, the intermediate product would be sold on the outside market at the current market price. Divisional profits are therefore likely to be similar to the profits that would be calculated if the divisions were separate organisations.

Use of a market price removes some of the difficulties associated with alternatives, such as the use of prices negotiated between divisions, or the use of prices imposed by Head Office.

The negotiation route appears to be more consistent with the principle of divisional autonomy. There are significant disadvantages however.

- Negotiation is time-consuming.
- It leads to conflict between divisions.
- Negotiated transfer prices are unlikely to reflect rational factors.
- Negotiated transfer prices will reflect personality/status/skill.
- It requires the time of top management to oversee the negotiating process and to mediate disputes.

If an organisation really believes in divisional autonomy, divisions should be allowed to source goods externally if they can find a better price or quality outside the group. This is a genuine advantage of using market prices: it enables comparison of our own prices with those applying in the wider market. But this could lead to an internal company losing 'sales' and having to operate below maximum capacity. Many organisations would refuse to allow this and would insist on internal 'trading'.

SOLUTION 6

Tutorial note: Once again it is possible to construct a solution largely by drawing on material in the Course Book, in this case Section 3 of Chapter 11.

In view of the large sums involved, capital investment decisions are an area where risk assessment is particularly important. Risks arise from the lengthy timescales involved (making forecasts difficult and possibly unreliable), the possibilities of economic changes during the life of the investment, and the possibility of technological obsolescence.

Traditional investment appraisal techniques are based on the assumption that predictions can be made about future outcomes. For example, we might estimate that the adoption of Projects A and B will give rise to certain cashflows over a future period of six years.

In reality, of course, there is no way to be certain that such cashflows will materialise. In other words, there is risk attached to our forecasts. A problem that managers must address is how to analyse the amount of risk involved. This obviously has an impact on the attractiveness or otherwise of any project we are considering.

One way of dealing with risk is simply to adopt very prudent criteria in deciding whether to make an investment. For example, if we think the likely positive cashflow in Year 3 is £120,000, we could scale this estimate down by, say, a factor of one third, to £80,000. If the project continues to look attractive on these pessimistic forecasts we can invest in it with some confidence: we have left ourselves a good margin for error.

A similar technique would be to impose an overriding criterion for acceptance of a project, eg a maximum payback period. For example, we might adopt a rule of never investing in a project that will take more than three years to pay back. Using this criterion we would reject even very attractive projects unless their positive cashflows were expected to arise in the first three years. Of course, this means we may lose out on high payouts further down the line, but we minimise the risk of expensive disasters.

Another possible technique would be to calculate not just one net present value, but a range of NPVs based on different discount rates and different estimates of future cashflows. For example, instead of forecasting that the positive cashflow in Year 3 will be £120,000 we might forecast that (with a high degree of likelihood) the amount would lie between £90,000 and £140,000. We could then compute the consequences at these extreme values and estimate how our decision would be affected in each case.

More sophisticated than all of these approaches would be the use of **sensitivity analysis**. This is defined as 'a modelling and risk assessment procedure in which changes are made to significant variables in order to determine the effect of these changes on the planned outcome'. This is essentially an extension of the technique described in the paragraph above.

As an example of sensitivity analysis, we could focus on one factor influencing our estimates of future cashflows. For example, we might consider the likely unit production cost of a new product that we intend to produce on a machine we contemplate purchasing. Our initial estimate of the unit production cost might suggest that the new machine is well worth buying, because it enables us to produce a product that can be sold profitably.

Use of sensitivity analysis would allow us to probe more deeply. By setting up the formulae on a spreadsheet we could estimate the degree of 'tolerance' in our forecasts. For example, in a particular case it might turn out that the production cost is absolutely critical, and even a small mistake in our estimate would make a big impact on the investment decision. In such a case, we would revisit our estimate and look at it very carefully indeed.

In another case, it might turn out that our decision is barely affected by the production cost. Even if our estimate understates the true production cost by 20 per cent the machine is still worth buying. In this case we would conclude that we are not much at risk from a mistake in forecasting this particular variable, and we should therefore concentrate our attention on other factors involved in the forecast (eg the volume of sales we might achieve).

Subject Index